2.50

E. Bays.
March 1950.

D1550751

Bulbs for Beauty

Simplicity and Charm. White and yellow tulips with an old-fashioned lilac bring nostalgic appeal to this small garden.

Bulbs for Beauty

By
CHARLES H. MUELLER

Drawings by
Else Bostelmann

M. BARROWS AND COMPANY, INC.

PUBLISHERS   NEW YORK

To

Janet

Who Remembers Every Bulb We Ever Grew

Acknowledgment

Sincere thanks are due Helen Van Pelt Wilson for advice and assistance in preparing this manuscript. For the history of bulb growing in Holland during World War II and information as to current trends there, acknowledgment is made to Messrs. Henry Langeler, Leo Van Zyverden and Dominicus Grullemans. I am also grateful to many gardening friends for countless bits of information given me over the years, particularly to Mrs. David L. George, who shared the wisdom of her gardening experience and for many years provided the space for display and trial bulb growing.

Foreword

Some years ago, my wife and I were standing on the platform of one of those observation towers which crown most mountain peaks approachable by car. As we gazed over the panorama of mountains and valleys around us, my eye caught a silver thread winding among the wooded slopes below. Nodding toward it I asked a near-by attendant, "Is that the Deerfield?" "The answers are all there," he replied promptly, indicating an adjacent counter stacked with guidebooks.

Although annoyed at the time, years later I recalled this incident with amusement when confronted by thousands of questions from visitors to my spring display of tulips and daffodils. So frequently the same queries were repeated: Can you tell me the difference between a daffodil and a narcissus? Must I take up tulips every summer? How many years will a hyacinth last? Why have my daffodils stopped blooming? Those who ask these questions expect concise answers. But it is impossible to give them. A true understanding of such problems requires some knowledge of the botanical nature of the bulbs and their means of reproduction.

To provide useful information about bulbs is, then, the purpose of this book. The discussion of culture is designed to help you obtain better flowering results. The descriptions of varieties and ways of planting them will suggest to you greater possibilities for enjoying them.

The point of view from which this is written is not alone that of the amateur gardener, but also that of the dealer. For this reason I have kept two factors in mind—ease of culture and market availability. We have all had the experience of reading about a new flower only to discover that the entire world stock consisted of twenty bulbs owned by a grower in distant Johannesburg. Or, it has become obvious after trial that some extraordinarily beautiful variety will not stand winters north of Atlanta or summers south of Bar Harbor.

In the matter of variety, gardeners often have violent opinions. Some do not like red, or orange, or a combination of both; others think that double-flowered tulips and daffodils are vulgar and plainly say so. A dealer rises above such prejudice. If you want a row of pink and orange tulips around your red brick house, by all means indulge this fancy without the uncomfortable feeling that you are violating the dictates of some self-appointed arbiter as to what is artistic.

Although my personal preferences are often shown in the following pages for particular varieties and for certain ways of planting them, I hope the dealer's tolerance for your preferences will always be taken for granted. For after all, they are *your* bulbs. And your constant and greater enjoyment of their beauty is the only reason for the existence of the bulb industry—and of this book.

CHARLES H. MUELLER

Lenteboden
New Hope, Pennsylvania
July 1947

Contents

Illustrations

LINE DRAWINGS   *Page*

Bulbs for Beauty

CHAPTER ONE

This World of Bulbs

In every land where plants are grown for the beauty of their flowers, and in almost every garden, you will find bulbs. In nature you will discover them all over the world, from the tiny dogtooth violet growing in countless numbers over the American countryside to the lovely lily rising on the remote slopes of Western China.

This happy circumstance follows from the basic character of the bulbous (or cormous, or tuberous) plant itself. Nature has endowed it with the faculty of storing up food energy so that it can make an early growth before trees, shrubs, annuals and herbaceous perennials get a fair start in the scramble for the soil's nourishment. And when man wishes to bring the bulb plant into his garden it is a relatively simple matter to pick up the storehouse and move it to a new location.

The flowers from bulbs are spectacular and beautiful. The fragrant hyacinth, the colorful tulip, the stately lily, the flaming montbretia and scores of others described in these pages, gardeners would want even if they were scarce and of difficult culture. But no group of plants can be more easily grown. "Plant a good bulb and you will have a good flower," is an almost invariable rule. Of course you do have to plant in well-drained soil, but that is about all—no pruning and little tending are necessary while bulbs are growing. And if that little be faithfully done, what rewards you reap!

Bulbs are adaptable. While they respond to favorable factors of climate, weather and soil, they flourish under a wide variety of these environmental conditions. If you come upon an exotic and beautiful flower during a visit to the African Veldt, or to mid-Korea, find out if it grows from a bulb. If it does, it will probably grow and bloom in Connecticut and Tennessee as well. With the prospect of increasing travel to little known parts of the world, it is exciting to think of the new treasures which await everyday gardeners in the flora of distant lands, particularly in bulbs, since they may be so easily transplanted and transported.

Bulbous plants are invaluable for extending garden bloom, both in time and space. They not only add their glory to the garden when other plants are flowering, but they lengthen the season at both ends. In early spring snowdrops, scillas and winter aconites break into color when the perennial garden is only a stretch of brown earth and there is but a touch of green on early shrubs. After tree foliage has turned brown in the fall, colchicums and autumn crocuses still dot the ground with color. Not only do bulbs share with annuals and perennials the task of filling the cultivated garden, meadow and woodland with appealing bloom, but they frequently flower where other plants falter. Who does not know the shady corner by the house where zinnias and marigolds languish, but where crocuses are bright in spring and tuberous begonias colorful all summer?

The flowers of bulbs are also fine and lasting for bouquets. The long life of tulips, daffodils, gladioli and many others makes it well worth while to plant bulbs in rows just for cutting. Indoors, too, they are dependable for both amateur and professional. Nearly every gardener has grown paperwhite

narcissi in pebbles and water, and from childhood associated Easter with lilies and hyacinths. The number of other bulbous plants that can be grown in window gardens will be told in a later chapter.

Bulbs are available. There are rare species and varieties, it is true, but no class of plants in general is so readily procurable or more easily brought to your door. The ease with which bulbs may be produced and handled has led to the establishment of bulb growing as an extensive horticultural industry. Their long dormant period makes it possible to keep them above ground a long time and to send them a great distance. Tulips from Holland may be shipped as safely to New York and thence to San Francisco, Hawaii or China as to neighboring Germany or Belgium. Gladiolus corms dug in Michigan will flourish under proper soil conditions whether replanted in their original beds or set out in Massachusetts or Florida. As a result, when you go to buy bulbs you find an abundant supply and a truly bewildering range of variety.

It is in the miracle of spring that bulbs play their most important role. This is the time when buds of deciduous trees unfold their brighter greens against the still dark verdure of evergreens, when magnolias, cherries, azaleas and dogwoods burst forth in a shower of colorful blossoms. We look up to all this beauty but some instinct within makes us look down as well, to see what the earth unfolds. For those of us who have planted bulbs in the fall, it brings forth a wondrous spectacle indeed.

The show begins with snowdrops, chionodoxas, crocuses, hyacinths, early tulips and daffodils while the buds of trees and shrubs are but burgeoning promises. It continues in a torrent of bloom from daffodils, tulips, scillas and camassias. Then the columbines, foxgloves and coralbells bloom, with iris and peonies awaiting their turn.

Although nearly every garden contains some spring-flowering bulbs, few gardeners realize their nearly limitless possibilities. One reason for this is that too many of us believe we must spread our efforts and energy over the entire growing season. We accept "continuous bloom" as our goal—and our dilemma! We have succumbed to the conviction that, while failure may attend our most slavish efforts to attain an all-season pageant of flowers, nothing less than disgrace is the lot of those who do not even try for it. How often you have heard the words, perhaps despairingly uttered on a blazing hot midsummer day, "My garden was lovely in the spring. Now look at it. I've worked so hard with so little to show for it. I've a good mind to give up gardening entirely and turn the whole place into lawn."

If these summer garden blues ever seized you, do not feel too depressed. You may be guilty of no other fault than attempting the impossible, led on, perhaps, by the boasts of others in speech or writing of how well they do it and how easy it is. The plain fact is that our summer climate, over a goodly portion of the United States—where most of us live—is ill disposed to many lovely midsummer perennials and annuals. We are apt to have long, searing dry stretches or protracted rainy spells. Of course you can water in dry weather. But when drought is so bad your plants will die of thirst without watering, you can expect a notice asking you not to waste the dwindling water supply on lawns or gardens. When the opposite occurs, and there are showers without end, the plants practically drown—all but the weeds which grow like mad, and if you pull them, mosquitoes pursue you like fury.

No, the effort to make our gardens burst forth in glorious bloom through all but the winter months, or even in recurrent stages all summer long, is a thankless task. How much more sensible—and you may have come to this conclusion

yourself—it is to let them do their utmost when nature is most willing that they should. If your gardening activities need be severely limited, this may call for no more than a bed or border of tulips and daffodils, to be filled later with friendly petunias which will cover the area with foliage and flowers up to heavy frost.

However, it is to be hoped that your time and garden interest will lead you to do more than this bare minimum. A satisfactory plan is to emphasize spring bulbs and the plants which associate well with them. Save room too for the succeeding blooms of iris and peonies and the June perennials. If space permits, grow roses separately. In your flower beds, during comfortable working weather, set out annual seedlings and tender bulbs for color through the summer. Somewhere plant hybrid daylilies for June to September flowering and of course chrysanthemums for fall display.

True, the main outpouring of bloom from such a garden will have ceased by July. But you will have had three wonderfully satisfying months. Then in July and August you can sit on the verandah watching the easy annuals grow, while you are flanked by great bowls of gladioli and montbretias produced from bulbs set out in April. When September comes you will have all the flowers you want from the asters, giant zinnias and marigolds growing profusely in the areas where your tulips bloomed in May.

In such a sensible program bulbs play a major part. Hyacinths, daffodils and tulips are emphasized in their turn by the gardener who concentrates on spring. They should be supplemented by such early little bulbs as snowdrops, crocuses and aconites and companioned by grape hyacinths, scillas, butterfly tulips, alliums and others whose acquaintance we shall make later. During the summer the gardener may again count on bulbs with lilies for every month. Then, to complement phlox and zinnias, there are hosts of such spring-planting bulbs as tigridias, cooperias and Peruvian daffodils, which freely bestow their blooms during the warm months. Finally, the gay blossoms of colchicums, autumn crocuses and stern-bergias stage a display until winter draws the curtain.

CHAPTER TWO

Matters Botanical

"TRUE *bulbs, corms and tubers,* when dormant except for storage growth, and when free from soil"—thus reads number one on the list of items which may be shipped without restriction under federal Japanese Beetle Quarantine regulations. Thus also are suggested, if we add *tuberous roots,* satisfactory groupings for this survey.

This definition excludes such fleshy rooted plants as mertensia, bleedingheart, daylilies and peonies, often called "bulbs" under too loose an interpretation. It also excludes rhizomatous plants such as German and Japanese iris which are called bulbous with more excuse, since rhizomes, like bulbs, are modified stems. Dealers increasingly tend to offer iris apart from bulbs and with perennials. And it certainly lessens confusion for the amateur if he thinks of rhizomatous iris as separate from bulbs, because there are important irises which do grow from bulbs!

Bulbs, corms, tubers and *tuberous roots* have this structural property in common: each is a form of modified stem from which the plant stalk grows up and roots grow down. They also have two common functions: to act as a food storehouse for carrying the plant over its dormant state and into its next growing period; and to serve as a means of propagation. They

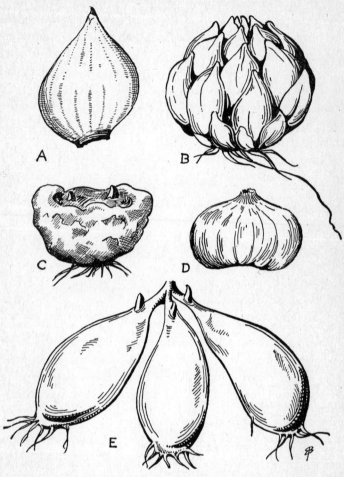

A. True bulb of tulip. B. True bulb of lily. C. Begonia
tuber. D. Gladiolus corm. E. Tuberous roots of dahlia.

differ from each other in some structural aspects and in their methods of reproduction.

In *true bulbs* the flesh grows in approximately concentric layers or scales. These may be firm and solid and tightly enclosed in a skin as in the case of the tulip and onion. Or like Scilla campanulata, they may have overlapping layers with no outside skin. Lilies are examples of bulbs composed of rings of separate but tightly held scales. Other familiar garden plants which grow from bulbs include hyacinths, daffodils, muscari, snowdrops and tigridias.

If you examine the bottom of your newly received tulip bulb in the fall, you will have no trouble in discerning the root base in the form of a ring of tiny nodules. These are called "root buds" by growers. It is important that they be healthy and clean. The top of the bulb plainly forms a tip from which a sprout often starts before planting. If you cut the bulb vertically in half, you will find the embryo plant in the center with foliage and flower already formed.

Bulbs usually reproduce themselves by some process of division. When you dig up a daffodil bulb in midsummer you will not find the large double-nosed bulb you planted the previous autumn. In its stead there will be a clump consisting of two or more medium-sized bulbs plus a number of offsets or "chips." Most of the offsets will not be large enough to produce flowers the next year but will require one or more years of further growing to achieve flowering size.

The growing on of offsets is the general commercial method of developing stock. In the case of certain lilies, the mature bulb sometimes is grown from the bulblets or bulbils formed in the axils of their leaves. Raising bulbs from seed—the process by which new varieties are born—is not possible for the growing of hybrids since hybrids do not breed true from seed. Also, for most kinds, propagation from seed is too slow a

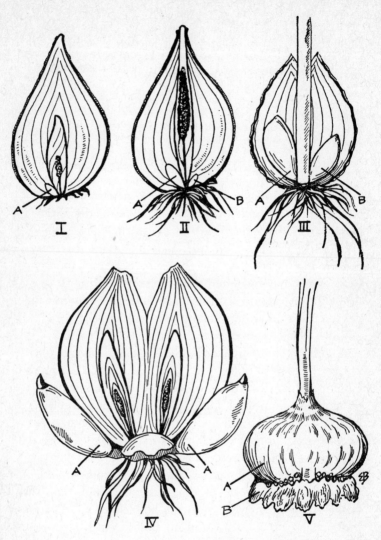

How bulbs multiply.

I. **C**ross section of a tulip bulb in October showing, at base of embryo foliage and flower, bud A which will develop into a new bulb within the membrane of the old.

II. Cross section of the same tulip in January showing the growth of bud A and the appearance of the second bud B, which will also develop into a new bulb. This illustration shows two. By January often three or four buds will have started progress into new bulbs and offsets. Note the upward growth of the foliage and flower.

III. Cross section of the same tulip bulb in March showing further growth of A and B at the base of what is now the plant stem.

IV. Cross section of double-nosed narcissus bulb in October showing two sections, each with embryo foliage and flower. Here still connected, these sections will be ready for separation at the end of the growing cycle the following summer. Note the offsets or chips A and A, each a potential mature bulb after two or more annual cycles of growth.

V. Diagram of gladiolus corm lifted after foliage has ripened in September. The new corm A has developed above the shriveled remains of the old corm B, which was planted in late spring. Note the evidence of tiny cormels growing between A and B.

method. There are certain exceptions to this, like chionodoxas, which produce flowering-size bulbs in the fall from spring sowings, and some species of lilies which even amateurs can grow successfully from seed.

Corms are solid growths in which the flesh is not arranged in layers or scales but is a uniform starchy mass. If you cut a gladiolus corm in half you will find no embryo flower in its heart, but you will discover an easily identifiable root base. The stalk sprouts from the center of the top or perhaps along its edge.

When you lift corms at the end of their growing season, you will notice at once how their means of reproduction differs from that of bulbs. Instead of divisions, you will find that the old corms have shriveled up, but growing right on top of them are new corms plus a number of little offshoots called cormels. All the cormels and some of the corms will need further growing before they reach blooming size. Growing on of cormels and small corms is the general commercial method of propagating corm-bearing plants, while seedlings are raised by hybridizers for the development of new varieties. Crocuses, gladioli and montbretias all grow from corms.

Tubers are uniform, fleshy growths which develop underground at the base of the old plant stem. New plants sprout from eyes located anywhere on the surface of these growths. Propagation consists of cutting the tuber into sections, each containing at least one eye. This is the method of propagating one of the best known tubers—the potato. Tuberous begonias also belong to this group.

Tuberous roots differ from tubers in that the eye, or bud, does not form on the tuber itself but on the neck, which joins the tuber to the old plant stem. The tuberous roots of dahlias are familiar to most gardeners. When dahlias are separated in the spring, the budded neck must be included with each root since a tuber which is planted without a bud will not grow.

Bulbs, corms and tubers—you will probably continue to think of them all as "just bulbs" and they will be offered to you that way too. This is probably just as well for all-around convenience. In fact you might think of a "bulb" as anything which can be cleaned off in its dormant state and carried around in your pocket like an English walnut.

Like other plants, bulbs are classified according to *family, genus, species* and *variety*. You will find them so listed in catalogues and other horticultural literature, although the name of the family may not always be given. *Genus* is indicated by the name tulip, narcissus, or scilla to mention a few. Plants of different genera having similar characteristics are grouped in the same *family*. Thus tulips and lilies are two genera of the lily family, or family of liliaceae, while daffodils belong to the amaryllidaceae. *Species* are plants as they are first found in nature. Species differ specifically from one another, yet belong to the same genus. Thus in the scilla genus are found the early, bright blue squill and the later, taller wood hyacinth, both of which, despite their difference of size and time of bloom, are scillas. The early one is known as the species sibirica, the later one as the species campanulata.

Variety is a classification applied to an individual plant which has identifiable differences from others of the same species, but yet is not sufficiently different to constitute a new species. Thus the bulb you may buy as Scilla campanulata, Excelsior, belongs to the *genus* of scilla, *species* campanulata and is known as the *variety* Excelsior.

Complications arise in a genus such as the tulip where centuries of hybridizing have produced tens of thousands of varieties distributed in commerce throughout the years. Other than botanical groupings have been made among these and accepted as necessary to bring order out of chaos. Sometimes

growers or dealers have made their own arbitrary classifications stick. Other classes have been named by general usage
in the trade or by horticultural societies and committees. Thus
in the case of "Darwin tulip, Pride of Haarlem," *tulip,* of
course, refers to the genus while *Pride of Haarlem* is the
varietal name. Although here the word *Darwin* stands in the
same relation as a species designation, it is not a species of
tulip, but a fairly recent and non-botanical classification. The
fact is that there is no satisfactory species name for those garden varieties which constitute the bulk of tulips that have
been bought and sold for hundreds of years.

Most flowers you buy today are not original species but are
hybrids. Most, yet not all. In many genera, original species are
still grown on a commercial scale, as in the case of tulips.
These are wild types collected in Southern Europe and what
is now called the Middle East. They differ from each other
and from the regular garden tulips so much that each is considered a separate species. Some of them, such as the beautiful clusiana and kaufmanniana, have been grown by the millions in our gardens.

The hybrids you buy today are grown from bulb propagation. Yet each variety once started out from seed. In some
bulb plants, the progress of the variety from seed pod to market covers many, many years and is a fascinating story.

For instance, the firm of E. H. Krelage and Sons, in Holland, hybridized the tulip known as King George V. Its in-
ception began when the pollen of one flower was carefully
dusted on the ovule of another. After the seeds ripened, they
were planted along with thousands of seeds from other pods
saved for hybridization. Each seed that germinated had the
capacity, of course, to produce a new variety of tulip. The
first year, the future King George sent up a tiny filament
carrying, in the manner of seeds, the empty seed shell at the

top. When the miniature plant ripened at the end of the first
season, a small bulb the size of a pea was formed at the base
of the stem. This was composed of but one layer of bulb flesh.

The next year it sent up a recognizable tulip leaf and added
another layer to the bulb. When four or five layers were
formed, the bulb was ready for flowering. What eager and
critical eyes examined its first blossom! The hybridizer had no
right to expect that more than a few of the thousands of new
seedlings first coming into flower would be worth keeping.
Here certainly was one of them.

The seed had done its work. From now on the plant would
increase through the multiplication of bulb and offshoots.
Now the variety would be tested for growing qualities. After
four to seven years of outdoor testing, the hybridizer had no
further doubts. Here was a fine new flower. At this time he
probably christened it and planned to show it at one of the
tulip exhibitions attended by growers looking for new stock.
At any rate, the record shows that the Darwin tulip, King
George V, won an Award of Merit at the Haarlem Show in
1912.

Other growers noticed it at Haarlem. Without doubt they
made Krelage an offer for some of his small stock of King
George bulbs. Perhaps he sold a few at a very high price.
Maybe he waited until his stock increased a bit. He sold
some eventually. By the early 1920's enough King George
bulbs existed for it to be offered to American gardeners as a
rare, new variety at fifty cents each. Here it proved its merit.

By 1939, growers had so increased their stocks as to bring
the price down to the level of popular varieties. By this time
hybridizers were probably offering small stocks of new varieties a generation improved on King George. At the same time
they were eagerly scanning the new crop of seedling flowers
for the best varieties two generations beyond it.

Now, except in the rare cases of sports or breaks, all the flowers produced by the new bulbs and offshoots of King George V were and are exactly like that of the very first seedling bulb. For that is the nature of bulbs. Botanically speaking, a plant together with all its asexually reproduced offspring is a *clone*. This name applies whether the reproductions are located beside the parent bulb in its garden bed or scattered all over the world. When you buy King George V bulbs, you are buying part of the same clone as other buyers of this variety in Canada, England, Finland, Holland or wherever Dutch bulbs are sold.

If in 1946 you acquire bulbs of a variety which was first seeded in 1896, you are buying part of a plant which is fifty years old even though the variety may be brand new to you. Some experts believe that, sooner or later, all varieties of bulbs lose their vigor. As proof, they point to the large turnover in varieties and the large number of older kinds which have passed out of existence. But there are other reasons than lack of vigor for varieties being discarded. One of these is the fact that growers, understandably, like to replace common and cheap varieties with better and more expensive kinds. Also, public tastes change and the grower must keep his stock abreast of changing demand. Yet there are varieties like Zomerschoon and Keizerskroon which for decades, or even for centuries, have persisted in holding both public favor and growing vigor.

It is also true that trouble will suddenly occur in the growing of certain varieties which have been hardy, popular and good commercially for years. Whether from age or weakness, strong growers sometimes go bad. Our American daffodil growers had great difficulty with some of the old Dutch varieties they brought over in large stocks before the quarantine. Golden Spur and most of the bi-colors behaved very badly.

Of course this may have been due to the unsuitability of their new environment, or to the lack of experience of their new growers, rather than to the age of the varieties.

Another case in point is that of Gladiolus, Picardy, of sensational history. From the first it won the favor of amateur and commercial growers with its fine size and substance and bright, shrimp-pink color. The corms reproduced faster than a colony of ants. Moreover, it took only a medium-sized bulb to produce a salable bloom. Stocks of Picardy multiplied until millions of corms were harvested annually. But lately Picardy has been giving trouble. Fusarium rot attacking gladioli has found Picardy vulnerable. Many stocks have been devastated and growers are planting less of this variety.

Fortunately for the amateur, the sudden or gradual debility of a standard variety is of little concern. There is small likelihood of any bulb stock you may have in your garden being affected by the problems which beset the commercial grower. But it may cause you to discover that some varieties are no longer available or are getting scarce. Here lies one explanation of the disappearance of some of your old favorites from the list, or of their relatively higher price.

Bulbs are sometimes classed as hardy and non-hardy according to whether or not they survive the winter in the ground. The hardiness of a genus naturally varies with the winter climate of the region in question. Not all bulbs are hardy everywhere in the United States, of course. Tulips, daffodils and others generally classed as "hardy bulbs," and so described in catalogues, will winter anywhere up to a point a little south of Hudson's Bay. Others like English iris may be hardy as far north as the Carolinas, while still others, including amaryllis and hippeastrums, will perish in a winter climate less mild than that of Florida or Southern California.

This does not mean that you cannot grow bulbs if you live

in the region where they are not hardy. In fact, many tender kinds, such as the corms of gladioli and the tuberous roots of dahlias, may be as familiar to you as the more winter-resistant genera. They have a dormant period long enough to permit their being dug before winter weather sets in, stored and planted out again each spring.

In general, hardy bulbs are planted in the fall, tender ones in the spring or summer. This division of bulbous plants according to time of planting clarifies the gardener's thinking about bulbs and indicates a good separation for this consideration of them. Discussion of culture and description of species of the fall-planting kinds will come first since they are the more numerous and more important.

CHAPTER THREE

Giving New Bulbs a Good Start

Each fall I look forward to bulb planting with genuine pleasure. The October air is crisp, the sun is warm, the earth inviting. Vivid pictures of spring flowers dance in my mind—of old friends grown before and new kinds sent from Holland. I try now to give my bulbs not tedious perfection, but reasonable care which will ensure good growth next spring and a fair chance for future development.

The care of new bulbs starts, of course, not with planting but with their delivery. True, most kinds are tough but they are living things. They need air and a livable temperature. If you deposit your carton of bulbs, unopened, upon a hot radiator and forget it for a few days, you may look in vain for bloom the following spring.

The proper handling of newly arrived bulbs is really as simple as taking a new suit or dress from the box, removing the price tag and a few loose threads, and hanging it up in the closet. You don't say, "I'm going to wear this next Wednesday, so I'll just leave it in the box till then." But how often the gardener thinks, "Tony comes Friday, so these bulbs can just wait as they are for two days." The probability of rain on Friday or Tony's not showing up is overlooked so that all too often the bulbs wait for weeks "just as they are" in the unopened box. Here is a simple routine which should not be varied:

1. Unpack box or carton immediately. Open all bags, if varieties are shipped in separate containers.

2. Place the opened bags on a shelf or table in any cool, dry place—an unheated garage or barn, a pantry, or the cool part of the cellar. Bulbs must be safe from deep frost and from mice or other rodents. If you have no suitable storage space, speed up planting.

3. Examine bulbs for damage in transit. If they feel soft and pulpy, instead of firm and solid, they are not worth planting. Report their condition to your dealer.

Sometimes bulbs sprout prematurely. Then they lose the hardness of dormancy but are still healthy. Notice whether growth has begun. If the bulb flesh gives a little as you carefully press it, it is likely that this softness is due to growth. Experience will soon enable you to determine this. If borderline cases puzzle you, you will be no worse off than the most experienced grower so give the bulbs the benefit of the doubt.

When to plant is the next question. Although bulbs vary in their preference, practically all have a high degree of tolerance for an earlier or later planting than the *best* time. The madonna or candidum lily is an exception. This should be planted at the end of August or by September twenty-fifth at the latest, for this lily makes a noticeable fall growth. Yet even with candidums, if October rolls around with your bulbs unplanted, or unbought, you may still plant them hopefully so long as sprouts are undamaged. Simply follow instructions as to depth and avoid injuring the developing rosette. Candidum lilies illustrate the wonderful quality fall-planting bulbs have of never demanding perfection, but always permitting an alternative.

Planting time also depends on when your dealer can make

delivery. Since most bulbs will probably continue to come from Holland or the West Coast, supplies will be available to you from the end of September to the end of November. And this is an excellent planting time. Perennials are now ready for cutting back while first frosts prompt the removal of annuals from spots destined for bulbs. The weather too is pleasant for planting.

Since daffodils have a much shorter period of dormancy than other bulbs, it is well to deal with them first so they may start making roots as soon as possible. This may not be as soon as you have been led to believe. Late August or early September is often said to be ideal. While this may be the best time to replant any of your old narcissi, previously lifted for summer rest, such early delivery of new bulbs would be highly inadvisable. It would mean that bulbs would be traveling across the ocean or continent during the hottest part of the summer when there would be maximum risk from overheating. If daffodils are to be safely shipped, they cannot reach you before the latter half of September. This is still sufficiently early for planting.

Tulips, in the middle latitudes, benefit by late October or early November planting. If set so late, they will be deterred from making that autumn top growth which may come from earlier planting. Tulip bulbs kept beyond the middle of November suffer so much from loss of moisture that many are likely to be too dehydrated for proper growth and bloom the following spring.

It is wise to divide your fall planting time into two periods: between September fifteenth and October tenth plant daffodils, winter aconites, erythroniums and other bulbs which your dealer's instructions say to get into the ground early; from October twentieth to November fifteenth set out tulips, Dutch iris and remaining bulbs. In the latitude of northern

Planting chart for familiar bulbs.

COVER WITH										
2 ins.										
3 ins.										
4 ins.										
5 ins.										
6 ins.										
7 ins.										
8 ins.										
9 ins.										
10 ins.										
11 ins.										

TULIP
4-5 ins. apart

SPECIES TULIP

TULIP deeply planted

NARCISSUS
5-6 ins. apart

SPECIES NARCISSUS
3 ins. apart

HYACINTH
6-8 ins. apart

SILLA MUSCARI
3 ins. apart

WINTER ACONITE
2-3 ins. apart

CROCUS

ERYTHRONIUM
rock
2-3 ins. apart

SNOWDROP
2-3 ins. apart

BASE ROOTING LILIES
8-10 ins. apart

GLADIOLUS
5-6 ins. apart

STEM ROOTING LILIES
10-12 ins. apart

New England work a week or two earlier than the latest of these dates.

If you must do all your planting at once, the middle of October is best. This will not be too early for tulips and will allow daffodils time for some fall root growth. It will also be safe for such little bulbs as crocuses, whose corms may dry up if kept out of the ground too long. When the place for your daffodils happens to be filled in September with profusely blooming summer annuals, by all means hold off planting until frost ends the display though it be late October. Although you may deprive the daffodils of some root growth and they may bloom a bit later and have shorter stems than if you had set them out earlier, they will eventually catch up. Indeed, if the spring weather is favorable, you may hardly know the difference.

There is an old saying that to prevent spring-flowering bulbs from blooming they have to be set in concrete. I suspect some gardeners of secretly wanting to put them to this test for I have seen many bulbs struggling up through soil which is but a step removed from cement. True, bulbs do succeed in overcoming handicaps, but *loose, friable and well-drained soil* offers the only proper medium for successful growing.

If by a miracle you have loamy, well-drained soil, full of humus and with a fair content of phosphorus and potassium, you have the ideal environment. Few of us, however, are lucky enough to have proper soil in every spot of the garden where we want to grow bulbs so we take care to improve existing conditions. How much improving is necessary depends on whether bulbs are to be planted in already existing flower beds, in soil never before used for flower growing but which is fairly good, or in soil hitherto untreated, naturally poor, and perhaps clayey.

Undoubtedly most bulbs are bought for existing gardens

rather than for new beds. In this case only the exact spots where they are to be planted need attention. If drainage and friability are satisfactory, you need only loosen the necessary area with a digging fork. If the planting spots are inclined to be hollow and depressed, they should be filled in with extra top soil until they stand a little higher than the rest of the bed.

How much fertilizer or what kind you may need cannot, of course, be definitely stated. For accuracy you would need to know the chemical content of your soil. Perhaps you already have more nitrogen than bulbs require, but this is not likely in beds which have produced flowers all summer. Since many soils are deficient in phosphorus, it is a good idea to keep on hand a 100-pound bag of superphosphate or bone meal. Commercial superphosphate makes an excellent general fertilizer for bulbs when mixed with equal parts of one of the commercial dried manures such as Bovung, Drichonure or powdered sheep manure. You will find this mixture satisfactory if used at the rate of one hundred pounds (fifty of superphosphate—or bone meal—and fifty of the dried manure) for one thousand bulbs.

You will probably want to plant some of your bulbs, perhaps all of them, not in flower beds, but along a hedge of evergreens, in a window corner or bordering a picket fence. Here, again, how much preparation your soil requires depends on its natural state. It may be good enough so that you can just spread the fertilizer mixture on the surface, fork it in and plant. Be sure the level of the planting area is somewhat higher than the surrounding earth. Fill in with top soil if this is not the case.

Too often untreated soil is hard and heavy especially near the house where the contractor, in excavating for your cellar, may have buried the original top soil under many feet of subsoil. Generally, in such circumstances, all you need do is to spread a two- to four-inch layer of peat moss or humus, plus the fertilizer, over the planting area and dig it in thoroughly before planting. This will not only improve consistency but also ensure a higher level for the bed.

Once in a while you will have a place which seems to offer a perfect setting for bulbs, but where the soil appears to be impossibly bad. Do not be discouraged. I have yet to see soil so poor it cannot be made excellent for bulbs, not excepting hardpan clay. Contrary to the common idea, red or yellow clay is not a bad bulb-growing soil, if it is properly conditioned. For it is not the chemical composition of clay which is harmful, but its thick, gluey, physical consistency which literally throttles plants. Change this and bulbs grow well and their flowers have good color.

In developing a good bed on the heaviest clay, do not rely on sand alone—it only makes the soil harder. The best way to start is to break up the clay with a digging fork—or a pick if necessary. A four-inch layer of sifted coal ashes (hard clinkers only, the soft ash is no good) should then be dug in. After this spread on a thin cover of sand and a three-inch layer of peat moss or humus, with fertilizer, and fork this into the bed by turning over the soil twice. You can now plant with confidence.

Above all, the site must be well-drained. If your soil is loose and friable to a sufficient depth, you will automatically have satisfactory drainage unless you plant your bulbs in a hollow where after each heavy rainfall a pond is bound to form. Although raising the bed several inches promotes drainage, do not suppose that drainage is good just because the bed is on a slope. If you have a clay bed on a hillside you may have completely bad drainage even though it would seem that the water must all run off down the hill. *Good drainage is measured by how well moisture seeps vertically down into the soil, not by how fast surface water runs off.*

Perhaps your home site is new, without a sign of a garden or flower bed, and the bulbs you set out in the fall are the first flowers you plant. Suppose you want them in a bed which is later to serve as your garden—for which you have high ambition. You'd better face it. Don't just plant the bulbs and postpone garden making until spring. You will only have to dig them up again. It takes hard work to prepare soil properly but it is well worth the effort. This is the best procedure:

1. Excavate two feet of soil. Then loosen the exposed area with a digging fork for a further six inches.
2. Spread a six-inch layer of coarse coal ashes, gravel or broken stone on the bottom for drainage.
3. Cover this drainage layer with a nine-inch layer of the excavated soil. If this soil is clayey, first thoroughly mix it with top soil, humus or peat moss. Then put it back.
4. Now add a three-inch layer of cow manure at least six months old, but not over a year old as by then it is little more than compost. When planting, do not permit the bulbs to come in contact with this layer.
5. Cover the manure with twelve inches of top soil. This will bring the level of the bed six inches above the surrounding ground but it will soon sink three inches or more, leaving just the right extra height to facilitate drainage. The bed should be constructed three weeks ahead to allow time for this settling before planting.
6. Finally, before setting out the bulbs, dig in superphosphate or bone meal at the rate of one pound per ten square feet.

In general there are two techniques for the actual process of bulb planting. One is to remove, to the required depth, the soil from the area to be planted. Bulbs are then set in place and the earth put back with due care not to disturb their position. The second method is to place the bulbs on the surface of the bed, after this has been loosened. Then each one is individually planted with a trowel.

For perfect evenness of bloom, so desirable when bulbs are formally planted at measured distances, the first method is undoubtedly the better. But it is certainly slower. I suppose to date I must have planted (or presided at the planting of) well over half a million bulbs and every one of them was set out the easier individual way with a trowel.

A trowel, incidentally, is much the best implement for surface planting. I never use anything else, since a trowel makes an opening in which I can firmly set the bulb base on the soil. No dangerous air space then remains below. If you lower a bulb into a space made by a dibble or sharp-pointed stick, especially where soil is heavy, it may be impossible to place it at the very bottom of the hole. Then a space remains which is a dangerous future container for water.

Even with trowel planting it saves time if the soil is first loosened with a digging fork. The looser the soil the faster and easier the planting. It also facilitates matters if the planting surface is raked bare before you set to work. Brown autumn leaves skittering over dark soil seem determined to hide tulip and daffodil bulbs. You will also find it helpful to place all bulbs before you plant one. Then you can rearrange without fear of placing some too near the ones already planted.

When you plant bulbs individually without removing the soil, you will have to gauge depth as best you can. Measuring each cavity with the trowel for the first few bulbs is a good precaution. After ten or twenty bulbs have been set, you can judge the proper depth and get each lot in at approximately the same level. To facilitate drainage many gardeners follow the practice of putting a handful of sand just below each bulb. Undoubtedly this theory is sound, but I have found that in properly prepared soil such a practice is unnecessary and far too time consuming to be worth while, even for lilies. After planting has been completed, smooth over the surface of the bed with a garden rake. Then your bulb tasks are finished for the year.

At this point, though, you may ask—how about mulching? The answer, for all but a very few semi-hardy bulbs like English iris and anemones, is—don't. The majority produce healthier growth without winter covering. Of course, if you have been planting in a bed which must be mulched for the sake of other plants in it, proceed as usual, but if possible cover the areas above bulbs lightly. Then in the spring remove the mulch gradually, starting early in the bulb sections. Salt hay, which is satisfactory for perennials, is also safest when you must mulch a bed containing bulbs.

A garden rake, a leaf rake, a digging fork and three trowels in different sizes for planting small and large bulbs comprise an adequate set of tools for the bulb planter. A mattock to break up roots may also be necessary when you do woodland plantings, and a pick to remove rocks or to attack very heavy clay. An extra digging fork and a couple of extra towels in the hands of willing assistants are to be highly recommended for easing the job!

Nothing brings a more comforting feeling of satisfaction than standing at the window, with the fire at your back, watching December's first snow cover flower beds well stocked with bulbs. And nothing will send arctic chills more swiftly up and down your spine than watching the same snow cover your beds while the bulbs still rest on a shelf! I hope this has never happened to you, but it does every year to many procrastinating gardeners. If you should ever get caught, don't get panicky and don't decide you will just keep the bulbs until it warms up in the spring. Bulbs don't keep!

They may be planted, however, after the first snow or after

the first freeze. Call this, if you wish, "winter" planting and be assured that it is much more uncomfortable for the planter than for the bulbs. The amount of difficulty for you will depend on the depth of frost. Perhaps you will only need to push a little harder than usual to penetrate a light crust with your digging fork. Perhaps, at the worst, you will need a mattock or pick to break up soil which will come up in large chunks. If the frost is too deep, you had better postpone planting and wait for a thaw.

Sometimes, of course, winter planting is forced upon us. There are a number of bulbs, particularly the late-maturing lilies, which cannot be dug early. Speciosums from Holland and Japan, and auratums from Japan, are not in proper condition for delivery before late November or early December. Even Oregon's regal lilies must sometimes arrive in the Midwest or the East after a freeze. Yet it is wiser to plant these on arrival, and under conditions not too comfortable, than to keep them in storage for spring planting.

The better procedure, if you have late lilies on order, is to prepare the soil for these bulbs ahead of time and to cover it with a foot of leaves or salt hay. Then, if a freeze comes, the mulch will keep the ground frost-free and it may be easily pushed aside when the time comes to set out the lilies. If you are reasonably sure bulbs will not be later than the first week of December, you may take a chance on the weather, unless you live far north of the latitude of New York. More than likely a freeze will come, but so will a thaw. At least it has been my experience in twenty-four years that a complete thaw always follows the first freeze.

Perhaps some year it won't!

CHAPTER FOUR

Spring Care That Looks Ahead

P<small>LANTING</small> new bulbs in the fall is the easiest part of culture. If you set out top size bulbs with a minimum of care, successful bloom will almost surely follow. It is in securing good flowers from the same stock year after year that the problem —and the work—lies.

It is true that the test of the bulb you buy is in the growth and flower of the following year. Other things are tested too, to the extent that new bulbs are affected by soil and drainage. If tulips bought in October produce vigorous foliage and beautiful flowers in May, you can credit your dealer with having given you good bulbs, for the flower you see was in the heart of the bulb you bought. But if, from the same bulbs the second year, weak plants arise bearing small, sickly blossoms, do not think darkly of your dealer. After the first year it is not *his* bulbs, but *your* bulbs you have in the ground. It is your crop produced by the preceding growth and ripening of plants in your garden.

Yet people will say, "If I buy good tulips, surely I should be able to count on fine blooms for a definite number of years." The answer is, alas, no, except in the sense that if you start with poor stock you can expect poor results the first season and thereafter as well. But, as gardeners discover for themselves, a fine first year showing, so necessary for future success, is no guarantee of it. This largely follows from the botanical fact that the individual top size bulbs you plant are, with the maturity of the first year's growth, replaced by offspring or divisions.

As a gardener you are more interested in practical effect than in botanical cause of bulb reproduction. You want flowers. "Multiplication" is "petering out" to you if it results in fewer and poorer blossoms. Your question is: What will these divisions and offspring do in the way of producing flowers? Must you buy new bulbs each year to get fine blooms?

The answer to this last question is, fortunately, no. Unless you require the uniformly perfect flowers only new bulbs assure—as parks often do and as gardeners sometimes do for certain special plantings—you need not consider annual replacement. For most of us it would be a needless expense, unthinkable in the case of crocuses, scillas, daffodils and other bulbs planted for naturalizing and unnecessary even where we want good individual blossoms in the border or perennial beds. Bloom in later years is conditioned by three factors: the quality of the bulbs you buy, the care you take with the original planting and the attention you give while they are progressing from the stage of dormant bulb to that of growing plant.

It is a good idea to keep a watchful eye on the bulb areas whenever winter weather permits you to go abroad in the garden. This is pleasure, not work. In fact, one of the greatest joys of gardening comes from the first glimpse of snowdrops, winter aconites and chionodoxas opening their buds at the approach of spring, or earlier when February days are mild. You will find it equally delightful on the same days to discover the sturdy green spears of daffodils and perhaps the first red shoots of tulips protruding from the ground.

In March comes the first light chore, the clearing of the

surface of the beds. If bulbs are sharing a mulch with other plants in a general border, the mulch should be gradually removed this month. Then at the end the surface should be raked clean: thoroughly, to remove all dead leaves or other bits of plants; carefully, to prevent injury to young bulb sprouts. Loose branches should be picked up, for if left knocking about in the March winds they might damage new shoots.

When the most advanced plants are four or five inches high, but after all have broken through, do the spring fertilizing and cultivating so important for future welfare. Dust the surface thoroughly but not heavily with the half-and-half mixture of superphosphate and Bovung and gently work it in with a small hand claw. If you do this for tulips before the leaves have spread too widely, you need not worry about fertilizer remaining in the leaf axils. If the plants get an extra week's growth fertilize anyway, but wash off the powder that adheres to the foliage with a fine hose spray unless rain does it for you within two days.

This plant food is not so much for the benefit of the flowers soon to open as for the new bulbs developing below. If your bulbs have spent the winter under a blanket of manure, omit the spring fertilizer but do the cultivating. After this task you may sit back and wait for blooms.

You have probably been told not to cut foliage when gathering flowers for the house. Technically, this is good advice. For absolute future welfare of the bulbs you should cut the stems not more than half an inch below the blossoms. Such restriction would be absurd since we grow flowers for our pleasure. A satisfactory compromise is to cut tulips so that only the top leaf is taken. When cutting daffodils, select spears for your bouquet from plants with heavy foliage. This may not necessarily be the same plant from which you gather the blossom.

Whether or not you cut flowers for bouquets, *never leave*

the blossoms until they disappear by themselves. This is important advice, too often disregarded. The best plan is to break off all blooms *before* the petals drop. If the dead blossoms fall before you get to them, pick up each withered petal wherever it lies, on foliage or ground. Then break off the stem to prevent formation of a seed pod. Decaying flower petals encourage the spread of disease. Ripening seed pods may rob new bulbs of strength.

But ripening of foliage is essential. This period of yellowing leaves is vital to the development of the new bulb. It is at this time that it stores the food which will carry it over to the next season. *Therefore never cut down the foliage of your spring bulb until it has completely ripened.* For daffodils, this will be about the middle of July; for tulips, the middle of June. If the sight of fading leaves is more than you can bear in prominent borders, by all means try to place the bulbs where other plants can conceal their retreat. Columbines may be conveniently set in front of the early daffodils, and shasta daisies to the fore of tulips. It is also a simple matter to keep daffodil foliage and hide it too. Just take one of the longer spears as a strand, wrap it around the others and firmly pin it to the ground with a bobby pin or bent hairpin. This is not done until two weeks after the flowering, for during that time daffodil foliage stands handsomely upright.

If you are deeply concerned with the future welfare of your bulbs, you will take a keen interest in the ripening process, during which the bulbs are building up fresh strength. You will not be impatient for its completion but disappointed, rather, if foliage ripens too quickly, since the longer it stands straight and sturdy and green the finer will be the bulbs forming below. In fact, it will become a matter of pride for you to say, "My tulips are still green," when others confess that the foliage of theirs has long since gone by.

A certain amount of post-flowering-season sun on foliage is essential to the proper ripening of spring bulbs. Many trumpet daffodils, like King Alfred, must have full or nearly full sun. Other bulbs, like camassias and the poeticus daffodils, require less. A few, like the wood hyacinth and English bluebell, seem to ripen with very little sunlight at all and Holland growers raise snowdrops and chionodoxas in shady orchards because they do not flourish in sunny open fields.

Thousands of times I have been asked the question, "Why have my naturalized daffodils stopped blooming when I never cut foliage before it ripens?" Although overcrowding, under-nourishment or the effect of a too acid soil are possible causes, the usual reason is lack of sufficient ripening sunshine. Many gardeners mistakenly discount shade of trees since daffodils bloom before trees are fully in leaf. Actually it is the amount of warm June sun when they are ripening which counts.

To avoid progressive dwindling of bloom, plant in shade only those narcissus varieties, like Alcida and Yellow Poppy, which require little sun for adequate maturing. If you already have tree-shaded plantings of daffodils which produce lush foliage but no flowers you can recondition them for blooming. Dig up such clumps early in the spring. Separate them and transplant them to rows in a vegetable or cutting garden. Permit all foliage to remain so that the bulbs will benefit from the current season's ripening. Then if you will give the needed fall and spring fertilizing, you can expect blooms from most of them in two years. Of course, you will have to balance the cost of this procedure in time and space with the expense of replacing with new bulbs.

Portfolio
of
Spring and Summer
Bulbs
Alone
and
in Gardens

1. *Invitation to Spring*. Narcissi edged by lavender pansies and deep blue grape hyacinths follow a path winding up a slope.

2. *Pickets and Tulips.* Tulips with pansies make a charming May picture as they follow a fence line and border the foundation.

3. *Drifts of Daffodils.* Short-cupped narcissi, thickly colonized, lend April enchantment to this slope beneath a rock ledge.

4. *Tulips Rising from Blue Foam.* Darwins in light and dark shades of rose find the perfect foil in a carpet of blue forget-me-nots running along the top of a low wall.

5. *Study in Checks*. A life-size portrait of the guinea hen lily,
Fritillaria meleagris, reveals the fascination of an unfamiliar April
flower.

6. *Angel's Tears.* The miniature beauty of this gem, Narcissus triandrus albus, is here increased one and one-half times actual size.

7. *Impact of Color*. Wide beds of bright May tulips outlined with boxwood bring beauty to a garden enclosed by hemlocks.

8. *April Scene*. Yellow narcissi, happily naturalized, combine with boulder, trees and lawn in a beautiful spring setting.

9. *The Candystick Tulip*. Clusiana, the favorite species tulip, is brightly striped in red and white.

10. *Fragrant Appeal.* Blue and white hyacinths and pale Single Early tulips grow in formal beauty between flagstones and well.

11. *Boundary Beauty.* Where the lawn ends bleeding hearts, May-flowering tulips and Scilla campanulata are pleasantly colonized.

12. *Late Summer Elegance*. The Formosa lily, Lilium formosa-num, brings fresh loveliness to gardens waning in late August and September.

13. *Ephemeral and Exotic.* The Mexican shellflower, Tigridia pavonia, spends the beauty of each blossom in one day but generously gives successive bloom.

14. *Brilliance in Summer*. Gladioli bordering a walk make an effective outdoor display and yield many flowers for cutting.

15. *Bowl of Beauty*. Single and double tulips with anemones and other flowers of spring are charmingly arranged in a copper vase.

CHAPTER FIVE

The Question—To Lift or Leave

A NUMBER of factors govern the decision as to whether or not to lift bulbs. There is no problem, of course, so far as the naturalized bulbs or the little, early kinds like scillas, chionodoxas, snowdrops and crocuses are concerned. They are left in the ground. In fact, they need no spring cultivation, watering or any special attention except that care is taken not to mow down their foliage before it ripens.

Only the tulips, daffodils and hyacinths, planted in beds by themselves, or with perennials, are sometimes taken up over the summer. If you are a perfectionist, or a gardener with plenty of time, you may want to lift these for the sake of the bulbs, despite the extra work involved. When you do, wait until foliage has ripened but take them up while enough of the stalk is left to guide you to the bulb. If the day is bright, do not expose the bulbs to the sun for more than an hour. In many sections of the United States the climate is such that tulip skins will get brittle and break if left too long in the ground, so the bulbs may have to be dug while the foliage still shows some green. Each gardener will have to determine this by experiment.

After the bulbs have dried, wipe off the soil and the old skins and store the clean bulbs. Save all the new bulbs and offsets, the larger ones for replanting in garden locations and the smaller ones for a special bed or bulb nursery for growing on. If you give the little bulblets proper culture, they will grow into blooming sizes in one to three years and these, in turn, will produce offspring. Thus you can benefit from nature's reproductive bounty for your original purchased stock of bulbs will increase and multiply instead of diminish.

Storage over the summer is another problem. Bulbs should never be piled into a deep basket or box, but spread out in flats or shallow trays to permit circulation of air. It is better if these have wire mesh bottoms or slats just close enough to keep bulblets from falling through. If there are a great many bulbs, special shallow bins may be constructed.

Under ideal conditions the air should have the right amount of moisture content and the temperature of the brick or stone storehouse be kept between sixty and seventy degrees throughout the summer. In Holland, where June, July and August are cool and damp, the natural climate provides these conditions. In fact, Hollanders have to use artificial heat to raise the temperature to the high eighties in rooms where certain curing processes go on. In most parts of the United States air conditioning would be required during the summer months for the perfect storing of bulbs.

Needless to say the average gardener will not want to go to the trouble of digging and storing, although some may. Others may want to do it for a few rare and expensive bulbs from which they wish to save the increase. For storing just a few bulbs over the summer, rayon or nylon stockings make excellent containers. They may be hung on nails in a dry cellar.

Most gardeners find it more convenient to leave the majority of their bulbs in the ground where they take care not to damage them when cultivating the beds in summer. There are times, however, when it is necessary to move bulbs after they bloom for reasons other than the desire to follow the perfect technique. Often the space is wanted for annuals. Sometimes bulbs are removed for this purpose when it would not be really necessary. Seedlings can be set among bulb stalks, even between tulips whose leaves are touching, by carefully holding the foliage aside without breaking it.

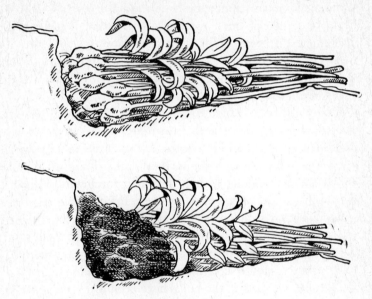

Tulips heeled in. Top: Plants placed in trench. Bottom:
Bulbs lightly covered with earth.

If you feel this is impossible, and want space for late spring planting, lift the bulbs as soon as they finish flowering, but remove seed pods. Raise the bulbs with exceeding care so that the plants will remain attached. Then heel them in in a trench with the foliage protruding, or place them in flats. The lower ends should be lightly covered with earth and the flats kept under high shade outdoors until the end of June. Bulbs so treated should be taken up and dried off during the latter half of June and stored for the rest of the summer.

There are other reasons for wanting to move bulbs. If growing conditions have been favorable, they will have made such an increase that every three or four years they will show signs of crowding. Or you may want changes in your garden, or wish to make room for new bulbs in the fall while saving old ones as a source of cut flowers. Do then what is obviously convenient. Lift your bulbs right after flowering and *transplant* them immediately either to the cutting bed or to their new garden location. Don't wait until fall—you will never find them then.

When bulbs are lifted for immediate transplanting, the stalk must be kept intact so that ripening foliage can continue to send strength down to the bulbs. If these have so increased that you actually dig up clumps, they should be separated so far as that can be done without breaking the plants. All the little bulblets and offsets can be saved for growing on, but if you have no suitable bed of rich soil to use as a bulb nursery, discard bulblets. They will take up valuable room and give you little or no return.

Whatever summer schedule you follow, when fall comes remember to fertilize. If the bulbs have been lifted and stored, dig in fertilizer before planting, as you did for new stock. If the bulbs have been left in the ground, spread plant food on top and rake it in lightly. The half-and-half mixture of superphosphate and Bovung you used for the original planting will be fine at double strength. You can overfertilize new top size bulbs but it is practically impossible to do so with their second year offspring. But no matter what you do, these smaller divisions will rarely produce quite as fine blooms as the new ones, so give them all the assistance you can.

With the fall fertilizing you will have completed a year's

cycle of spring-flowering bulb culture. The next spring you can again look forward to promising new shoots, but earlier this time from bulbs left in the ground. If your work has been well done, when flowering time comes you can say with pride, "Come, look at *my* tulips. Aren't they beautiful?"

CHAPTER SIX

How Deep to Plant

Much publicity has recently been given an old method of planting tulips for a long and fine-blooming future. This method is deep planting. The purpose of it is to prevent multiplicity of offspring.

When you plant a top size bulb under the ordinary four and one-half inch soil covering, it reproduces itself with, not one, but several new bulbs and usually a few offsets. The new bulbs, smaller than the parent, tend to produce smaller flowers, while the offsets rarely flower until the third year. In exceptional cases the progeny may consist entirely of seven or more little bulbs all below flowering size.

Tulips planted deep generally reproduce themselves with but one large bulb plus two or three offsets. You may have noticed that some of your tulips from a long-ago planted clump produce large flowers year after year. These have deeply planted themselves. You will discover this if you try to dig them up. Although you may have covered them with but four and a half inches of soil, they have worked their way down.

Deep planting, to be really effective, calls for a soil covering of nine to eleven inches, although some gardeners report excellent yearly bloom from bulbs covered only seven or eight inches. Although it is still new to most gardeners, deep planting has been successfully used for decades, perhaps longer, by some amateurs. If you wish to try it with some of your bulbs, do so with confidence, provided you meet the conditions the method requires.

To be safe for tulips the soil for deep planting must be rich, loose and, most important of all, well-drained for a full two feet. This involves considerable extra digging, since very few soils are naturally well-drained at such depths. If you are constructing a bed with this planting method in view, put the six-inch layer of hard, sifted coal ashes or other coarse material *three feet below the surface instead of two.* There must be plenty of rich soil beneath the tulips so that the roots will have at least six inches of good growing medium, the soil below the bulb being the most important part of the bed. If such digging is beyond you, avoid deep planting for it will almost certainly be ruinous to fine bulbs. Nor do I recommend deep planting for any kinds but tulips. Although many spring bulbs may work their way deeply into the ground when left by themselves, it would be rash to plant them there in the first place. Daffodils, for example, are likely to make poor, short-stemmed growth from plantings more than four inches under the surface particularly if soil is at all clayey. And if the bulb planted in clay does not make healthy growth the first year, better results cannot be expected thereafter.

It is obvious then that dealers cannot send out bulbs with indiscriminate instructions to plant them nine or ten inches deep since they might never see the light of day if the site were not adequately prepared. I recall the inexperienced gardener who asked me why three hundred top-sized tulips purchased from a reliable source had failed. No sign of leaf or sprout appeared on the bed which was of rather unimproved clay and somewhat sunken. Her gardener, she told me, had persuaded her to try deep planting. That clinched it. I explained to her that even at standard depth the best bulbs would have had a hard struggle but, deeply planted, they were gone for good. She smiled ruefully and said, "Well, my man was right in one way. He said if I planted bulbs eleven inches deep I could forget about them for eleven years."

Another advantage claimed for deep planting is that with the bulbs a foot underground you can safely cultivate above them with fork or spade. This is true only during the months that follow the ripening, for tulip foliage must be left to ripen just as long for the deeply planted bulb as for others. Caution in autumn and spring cultivating is also needed, since the sprouts of deeply set tulips reach the surface at about the same time as those from bulbs planted at standard depths.

In spite of the extra work involved in deep planting, you may wish to try it. After all, it is worth considerable original effort to have tulips come up year after year with nearly the same number and quality of flowers they produced the first spring. You might try deep planting, for example, in a place where you plan to grow begonias, geraniums or heliotrope in the summer. With this combination of bulb and bedding plants you can have May to November bloom. Space the bulbs at least six inches apart so that there will be room to place the seedlings of the summer plants between the still-green foliage of the tulips.

I once knew a gardener who for many years had tulips and cannas blooming successively in the same bed. Shortly after the tulips ceased flowering in May he planted canna roots among them. The tulip leaves ripened and disappeared before the cannas were very far above ground. Although these filled the bed with massive foliage and flowers, their spreading roots never interfered with tulips set eighteen inches below the surface! The cannas were lifted each fall for winter storage and spring replanting, but the deeply planted tulips remained in the ground for the six years that I knew this garden. I should hasten to add that this double-duty bed was perfectly drained and filled with loamy soil to a depth of more than three feet.

The very permanence of deep planting can be a disadvantage. Good gardening often requires change. If your tulips are deeply set, it will be onerous to move them as often as you want. Nor can you readily replace your old stock with better varieties. During World War II, with our main supply cut off, we had to use many outmoded varieties of which I thought we had long ago seen the last. I well remember one yellow variety we turned to in our extremity. It was Golden Crown, a shapeless bowl of mustard and cinnamon carried on a weak stem. I hate to think of anyone having to look at Golden Crown year after year simply because it was planted too deeply to warrant removal.

Another gardener solves this problem of permanence by compromise. His space for flowers consists chiefly of two long borders separated by a broad strip of sod. In the rear of these beds of rich soil and three-foot drainage are clumps of deeply planted tulips set among perennials. Groups of the dark purple Darwin, Black Eagle, are alternated with the white Darwin, Duke of Wellington, and the rose-blend Cottage, Marjorie Bowen. These have given good blooms for four years. The front tulip areas are saved for a wider range of varieties planted at standard depths to permit removal and change every three years.

This plan is probably the best one for an average gardener. Try it with a portion of your bulbs. Select varieties you think you would like to see for five or more consecutive years. Prepare the soil to the proper depth and plant the bulbs the required nine to eleven inches deep. Regard the matter as experimental both as to quality of first year blooms and of subsequent flowers. If your preparations are thorough, the experiment should be highly successful.

CHAPTER SEVEN

The Weather Plays a Part

No DISCUSSION of spring bulb growing would be complete without some reference to the weather. Obviously the gardener can do nothing about it, but he ought to know what to expect from its vagaries. Even at its worst he can appreciate it as an alibi which never lets him down.

Autumn throughout the United States is the best season. Practically all Europeans agree that our fall is superior to theirs. So far as bulb planting is concerned, the weather is usually favorable. There is enough rain to make the ground moist and crumbly while the brisk, invigorating air encourages the gardener to plant. Days of warm sunshine occur until quite late, keeping the earth warm enough to stimulate root growth.

Winter, no matter how cold, is never too severe for hardy bulbs. It is when bitter days come in March, after a mild season in January and February, that bulbs suffer. The flowers are seldom harmed but damage to advanced leaves is shown later in brown tips.

Spring is another matter. It has been said that Americans derive their notion of spring from English literature. Be that as it may, the European spring when each day the air is a little warmer, the earth a little greener, is not duplicated here. Our springs too often consist of alternate bursts of warmth and cold, with each warm spell a little hotter until suddenly, without transition, summer is upon us.

The way in which spring weather most obviously affects flowering is in the time of blooming. If you ever served on a garden club committee which had to choose a date for a daffodil or tulip show, you are well aware of this. Did you ever pick a date just right? I have known the flowering peak of certain varieties to vary a full month with the earliness or lateness of the spring. The season of 1944 was extraordinarily late, for example. I know one gardener who opened her garden of daffodils to visiting club members that spring. The date set was April twenty-eighth which, for this garden, would have been several days past its normal height of bloom. Actually on that day only one flower was in blossom, all the others still in green bud. The next year the weather reversed itself with an incredibly early spring and in this garden by the end of April there was hardly a daffodil left.

Early seasons are generally longer. The earliest warm spells which bring on bloom are usually not so hot as to hasten maturity, and they are apt to be interrupted by cool spells while the flower is still young. Cool weather while the flower is in blossom delays maturity and thus prolongs life. When the weather in the early part of the season is so cold that buds do not open, the succeeding warm spell is likely to be as hot as it is late, forcing bloom while stems are still short and rapidly aging the flower. If extremely hot weather continues, it will cause a shorter blooming span. Thus it is that in certain years a variety may stay in flower for three weeks while in others its bloom may last but eight or nine days. In any case I have never known a season so unfavorable that spring-flowering bulbs well cared for did not open to full perfection for at least a brief period.

Vagaries of weather are also responsible for variations in

color from one season to the next. This is particularly noticeable among red-cupped daffodils. Varieties like Francisca
Drake, Dick Wellband and Damson have much more red
in their cups in a moist, dull season while under cloudless
skies their crowns are so little colored that sometimes you
wonder if the bulbs can be true to name. Sometimes gardeners
believe they have stumbled on a particularly choice, or poor,
bit of soil for certain kinds, only to discover the next year
that it was the weather of the previous season which accounted for the abnormal presence, or absence, of color.

You cannot control the weather, but there are some things
you can do to offset its unfavorable aspects. Early spring
cultivating facilitates sturdy growth and quicker and longer
flowering. Then, if April rains are lacking, you can water your
tulips and daffodils. Any spray from the garden hose is sufficient so long as you do not knock down stalks with too heavy
a stream or spatter blossoms in the glare of the sun. You need
not be concerned about even watering or fearful of encourag-
ing shallow roots. Thorough watering in a very dry season
sometimes lengthens the blooming time of tulips by as much
as a week.

Also, for longer blooming, select a site for your bulbs with
some protection from full sunshine. Sun half the day is better
than all day, and morning sun better than afternoon. Bulbs
set in the partial shade of the house or under the shadow of
high-branching trees far enough away for their roots not to
interfere will have the benefit of protection from hot sun.

The best way to insure a long spring season from bulbs regardless of weather is to broaden your selection to include
genera which bloom at different times. Then choose several
varieties within each genus so that you may get the most
bloom through the season. Start the year with snowdrops,
chionodoxas, crocuses and hyacinths. Add early, midseason

and late varieties of both daffodils and tulips. Plantings can be made of the same variety under different conditions. Place some in full sun, others in partial shade; some at a southern exposure, others to the north.

Watch, also, the post-flowering-season weather, for it has an important bearing on your future bulb crop. A cool moist month after blooming prolongs ripening and sends increased strength down to the bulbs. A prolonged hot, dry spell practically burns up tulip foliage. While you may think this early disappearance convenient at the time, it is a poor augury for next spring's bloom. When watering your garden during late May or early June dry spells, do not neglect the areas where bulb foliage is ripening. Excessive wetness is not good either. If rainy stretches follow flowering, they will test your previous provisions for drainage. There is little you can do during wet weather except keep the bed surfaces free of leaves or dead foliage.

It pays to be weather conscious. Then you know what to expect and how to explain changes in time, height and coloration of flowers. But never worry about the weather. If you plant a wide range of bulbs in varied locations and take care of them you can expect fine blooms.

CHAPTER EIGHT

Bulb Enemies Outwitted

SPRING-FLOWERING bulbs are subject to parasites and diseases which occasionally present a problem to the commercial grower. It is a problem which can be solved by prevention or quick eradication. Indeed, it is accurate to say that wherever commercial propagation is successfully carried on disease-free stock is the rule and so excellent is inspection that affected bulbs practically never enter the market.

Happily for the amateur, spring-flowering bulbs are rarely affected by disease in his garden. Indeed, if you grew nothing else, you would have little use for insecticides or sprayer. Continued freedom from disease for originally sound stock is further insured by observing a few simple precautions:

1. Discard new bulbs which have soft areas.

2. Examine new shoots before the first spring cultivating. Brown-tipped leaves indicate nothing more than frost damage. Remove immediately any plants with withered, stunted growth, or any with sickly brown or blue foliage. Lift such bulbs with a little of the surrounding soil. Destroy the whole plant and discard the soil. Let no sentimental hope stay your hand. Just as colds attack tired humans, parasites and microbes fasten on weak plants. Here they start the diseases which infect healthy specimens.

3. Practice principles of sanitation. Keep the surface of the

bed clean and free from decaying bits of foliage. Avoid planting so thickly that sun and air cannot penetrate.

Daffodil enemies include the narcissus nematodes which cause the so-called eel worm disease. Although serious it is kept under such strict control by growers that it has all but disappeared. I have observed millions of daffodils growing in gardens but have never seen any which could definitely be considered affected by the eel worm disease. It is famous however because it was the reason given for the ban against importing narcissi which was enforced from 1926 to 1939.

Basal rot presents a more serious problem. This appears as a brown discoloration near the base of the bulb. Unchecked, it spreads until the bulb is rotted. It most frequently appears among bi-color trumpet varieties of narcissi. Growers control basal rot by ensuring perfect drainage in the fields and by destroying affected bulbs. Amateurs should examine the root bases of new bulbs for evidence of rot and destroy any obviously diseased. Bulbs which seem perfectly hard in September will sometimes start to go soft if kept out of the ground too long. The surest means of avoiding this is to plant the bulbs promptly on arrival.

Tulip fire or botrytis blight is the most serious affliction of these flowers. This is a fungous disease causing stem lesions and decay of leaves followed by a general withering of the plant. Once started in a thick field of tulips it can quickly spread over a large area. Hence comes its name, and hence the watchfulness of commercial growers to prevent it and to stamp it out at its first appearance. In all my experience, I have known only six private gardens where botrytis caused tulip failure. I suspect it occurs, however, in many places but is limited to so few plants that it may not be evident to the gardener. Moist air and a moist ground surface, such as is provided by a warm winter mulch, are ideal, in fact almost requirements, for the spread of this disease. The gardener whose bed surfaces are clean and dry need give it little thought.

When tulip fire occurs, spores survive on bulbs and in soil. Evidently it works itself out of the soil in several years. Holland growers never plant tulips in the same field oftener than every four years, a practice naturally impossible for the amateur limited to the same garden beds. Gardeners used to be advised when this infestation occurred to change their soil or not to plant tulips for four years. Now, a product called Brassicol may be depended upon for disinfection. All plants are removed from the affected area and Brassicol is dug in three weeks before autumn planting at the rate of one ounce per ten square feet. Old or new bulbs may then be planted with expectation of health the following spring.

Perhaps I should emphasize the fact that general freedom from disease and pests may be expected only from the spring-flowering bulbs. Lilies and gladioli have frequent troubles. These will be discussed in the chapters dealing with these flowers.

Far more dangerous than invisible microbes are the enemies of bulbs which scurry about on four feet. Moles, mice, rabbits, chipmunks and squirrels account for more depredations than all diseases and parasites put together. In suburban or rural areas where these animals abound they sometimes become so serious a menace that pusillanimous gardeners give up growing certain bulbs. Fortunately one big genus is exempt—the narcissus. Daffodil bulbs are poisonous, or at least inedible, so the predatory quadrupeds leave them alone.

Moles tunnel under the ground and mice find their passageways an easy means of reaching succulent bulbs. Tulips are a favorite delicacy of mice. They enjoy lilies too, but most lilies are planted too deeply for convenient access. Mice can completely clean out a tulip bed without your being aware of their nefarious work. Chipmunks eat crocuses and also tulips but they dig a hole for each bulb so that you see what goes on. Squirrels seldom bother anything but crocuses, which they find tastier than nuts. Rabbits chew fresh and tender crocus leaves and tulip sprouts when these first appear—and so do deer. Deer seldom destroy the tulip flower, but chewed leaves are unattractive and also able to manufacture less food for developing bulbs.

The mole-mice combination does the most damage and the best way to combat this team is to go after the makers of tunnels—moles. Most advertised methods of mole destruction are effective. These include setting traps or putting tablets in the runs to release poisonous gas. When they do not succeed it is usually because the gardener lacks persistence. It is not enough to catch one mole in a trap or put a few tablets in one or two runs. Follow up the runs every day for a week, especially in areas near the tulip beds. Then if they seem to have disappeared, look out for new runs. Moles will not use a run once it has been disturbed, but they have main runs and branches and it is the main run you must get in order to discourage them thoroughly. Slapping the runs with a fork or a stick is better than nothing—but not much better. Some gardeners have reported success through flooding the runs with water from the garden hose.

Fighting moles has brought varied experiences to gardeners. Sometimes you can catch them as you come upon them burrowing their way along under the sod. The technique is to drive a stick quickly down in the run right back of the spot where the mole is evidently working. Drive another just ahead of him. You can then spear him with a fork or sharp stick. This horrifies some gardeners; others harassed beyond pity derive satisfaction from the act. A friend of mine with several acres of mole-ridden ground was once told that if she scattered a barrel of fishheads around the place the moles would leave. She did so. The moles remained. The family took a brief vacation.

If you feel that you cannot cope with mice and moles, you can still grow tulips by planting them in home-made wire baskets. Small mesh wire should be used. When planting be sure the sides of the basket come up to the surface of the bed. Gardeners have also reported successful protection from mice by burying large handfuls of naphtha flakes around the bulb clumps.

As for rabbits, chipmunks and squirrels which operate from above, human activity is the best protection. It simply drives them away. That is why you will seldom find them disturbing bulbs planted close to the house. To protect bulbs beyond the immediate field of your movements you will have to take special measures. A couple of small terriers can be very discouraging to the little rodents. A couple of small boys are better.

If you have neither dogs nor boys, go to it yourself. Try to clear out the nests of rabbits and chipmunks. Of course success in ridding your garden of enemies depends on the attitude of your neighbors. If they are soft, you are lost! But eventually suburban communities may change the foolish laws which now protect such nuisances.

Not all things hostile to bulbs are animal or mineral. You must guard against plant rivals too. The encroaching roots of such sturdy perennials as phlox and peony must be checked and such rampant root-makers as iris and daylilies need to be hacked into submission since they have an insatiable appetite for garden space. Adequate pruning of shrubs is necessary, too, to keep bulbs planted near them from being smothered.

Trees can be another problem. When houses are built in woodland, too many trees are often left standing. Tall and magnificent though they be, there are sometimes too many not only for bulbs or the garden generally, but also for the house and the people in it. Man cannot make a tree but he can cut it down when it shuts out necessary sun and air. Or perhaps he need only saw off some of the lower limbs—a fair compromise.

Perhaps the present excessive American awe of trees is atonement for the disregard of past generations. I remember a teacher inculcating love of trees in her pupils. I recall the scorn in her voice as she read, "It didn't bear, so I cut it down." These words were supposed to have been uttered by a skinflint farmer, whose trees had to produce or become firewood, no matter how artistic were the gnarled branches. It was our teacher's pious hope that we children would not grow up so indifferent to beauty. Nowadays garden lovers know that sick trees must be doctored or cut down for the good of their companions, and healthy ones must be judged by the good they do and the beauty they give.

I should quickly say I advocate no indiscriminate cutting down of trees, even if they do occasionally cast too much shade. In most places, perhaps, there are still too few. But in all the gardens I have visited, I have never known a single tree to be cut down unnecessarily. I can think of hundreds left standing whose owners would be better off without them.

CHAPTER NINE

Your Tulips—How to Know Them

A HOLLANDER once said to me, "You Americans are so fond of the tulip, you ought to make it your national flower." Whether we would want to go as far as that is a question, but certainly tulips are flowers which arouse tremendous enthusiasm. Indeed, about half of all spring-flowering bulbs sold annually are tulips.

Tulips always give pleasure but when planted in named varieties they provide ten times more enjoyment than if set out in mixture. Knowing the name of each variety you grow also adds to your interest in it. Considerable confusion exists among gardeners regarding classes of tulips. They know there are Darwin, Breeder and other categories, but are not sure exactly what these names mean. Catalogues add to the confusion with their lack of uniformity. Registered names are, of course, adhered to, but varieties are classed differently by dealers. Thus Yellow Giant has always been sold under that name but sometimes it is catalogued as a Cottage tulip, sometimes as a Darwin.

The background of the present classifications of tulips lies in their history. As flowers go, this history is not ancient. Tulips only came into western European gardens in the latter half of the sixteenth century. Since that time they have not only furnished beauty, but exciting moments in commerce and politics, too.

Busbequius, a Viennese ambassador to Turkey, was the first European on record to introduce them to Europe. He admired them in Turkish gardens where they had been cultivated for many years, originally having been brought there from Persia. The name, tulip, probably comes from the word dulban or toliban, meaning turban, since the shape of the bloom suggests an inverted turban. Flowers grown from seed sent back by Busbequius were so pleasing in Vienna that seed and bulbs were soon sent to all parts of Europe.

The botanist Clusius of Leyden was one of the earliest European growers. He developed a collection which he proudly displayed to his fellow townsmen. He also offered bulbs for sale at very high prices. Whether he sold any or not is a question. According to some accounts his neighbors refused to pay the excessive price Clusius asked and stole the bulbs from his garden instead.

In any case countrymen of Clusius in the 1590's somehow acquired stock and commenced the tulip growing which is such an important industry in Holland. From the very beginning tulips became collectors' items. Rich men paid high prices for bulbs of the new flower. Speculation surged until it reached a peak during the famous tulipomania of 1634 to 1637. During this period men dropped everything to speculate in tulips. It was not uncommon for thousands of dollars, or fortunes in land, stock and houses, to be exchanged for a single bulb of a new variety. People mortgaged their homes to invest in stock of companies formed to control one or more bulbs. They speculated in varieties not yet planted or still in the seedling stage.

If these fantastic prices were paid to acquire beauty they might seem comprehensible to tulip lovers of today. Adorable,

Glacier, Indian Chief, Mayflower, Treasure Island and a host of other new and old varieties possess such loveliness that too high a price could scarcely be set on them. But, alas, in the tulipomania, buyers were not seeking beauty. They were hoping for quick profits through resale of the bulbs at still higher figures. Like all speculative bubbles this one collapsed, bringing not riches, but ruin to the hapless investors.

It may surprise modern gardeners to learn that the tulips for which people once paid fortunes were kinds now little grown or appreciated. The tulips sought in the 1600's were not the self-colored Darwins or Breeders of present day favor, but the broken sorts known as Rose and Violet Bybloemens and Bizarres. These are rose, scarlet, purple or brown, feathered and flamed on a background of white or yellow.

Broken tulips cannot be produced by seed. Seedlings are not always uniform, often being blends of two colors, but they never are broken. Something is needed for a self-color to break. Modern scientists claim that it is always the virus disease, mosaic, which causes this breaking. Dutch growers maintain that while certain Bybloemen and Bizarre tulips are mosaic-infected, others are not.

Be that as it may, if a red tulip in your garden comes up some year with a patchwork blend of red and white, it has acquired mosaic. Henceforth this bulb and each of its progeny will produce broken flowers in the identical new pattern. Others of the same clump will also be likely to change color, each with a similar but slightly different combination and each a new variety capable of indefinite future propagation through bulb offspring.

Some gardeners allow tulip mosaic to continue when it occurs in their plantings, rather liking the new broken flowers. The disease does not kill the bulbs, although the new "broken" blossoms tend to be smaller and shorter-stemmed than the self-colored originals. Personally, I dislike these feathered tulips and so check mosaic whenever it appears by removing the affected plant and bulb immediately. I have never had to do more than this. Sometimes, to stop a breaking process which has gone unhindered for several years, it is necessary to lift the whole clump and change soil before planting tulips in the same place.

Whatever his ignorance of the actual cause, the older grower knew that in order to induce his self-colored tulips to break he had to plant them near others which had broken or else in the same soil. He needed stock of the plain varieties as "breeders," to plant with the hope that they would be transformed into the much desired broken tulips. He also raised seedlings so that they would in turn produce feathered and flamed kinds of ever newer design.

In time, some of the self-colored breeding tulips became popular and were grown and sold for their own sake. Particularly favored were the rich purple, mahogany and bronze shades. These were the direct ancestors of the modern class of tulips known as Breeder, whose present representatives include such varieties as Autumn Glow, Dixie Sunshine, Indian Chief and Simon Bolivar.

Darwin tulips also have their origin in the plain colored varieties kept by Dutch growers for breeding. Darwins were introduced as a new race by the great bulb nurseryman, E. H. Krelage, of Haarlem in 1887. Some time prior Krelage secured a collection of seedlings developed by a Flemish grower from a particularly fine strain of breeders. After growing them for some years, and making further improvements, he selected and named the best varieties which he then offered in commerce under the group name, Darwin.

The new Darwin varieties immediately caught on. So popular are their descendants that a large section of the garden-

ing public today mistakenly applies the word Darwin to any
tall May-flowering tulip. The Krelage introductions had tall,
fairly slender stems and large cup-shaped flowers with petals
squared off at the top. They were uniformly colored in tones
of red or rose, purple or lavender. Each had an inside base of
blue.

Other hybridizers bought stocks of these varieties and
raised new seedlings so that Darwins today are many generations improved over the originals. But for years all new varieties registered in this class retained the form and color range
of the first ones. Since the 1920's, however, new white and
yellow tulips have been assigned to this class because they
have the characteristic form. A large group of new kinds containing white and yellow as well as rose, red, lavender and
purple shades were offered as Ideal Darwins by a firm of
hybridizers who felt that they embraced so many fine new
color tones as to deserve a separate category. Some retail catalogues still list varieties in this group although it has not won
universal recognition as a separate class. Probably it is better
in the interests of simplification for all the tulips in this division to be thought of merely as Darwins. The cherry Pride of
Haarlem and the rose Princess Elizabeth are examples of
Darwin tulips of the original color range. The white Glacier
and the yellow Niphetos are newer shades.

A third classification, the Cottage, came into the hands of
modern Dutch nurserymen by way of England. The tulip
craze of the sixteenth century had spread to that country also.
There it was likewise the broken tulips for which wealthy
fanciers paid enormous prices. Indeed, violent controversy
flared up at one time over what degree of feathering and
flaming was required before a tulip could be considered beautiful. The plain breeders were kept only for propagation.

Many passed into the hands of poorer folk in whose cottage gardens they were grown for generations.

Many of these old varieties were being gathered from English gardens by the British nurseryman, Peter Barr, and from Irish gardens by W. B. Hartland at the same time Krelage was developing his Darwins. Later these English and Irish kinds were introduced to commerce as Cottage tulips. The first members of this class and their later successors were whites, yellows, pinks and reds or beautiful blends of rose and amber. The stems of the earliest Cottage tulips, while tall, were a little shorter than the typical Darwin, but the later hybrids which belong to this class are tall, often reaching thirty inches. Inglescombe Yellow and the rose-blend John Ruskin are examples of older Cottage varieties. The white Mount Erebus and the crimson Mayflower are two of the newer hybrids.

Certain Cottage tulips, hybrid descendants of the variety, Retroflexa, have long, pointed and markedly reflexed petals. They are often listed separately as a subdivision of Cottage tulips and are called Lily-flowering. The garnet Captain Fryatt and the light yellow Fascinating are examples of this type.

There is today more public confusion about Cottage tulips than any other class. Many gardeners mistake these tall, late varieties for the really short, early-flowering kinds like Keiserskroon and Lady Boreel which belong to the class whose only correct name is Single Early. I have always suspected this confusion persists because the word "cottage" suggests something small. If these same tulips had only been collected from "palace" gardens and named accordingly, I doubt if there would have been any misunderstanding.

Misinformation on this point can be a real problem. Gardeners sometimes turn down giant hybrid tulips, correctly listed as Cottage, saying "No, I want only the tall Darwins." I have had long distance telephone calls from gardeners who, on receiving new bulbs, protested, "I bought *tall* tulips. The label on the bag says they are *Cottage*. What shall I do?"

Some try to avoid the problem of the Cottage tulips by classifying them as May-flowering. This, it seems to me, is deplorable, since the term applies to all the kinds which flower in May and is valuable as a name designating a number of classes of which Cottage is only one. The only thing to do is to adhere to correct terminology and trust to the gradual spread of accurate information.

Tulip classification is further complicated by growers who practice occasional introduction of new varieties under trade class names for promotion. These designations are not official but they find their way into catalogues to add to the confusion of gardeners. The whole problem could well be given attention by those interested in the flower. Perhaps a committee representing horticultural societies, dealers and growers could draw up classifications which would be universally accepted. A not too complex system, generally adopted and adhered to, would be a boon to both sellers and buyers of tulips.

When you are familiar with the genesis of the modern categories of Breeder, Darwin and Cottage tulips, it is still not easy to classify these tulips on sight. Generally speaking, the Breeders have tall, stout, stiff stems. Orange, bronze and purple-bronze tones predominate. There are no white Breeders. Pink Pearl and Yellow Perfection, unattractive varieties both, seem happily to have passed into oblivion leaving the class without representation in those colors. However, many of the pale bronzes like Tantalus and Golden Buff have a good deal of yellow overlaid with lavender and there are new varieties like Katherine Thruxton with definite pink tones. An orange tulip like Simon Bolivar or a bronze like Autumn Glow could never be anything but a Breeder.

The tall, thin stem and cup-shaped flower is still characteristic of the Darwin. Reds, rose tones, purples and lavenders predominate, although the class now contains varieties of every tulip color but bronze. If a tall, red tulip discloses a bright blue base with purple anthers when you peer inside, you may be sure it is a Darwin, possibly Eclipse. If it has a white base with light yellow anthers it is certainly a Cottage, perhaps G. W. Leak.

The petals of Cottage tulips are generally long and pointed. The stems are thin and their average length is a little less than that of Darwins and Breeders, although there are many exceptions such as Vesta, Dido and Marjorie Bowen, all taller than the usual Darwin or Breeder. Most of the good yellows, like Mrs. John T. Scheepers and Golden Duchess, still belong to this class or to its Lily-flowering subdivision. Whites, pinks, flaming scarlets and blends of buff, apricot and rose abound in the Cottage division. The apricot-orange Good Gracious and the rose and amber Astor are examples of Cottage and Lily-flowering blends. There are no lavender, purple or bronze varieties in this class.

There are other classes of May-flowering tulips to be found in catalogues, besides the Breeders, Cottages and Darwins which constitute ninety per cent of single late varieties sold in this country. Broken Breeders are still sold in modern kinds as Bybloemens and Bizarres, while the flamed and feathered Darwins are classed as Rembrandts. Broken Cottage tulips are simply listed under that name. Then there are the Parrot tulips.

Parrot tulips are also the result of a sudden physiological change, not breaking this time, but sporting. Again the newly changed individual will produce bulb offspring—but not seed-lings—each with the identical color pattern of its altered parent. Parrot tulips have long, laciniated petals, exotic markings and usually a green sheen on the outer petals. Some varieties, such as Fantasy, the sport of Darwin tulip, Clara Butt, have been grown commercially in tremendous quantities. Not all are May-flowering; Gemma, for example, being a sport of Single Early, La Reine, flowers in late April. But most Parrots saved for commerce are sports of May-blooming varieties so that it is reasonable to include this division among kinds which flower then.

Dutch growers love to gamble with Parrots. They often pay a big price for one or two bulbs. If they pick a winner which turns out to be both a good grower and a public favorite, returns are large. Of course, few Parrots have a career like Fantasy. Sporting is rare, only an occasional individual tulip out of millions of the same variety will do it. But it can occur anywhere, in the fields of Holland, in a park planting or in your garden.

Besides the tall late varieties, early short-stemmed tulips are grown today, as they have been ever since their introduction to western Europe. Indeed, the Turks preferred the Single Early kinds to the taller ones, although in Europe and America it has been the long-stemmed May tulips which drew most attention from both gardeners and hybridizers. Large, bright colored flowers with stocky stems of ten to sixteen inches are characteristic of modern Early tulips. Bright yellow Rising Sun, orange De Wet, crimson Couleur Cardinal and the old vivid red with yellow border, Keiserskroon, are typical.

Two new and similar classes of tulips have been developed during the twentieth century. Mendel tulips are the result of crossing May-flowering varieties with hybrids of the Single Early Duc Van Thol. Triumph tulips are crosses between

May-flowering kinds and other Single Earlies. Both Mendels and Triumphs flower somewhat later than the Earlies but a little before the Breeder, Cottage and Darwin kinds. Both are taller than the Earlies and shorter than the May-flowering, with stems averaging twenty inches. Mendel tulips are used mainly for forcing. The Triumphs, with the bright tones of their Single Early parents, include such garden favorites as Lord Carnarvon, Dembola and Johanna.

Double forms of the different classes have been grown continuously from the early days of tulip culture, although they play a minor role compared to singles. Double Earlies are bright colored favorites for bedding and for pot plants. Murillo, Peach Blossom, Vuurbaak and Schoonoord are all familiar. Double Triumphs and double varieties of the May-flowering tulips are also grown. Both are frequently listed as Double Late. New varieties of these later flowering doubles have been developed by hybridizers and are becoming so popular that the class as a whole is playing a larger part in May gardens. Wine-colored Uncle Tom and orange Avondzon are examples of Double Triumphs, while soft rose Eros and snowy Mt. Tacoma are two of the Double May-flowering tulips.

All of the foregoing are sometimes called "Garden Tulips," to distinguish them from tulips found growing wild in Asia and Europe. These are known as Species Tulips, Botanical Tulips or simply as Tulipas. Actually, so far as their use is concerned, some of the Species, like kaufmannia and fosteriana, are just as much "garden" tulips as any others. But while other tulips are hybrid descendants of an unknown species ancestor, each distinctive wild tulip is a species in itself. Sometimes a species will occur in different forms to which varietal names are given. Thus we have Tulipa Kaufmanniana, Brilliant and Aurea, as well as the type.

To summarize, here is a chart of the various tulip classes arranged chronologically according to blooming times:

April-flowering (April 15–30 for New York Latitude)
   Single Early
   Double Early

Late April-flowering (April 20–May 5 for New York Latitude)
   Mendel
   Triumph
   Double Triumph

May-flowering (May 5–25 for New York Latitude)

Self-colored Varieties	*Broken Varieties*
	Rose Bybloemen
Breeder	Violet Bybloemen
	Bizarre
Cottage	Broken Cottage
Lily-flowering	
Darwin	Rembrandt
Double May-flowering	
Parrot	

Species Tulips (April 1–May 25 for New York Latitude)

CHAPTER TEN

May-flowering Tulips—
Glory of Spring

"I wonder often what the Vintners buy
One half so precious as the stuff they sell."

PERHAPS Omar Khayyam was right. Perhaps he gave no more than its due to the beverage he so often praised. But with what a finer sense of value could he have written lines on the intoxicating loveliness of tulips blossoming in May. Surely the beauty of these majestic flowers with their vibrant colors provides more lasting exhilaration than the quaffing of the finest wines of Arabia.

The spring pageant reaches its climax with the blooming of Breeder, Cottage and Darwin tulips. If you have only a square yard of soil in which to grow them, they should not be overlooked. When these flowers are in season your garden can be at its most colorful peak. In every color but blue, in every tone from blazing scarlet to the subtlest blush of rose, they display their loveliness.

Preferences in colors and shades are personal but individual tastes are influenced by trends. Some years ago there was a vogue for pale tulips. The reds, oranges, bright yellow and rose tones were banished. You were a vulgar fellow if you

suggested them. Each garden maker seemed bent on achiev-
ing a color symphony entirely pianissimo. Whenever I en-
tered one of these pallid creations, it always reminded me of
the interior of Grant's Tomb, so cool for a hot summer day, so
unexciting on a fresh spring morning. The brightly colored
birds flying across the lawn seemed out of harmony.

Happily this penchant for color anemia seems to have run
its course. Gardeners now follow the natural human longing
for brightness after winter's brown and gray. They derive
special pleasure from a tulip planting in which vivid varieties
bloom in contrast to the pale ones. They like to see a pale yellow like Niphetos next to the deeper Golden Age and the
light blush of Dresden China with the warm, wine-rose of
Margaux.

You will find that dark varieties like the purple Black
Eagle and Mark Anthony, the mahogany Indian Chief and
the bronze Autumn Glow set off bright tulips, and that it pays
to use plenty of whites. They are vivid in themselves, yet
provide relief and contrast for other bright colors. Above all,
never deny your husband's passion for red, or your own secret
yearning for it. The tulip kingdom is bursting with glorious
varieties of scarlet, rose-red, cherry and wine. Surely one or
more of them will fit into your garden. If not, make a separate
planting. I shall never forget the sight of a large pool of deep
red Eclipse beneath the soft rose blossoms of a Bechtels flowering crab apple tree, or of a colony of the deep rose Eggink's
Ideal backed by the bright green foliage of an espaliered
pyracantha.

Your home probably provides many excellent locations for
the tall tulips though you may have no formal garden. Plant
them for a feast of May color in a bed by the side of the house
where there is full morning or afternoon sun. Group them
in indentations made by the foundation planting or shrubbery

border. Arrange clumps of bright-hued varieties by a white picket fence, or soft colored kinds along a privet hedge, but with the bulbs planted at least twelve inches away from the privet roots.

Tulips always look well at the foot of a stone wall. They are equally charming in a bed at its top. If no background exists, let them rise from a foam of blue forget-me-nots thickly interplanted among their stalks.

A single line of tulips marching up the path or drive which leads from the sidewalk to your front door is not effective. Flank such paths with borders wide enough to permit plantings in repeated groups of your favorite varieties and you will have a fine display. Set seedlings of annuals among the individual tulips as their flowers fade to provide succeeding summer blossoms.

May tulips often bring beauty to areas seemingly unsuitable for any kind of garden. One small Manhattan backyard enclosed on three sides by a five foot wall, whose rear section faces north, is lovely every spring. The sun climbs over the barrier in sufficient strength to encourage tulips planted along each wall. The white Cottage Carrara and soft primrose Arethusa are there combined in pleasing harmony with the Darwins, Golden Age and Blue Perfection. Annual Impatiens holstii fills the beds with summer foliage and flowers.

Another gardener, away during the summer months, uses her space for a crescendo of bloom in spring and fall. At the rear of the house is a rectangular stone terrace porch. A fifty-foot border six feet deep stretches from one corner to form a right angle with the terrace edge. Backed by a yew hedge and bisected into two twenty-five foot sections by a strip of lawn, it can be seen in full perspective from the porch.

In this border May-flowering tulips display their full charm and beauty each spring. Down its length are planted repeated colonies of the mahogany Indian Chief and the lavender Georges Grappe, both Breeders, the salmon-orange Cottage, Good Gracious, and the creamy yellow Darwin, Niphetos. Forget-me-nots and coralbells are planted in front of the tulip groups, while to their rear foxgloves add variety of form and color.

After the tulips bloom, this border carries on through the first week of June, with clumps of German and Siberian iris providing the centers of interest. In the background are on-coming plants of hardy asters. These, with wide strips of chrysanthemums down the center and small groups of the late formosanum lily, furnish another floral peak in autumn.

Formal gardens are always resplendent in May when tulips are featured. I know one where they are planted in sufficient quantities to be effective, yet they cover only a limited portion of the beds. Here is achieved that elusive goal—continuous bloom from spring to fall. In May much of the garden space is covered by the early green foliage of later blooming peren-nials.

In design and planting this large garden is a pleasant combination of the informal and the formal. Rectangular in shape, it is enclosed on the front and sides by a vine-clad balustrade. In the rear a low myrtle-covered bank, naturalized with montbretia and Narcissus triandrus, Thalia, slopes up to a hedge of hemlocks. The balustrade is broken in the front by the garden entrance which is approached by a short flight of wide stone steps.

At either end of this garden two long beds face each other across a middle strip of lawn. In the center of each is a wide-spreading clump of bleedingheart with colonies of the soft rose Darwin, Caroline Testout, and the deeper blush Darwin, Adorable, on opposite sides. A planting of the creamy white

Glacier, of the same class, is charming at the inside corners of these beds.

The middle section of this garden, on a lower level, consists of four beds focused around a sun dial set in a center circle of lawn. In these colorful groups of tall tulips are placed behind edging plants of myosotis and pansies. The dark rose Darwin, Margaux, contrasts with the soft pink Darwin, Van Zyl. Cottage varieties, Golden Harvest, a lemon yellow, and Mimosa, cream with a brushing of rose, are grouped with the violet Darwin, Madame Butterfly. Dwarf iris and hardy candytuft at the corners, Phlox divaricata and Anchusa myosotidiflora a little to the interior of the beds pleasantly associate their flowers with the tulips. From late May on perennials take over with their colorful blossoms, each in its season, while portions of the tulip areas not covered by the spreading foliage of these plants are filled with petunias and the white miniature dahlia, Helly Boudweijn.

May-flowering tulips are best planted where their beauty is enhanced by association with other plants. In the border they are lovely with such early perennials as Anchusa myosotidiflora, Phlox divaricata, columbines, coralbells and foxgloves. Foreground plantings or low interplantings are also effective. For this purpose pansies are ideal, either in separate colors to combine with each tulip variety, or in one variety to accent a general color scheme. I have found the blue-purple pansy, Lord Beaconsfield, a particularly admirable foil for tulips in soft shades and blends. Both annual and perennial forget-me-nots are also excellent as a general foreplanting with all varieties of tulips.

When tulips are planted in a long border or bed especially made for them, a scallop design is attractive with groups of them on the outward curves and Scilla campanulata filling the indentions. White scillas make a pleasing contrast for such red tulips as Charles Needham, Scarlet Beauty, Mazeppa and G. W. Leak. Blue scillas combine with practically any shade but are especially effective with rose varieties like Caroline Testout, Adorable, Mayflower and Pride of Zwanenberg.

Foreground plants selected for edgings should be so used that they do not overplay their part. Modest flowers like forget-me-nots never usurp attention, but the bold blossoms of ageratums and the profuse blooms of pansies occasionally try to play the stellar role. I remember an allée with long borders filled with pale-hued tulips and edged with ageratums. The ageratums seized your eyes and made them race down parallel tracks of dazzling blue before you could so much as glance at a tulip.

I know from experience how distracting these edging plants can sometimes be. Occasionally a visitor's first remark on the sight of one of my tulip beds would be, "What stunning pansies! Where did you get them?" Whenever this happened you may be sure the pansies were promptly thinned out or their blossoms heavily picked.

In creating tulip compositions for your own gardens, do not be bound by class divisions. Choose varieties for color, height, size and flowering quality, regardless of whether they are Breeder, Cottage or Darwin. It may happen that all the kinds you prefer for a given season belong to one class, although usually they are drawn from all three. One of my favorite combinations includes the tall mahogany Breeder, Indian Chief, planted as a background for groups of the soft rose Darwin, Mr. Van Zyl, and the primrose yellow Cottage, Mongolia.

To describe May-flowering tulips adequately is always difficult. For the tulip seldom holds its blossom like a single-colored torch of purple, pink or yellow. Each bloom is a two or three weeks drama of unfolding beauty in color and form. To tell its story properly would require a paragraph or a page. To keep a catalogue from running into hundreds of pages we use brief terms like "rose, edged silver," or "yellow with cream stripe." But these are merely code words barely hinting at the loveliness of each flower.

You who have grown them are familiar with the fascinating way in which tulips change during their blossoming. You may have watched the Lily-flowering Captain Fryatt, for example, from the time it begins to show color at the tips of its long, green bud. Will it be purple or red, you wonder. Slowly the color spreads. Beet red, you decide. Then the tone deepens to rich garnet as the petals open in expanding glory.

You may also have been entranced by the spell of Cottage tulip, Mayflower. The outer petals open crimson and slowly take on an ashy bloom. The inside opens salmon, turns rose, then brilliant salmon-scarlet. Meanwhile the blossom develops until you are conscious only of the enormous size and dazzling interior. The charming Astor, as you may already know, beguiles you into paying it a daily garden visit. Also Lily-flowered, this wasp-waisted variety does not open as widely as Captain Fryatt, but delicately turns back its pointed petal tips. At first a blush of pink on a background of cream climbs up to a buff border. The color deepens to amber-orange, then, before the petals drop, softens to pale rose with a border of beige. Those who first come upon it in its final stage frequently declare it to be one of the most beautiful tulips they have ever seen.

Changing colors in tulips can bring delightful surprises. Well do I remember the first time the new Darwin, Demeter, bloomed in my garden. Sent to me for trial by a grower who hailed it as a marvelous deep purple, it had been planted in a border where daffodil groups were placed to the rear of

Darwin tulip colonies. To my horror it opened in mid-April on a jarring note of reddish violet with two clumps of golden daffodils in full flower behind it. What a grim joke or lack of color sense, I thought, on the part of the grower. Obviously this ugly duckling was no purple Darwin but a magenta-hued Triumph instead. But wait, I told myself, the season is young. Surely enough, as the flower expanded the color slowly deepened to the most beautiful royal purple imaginable, and the blossom lasted to the middle of May, right through the height of the Darwins.

This quality May-flowering tulips possess of slowly unfolding their beauty emphasizes the fact that to know them you must live with them. I think that to really know a variety you must grow it for three seasons. Where tulips are planted by thousands in parks or public grounds, their tapestries of color make beautiful pictures for the casual beholder. But for all their impressiveness these mass displays will not give you as much real pleasure as a single tulip unfolding its loveliness in your own garden.

Among the Breeder, Cottage and Darwin tulips I have grown, my favorites are almost as numerous as Solomon's children and I find it hard to be partial to this one or that. So successful have hybridizers been that every shade or tone boasts a dozen fine varieties. Yet gardeners frequently ask me to name the best one or two varieties of each shade, and I have made up such a restricted list. Here are my present choices which I will change as new varieties appear. You may prefer other kinds to some listed here but I believe you will agree that all these are beautiful. They are not recommended as a combination to be planted together but as best varieties in their respective color groups.

Starting with the palest of those with rose or red in their color, I would choose the Darwin, Dresden China, and the

Cottage, Rosabella. From those with a little deeper color I would choose Darwins, Adorable and Caroline Testout; then, passing on to still brighter ones, Tubergen's Glory, a worthy salmon successor to Clara Butt, and Erfordia, which has a lilac tone in its rose. Among the brighter roses I would select Darwins, Eggink's Ideal and Pride of Zwanenberg. The Darwins, Wagram and William Tell, are the ones I would grow among the raspberry shades, and Margaux and Arabian Nights among the wine-rose or maroon varieties. For vivid scarlet-red the Darwin, Charles Needham, cannot be excelled, while for deep red either Eclipse or Peter Barr are unsurpassable.

The foregoing kinds have no yellow in their rose or red pigmentation. I call them "dry" rose tones or reds. The many beautiful "yellow" rose tones start with the pale blends and intensify to the deep orange sorts. The Cottage tulips, Mimosa and Queen of Spain, are my favorite creamy blends. These are followed by Lily-flowering Astor. Then come the rosy-orange Cottages, Good Gracious and Alice Tiplady, the latter a particularly luminous color. The salmon-scarlet Cottage tulip, Mayflower, is in a color class by itself. Deeper and more rosy-scarlet are the Cottage varieties, Mazeppa and G. W. Leak. Of vivid orange tone are the Breeders, Sonate and Simon Bolivar. The new Breeder, Monte Cristo, is hard to classify. Mainly crimson-scarlet, it has a definite tone of orange, but it certainly belongs among first choices.

Many handsome white varieties have recently been introduced. The Cottage, Ivory Glory, and the Darwin, Glacier, are magnificent whites with yellow anthers, while White Giant is a splendid variety for those who like the contrast of black anthers. The Cottage, Delbay, and the Darwin, Niphetos, are my choices among cream shades. The search for pale yellows which do not fade seems at last to have met success with the new Cottage, Treasure Island. Cottage tulips, Mongolia and Mrs. John Scheepers, are the best of the chrome yellows, while the Darwin, Golden Age, is the finest deep yellow.

The Breeder, Georges Grappe, and the Darwin, Cote d'Azur, are fine light lavenders. Two new Darwins are the best of the deeper tones of the lavender to purple group: Gloriosa, a wonderful blue-violet without any tone of rose, and Demeter, a royal purple. Black Eagle is still my favorite maroon-purple, while Queen of the Night, another Darwin, is the best of the so-called "black" tulips.

The bronze shades, ranging from café-au-lait to chestnut brown, are all Breeders. Tantalus and Dixie Sunshine are the best of the light group and Madelon the finest buff-bronze. Huchtenburg and Hirschbrun are choice purple-bronze combinations, while Indian Chief and Indian Sunset are favorites among those classed as mahogany-bronze. The finest deep bronze is Don Eugo.

The following more general list of varieties is also offered frankly as my personal selection. These are kinds I should always like to grow. None is included because of current popularity or heavy sale, although availability is considered. Unless a variety is specifically noted as blooming early or late, it may be assumed that its flowering time coincides with the average of its group.

Individual heights are given but it must be emphasized that these figures are approximate, even as to relative height. Growing conditions so affect stem length that I have known a 26-inch variety planted in shade to top a 29-inch variety planted in sun. Other factors affecting height are quality of soil, and depth and time of planting in relation to weather of the following spring. Knowledge of height should be used by the gardener, in general, *to avoid uniformity*. A succession of level blossoms through the border is monotonous but nothing emphasizes individual charm like the juxtaposition of tulip groups with different stem lengths.

These are the May-flowering tulips I recommend listed by class and color:

BREEDER TULIPS

CAFÉ-AU-LAIT TO DARK BRONZE

Cunera. 31 inches. Light bronze, flushed lilac, with lighter edge.

Dixie Sunshine. 28 inches. Light yellow-bronze, flushed blue-lavender.

Don Eugo. 26 inches. Rich chestnut brown. Large egg-shaped blossom.

Hercules. 30 inches. Light bronze, flushed plum, deepening to dark bronze at edge.

Madelon. 30 inches. Warm rosy bronze, shaded violet.

Tantalus. 28 inches. Café-au-lait, flushed lavender.

MAHOGANY TO DARK BROWN

Autumn Glow. 28 inches. Reddish mulberry, suffused dark bronze. Inside chestnut bronze.

Hirschbrun. 28 inches. Deep mahogany-brown with plum bloom on outer petals.

Indian Chief. 32 inches. Rich brownish mahogany, flushed purple.

Indian Sunset. 29 inches. Outside dark mahogany red, inside deep copper red.

Mahogany King. 27 inches. Deep brown-red, flushed rosy purple.

ORANGE

Dillenberg. 27 inches. Rosy orange, edged bronzy yellow.

Katherine Thruxton. 28 inches. Slaty rose, edged golden bronze. Inside orange-bronze.

*Monte Cristo.** Scarlet, deepening to orange-scarlet, overlaid with rose. Outside covered with ashy bloom.

* See footnote on page 95.

Simon Bolivar. 29 inches. Clear, vivid orange-red.
Sonate. 27 inches. Deep orange-red with a fine edge of gold.

PURPLE WITH BRONZE EDGE

Crusader. 30 inches. A deep purple overlaid with bronze, shading to dark brown at edge.
Huchtenburg. 32 inches. Plum purple overlaid with bronze, edged chestnut.
Jessy. 30 inches. Coffee-bronze, flushed purple with a margin of golden bronze.
Louis XIV. 30 inches. Violet purple, edged warm bronze. Fragrant.

LAVENDER TO DARK PURPLE WITH NO BRONZE TONE

Barcarolle. 27 inches. Dark maroon-purple.
Blois Van Amstel. 29 inches. Uniform light violet-blue.
Denver. 30 inches. Rosy lavender, shaded lighter at edge.
Georges Grappe. 32 inches. Clear tones of lavender-blue. The most nearly blue tulip.
Mrs. Beecher Stowe. 25 inches. Clear violet purple.

COTTAGE TULIPS

(Not to be confused with short-stemmed Single Early Tulips)

WHITE OR CREAM

Carrara. 25 inches. Pure white with yellow anthers. Bowl shaped. Early.
Delbay. 26 inches. Rich creamy yellow, maturing to cream. Bell shaped. Late.
Ivory Glory. 29 inches. Creamy white with yellow anthers. Huge, egg-shaped flower. Late.
Mount Erebus. 30 inches. Snow white with yellow anthers.

SULPHUR TO GOLDEN YELLOW

Arethusa. 27 inches. Primrose with creamy stripe up center of outer petals.
Golden Harvest. 28 inches. Bright lemon yellow.
Mongolia. 29 inches. Soft butter yellow. Large globular flower.

Mrs. John T. Scheepers. 28 inches. Pure chrome yellow. Egg-shaped.

Sulphur Pearl. 27 inches. Pale yellow, passing to creamy yellow.

Treasure Island.* 30 inches. Silver yellow, deepening to primrose at edge. Does not fade. Huge open blossom with pointed petals.

Wall Street. 29 inches. Outside pale primrose, inside golden yellow.

CREAM OR YELLOW BLENDS

Conde Nast. 28 inches. Creamy yellow with faint rosy blush deepening with maturity.

Mimosa. 28 inches. Creamy yellow with a brushing of rose on outer petals.

Queen of Spain. 28 inches. Soft cream, very delicately brushed rose near edges of outer petals.

SALMON AND ORANGE BLENDS

Alice Tiplady. 29 inches. Luminous, rosy apricot. Bell-shaped.

Dido. 29 inches. Deep salmon-rose with amber border.

Good Gracious. 28 inches. Lively, but not hard, salmon-orange, shaded pink.

Marjorie Bowen. 28 inches. Salmon rose with delicate buff lights.

Orange Ophelia. 27 inches. Warm, mulberry rose, edged amber-buff.

ROSE WITH NO YELLOW TONES

Geisha. 27 inches. Soft lilac-rose with grayish tones. Long, loose petaled blossom.

Rosabella. 26 inches. Rosy pink with edge of light silver-rose.

SCARLET

G. W. Leak. 28 inches. Vivid rosy scarlet. Long petals.

Mayflower. 29 inches. Outside scarlet, flushed rose, with ashy bloom. Inside dazzling scarlet. Largest May-flowering tulip.

* See footnote on page 95.

Mazeppa. 27 inches. Rosy scarlet. Much the same shade as G. W. Leak, but bowl shaped.

LILY-FLOWERING TULIPS

(Subdivision of Cottage with long pointed, reflexed petals)

Astor. 25 inches. Soft amber-orange, shaded rose. Edged buff-amber.

Captain Fryatt. 26 inches. Rich garnet with pale yellow anthers. Petals open wide with maturity.

Elegans Alba. 20 inches. Creamy white with fine picotee edge of carmine-rose. Rather small, dainty flower.

Fascinating. 26 inches. Sulphur yellow, passing to cream. Narrow waisted flower with ruffled petals.

Golden Duchess. 22 inches. Deep yellow. Large blossom, opening out widely with maturity.

Golden Emblem. 22 inches. Deep chrome. Much the same color as Golden Duchess but blooms a little earlier.

Greta. 20 inches. Orange-scarlet. Purple bloom on outer petals.

Martha. 28 inches. Warm cherry-rose.

Painted Lily. 18 inches. Golden yellow with picotee edge of rose.

Rhodes. 29 inches. Clear, soft rose.

The Bride. 25 inches. Creamy white with yellow anthers. Medium-sized, bell-shaped flower.

White Cross. 27 inches. Pure white, yellow anthers.

White Duchess. 28 inches. Snow white with yellow anthers. Outer petals tinged green. Petal edges laciniated.

DARWIN TULIPS

White and Cream

Annie Speelman. 28 inches. Creamy white. Yellow anthers. Long tubular flower.

Duke of Wellington. 30 inches. Pure white with yellow anthers.

Glacier. 29 inches. Rich, creamy white. Yellow anthers. Blossom keeps its long tubular shape for weeks as petals never open widely.

Helen Eakin. 30 inches. Snow white with black anthers. Bowl shaped.

Mrs. Grullemans. 28 inches. Creamy white with yellow anthers. Long, slender flower.

White Giant. 31 inches. Pure white with black anthers. Large, cup-shaped blossom.

Light to Deep Yellow

Golden Age. 29 inches. Chrome yellow with a border of warm, deep yellow. Long, pointed petals.

Helen Gahagan. 29 inches. Sulphur yellow, changing to cream.

Niphetos. 28 inches. Silver-yellow. Long tubular flower.

Sunkist. 28 inches. Warm yellow, deeper at edge.

*Treasure Island.** 30 inches. Silver yellow, deepening to primrose at edge. Does not fade. Huge, open blossom with pointed petals.

Lavender, Violet and Purple

Black Eagle. 29 inches. Lustrous, bluish maroon-purple. Wide open flower.

Cote d'Azur. 26 inches. Lavender-blue, with white base.

Demeter. 30 inches. Opens reddish purple, matures a deep royal purple. Large bowl-shaped blossom which opens a week earlier than the May-flowering tulips but lasts through the season.

Faust. 28 inches. Purple-maroon. Long flower.

Gloriosa. 30 inches. Very bluish violet-blue with no tone of rose.

Madame Butterfly. 29 inches. Violet with faint buff lights.

Mark Anthony. 30 inches. Dark wine-purple. Same color inside and out.

Queen of the Night. 29 inches. Very blackish maroon-purple. None darker.

* See footnote on page 95.

Scotch Lassie. 29 inches. Bright, violet-purple. Wide open, bowl-shaped flower.

The Bishop. 29 inches. Clear, deep bluish violet. Rather late.

PALE TO DEEP ROSE

Adorable. 30 inches. Deep blush in center of petals, creamy rose toward edge. Perfect with bleedingheart. Late.

Caroline Testout. 28 inches. Uniform color of clear soft pink.

Councillor. 27 inches. Warm rose, edged American Beauty rose.

Dresden China. 28 inches. Faintly brushed rose on creamy background.

Eggink's Ideal. 30 inches. Deep rose, edged lighter. Large, oval blossom.

Erfordia. 28 inches. Lilac rose, broadly margined silver.

Eunice. 29 inches. Deep silver-rose, lighter at edge.

Kathleen Parlow. 28 inches. Bright silver-rose, paling toward ends of petals.

King George V. 30 inches. Uniform, bright cherry rose.

Mr. Van Zyl. 28 inches. Light rose paling to flesh at petal edges.

Orange Perfection. 28 inches. Clear tone of vivid salmon-rose.

Pride of Zwanenberg. 30 inches. Bright rose with deeper flush at center.

The Peach. 27 inches. Bright salmon-pink above broad white base.

Tubergen's Glory. 28 inches. Uniform color of bright salmon-rose. A better-colored successor for Clara Butt.

Wagram. 28 inches. Deep rose-pink with lighter edge.

William Tell. 27 inches. Uniform color of bright raspberry-rose.

WINE TO MAROON

Arabian Nights. 29 inches. Deep chestnut-red.

Bourgogne. 29 inches. Dark burgundy-rose.

Mahogany. 27 inches. Raisin. Egg-shaped blossom.

Margaux. 30 inches. Color of Margaux wine with sun shining through it. Long, oval flower.

SCARLET AND RED

Charles Needham. 27 inches. Dazzling scarlet, flushed carmine.

Eclipse. 30 inches. Deep blood red with blackish sheen on outer petals.

Masterpiece. 26 inches. Deep scarlet, dark bloom on outer petals.

*Monte Cristo.** Scarlet, deepening to orange-scarlet, overlaid with rose. Outside covered with ashy bloom.

Peter Barr. 29 inches. Dark red, margined bright red.

BLEND

Lady Hillingdon. 30 inches. Bright rosy orange, overlaid with terra-cotta.

Sunset Glow. 24 inches. Salmon-scarlet overlaid rose, deepening to orange at edges.

PARROT TULIPS

Petal edges laciniated and outer petals usually covered with green sheen.

Blue Parrot. 28 inches. Bright blue-violet. Enormous, open flower.

Fantasy. 27 inches. Salmon pink sport of Clara Butt.

Gemma. 16 inches. White, delicately tinted pink. Flowers in April.

Red Champion. 24 inches. Carmine shaded rose.

Sunshine. 18 inches. Golden yellow.

Therese. 28 inches. Rosy scarlet with bright blue base.

DOUBLE LATE TULIPS

Bleu Celeste. 24 inches. Blue-violet.

Eros. 22 inches. Soft old rose.

Mt. Tacoma. 22 inches. Pure white.

Pavo. 22 inches. Bright rose.

* The new tulips Monte Cristo and Treasure Island are officially registered in Holland as Breeder and Cottage respectively. However, you may find them catalogued for trade promotion purposes as Darwins or Ideal Darwins.

CHAPTER ELEVEN

Early Varieties and Species Tulips

Hundreds of colorful tulips come into bloom weeks before the May-flowering varieties unfold their green buds. Familiar to all are the Single and Double Earlies so frequently misnamed Cottage tulips. These blossom by mid-April in the New York area, lasting for two to three weeks. The flowers are large and bright, and are borne on short, stocky stems.

Early tulips, in beds or colonies by themselves, make brilliant patches of color. Pink Beauty, Couleur Cardinal or the double red Vuurbaak offer a bright splash by themselves or when contrasted with the white Lady Boreel. The orange Sunburst and the yellow Rising Sun are a warm combination.

Short-stemmed tulips in the border are attractively set off by pansies, forget-me-nots, ajugas, primroses and other low plants which blossom at the same time. One garden I know has the double soft pink Peach Blossom interplanted with myosotis and several shades of blue and purple pansies. Another colorfully combines the dark blue hyacinth, Duke of Westminster with the orange Single Early, De Wet and the primrose daffodil Aerolite. Morning sun reaches the hyacinths last so that all three bloom together.

One mid-April garden features a combination of yellow and coral. Forsythia has been trained in espalier form over an arbor. When the flowers of this shrub are fully open, flat-sheared bushes of Viburnum carlesi, planted at the base of the trellis, are covered with clusters of bead-like coral buds. A bed of the orange tulip De Wet edged by clear yellow pansies, Coronation Gold, completes a bright and unusual picture.

The two newer classes of tulips, Triumph and Mendel, follow close on the heels of the short-stemmed kinds. In height intermediate between their Single Early and May-flowering parents, but with stems long enough for cutting, they may be planted freely with the Breeder, Cottage and Darwin varieties to lengthen the season of tall tulip bloom. They are invaluable for a border where tulips taller than the Single Early varieties are desired but where space is wanted for other plants before the May-flowering tulips cease blooming. Since the Triumph-Mendel season usually ends the first week of May, the bulbs may be lifted then and heeled in to make room for summer plants. In such a border an edging of Muscari armeniacum is effective with the tulips.

For complete enjoyment of the tulip season, some of the more easily grown Species tulips should also be used. Although included here with the earlier flowering varieties, these wild types collected from Europe and Asia have the widest blooming range of all. Tulipa kaufmanniana which blossoms in late March or early April is the first of the genus to flower; sprengeri, opening in late May is the last. If only these two Species are added to a collection of Early, Triumph and May-flowering tulips, you can revel in seven or eight weeks of bloom.

Do not limit yourself to these two. You will find many fine tulipas catalogued at moderate prices since they are propagated in sizable quantities in Holland. Give them the same culture as other tulips but plant them deeper and earlier. Planting by October twenty-fifth under a six-inch soil covering is a good general rule for these. Let them naturalize but be sure their foliage gets plenty of warm ripening sun.

The interesting variations of form and color among the Species endear them to the collector's heart and the attractive plantings they make endear them to the average gardener, too. Tulipas range in size from the small cups of chrysantha and clusiana to the large fosteriana forms which measure ten inches across. Most of them have striking basal patches inside black or dark green. Stem lengths vary, but none is too long for a sunny spot in the rock garden.

You should, of course, start your collection of Botanical tulips with a colony of kaufmanniana beside drifts of blue chionodoxas or squills, then add other tulipas as space permits. Be sure to include a planting of eichleri or fosteriana, Red Emperor. Either will stand the light shade afforded by the edge of a birch or hemlock grove and either will show off in dazzling scarlet brilliance against this background. Plant thick groups of clusiana, marjoletti and australis in front areas of the perennial borders, or in colonies behind hardy candytuft for garden charm and cut flowers as well.

The following Early, Triumph and Mendel varieties and individual Species tulips are recommended:

SINGLE EARLY TULIPS

(Not to be confused with Cottage Tulips)

Apricot Yellow. 13 inches. Primrose, flushed carmine.
Couleur Cardinal. 15 inches. Crimson with purple bloom on outer petals. Long, pointed flower. LATE.
Cullinan. 12 inches. Cream, edged pale rose.
De Wet. 16 inches. Orange-yellow, deepening to orange. Large, loose blossom.
Diadem. 14 inches. Clear, soft rose. LATE.
Hobbema (Le Reve). 15 inches. Lilac-rose, flushed buff. Large, globular flower blooming so late it may be combined with May-flowering kinds.

Keiserskroon. 15 inches. Crimson-scarlet, broadly margined bright yellow.

Lady Boreel. 13 inches. Snow white. Large, bell-shaped flower.

Madame Gevers. 12 inches. Clear lemon yellow.

Pink Beauty. 15 inches. White with broad margin of cherry-rose which later suffuses the blossom.

Rising Sun. 14 inches. Rich golden yellow.

Sunburst. 14 inches. Yellow, suffused orange.

DOUBLE EARLY TULIPS

(Not to be confused with Cottage Tulips)

Marechal Neil. 14 inches. Canary yellow gradually suffused orange.

Mr. van der Hoeff. 12 inches. Deep primrose. Very full double.

Murillo. 12 inches. Opens white and is slowly suffused rose.

Peach Blossom. 12 inches. Clear rose, brushed creamy white.

Schoonoord. 13 inches. Pure white.

Tearose. 12 inches. Pale yellow, tinged rose. Gradually suffused rose.

Vuurbaak. 12 inches. Deep scarlet.

TRIUMPH TULIPS

Alberio. 19 inches. Raspberry-red, flushed rose, with a narrow margin of buff.

Dembola. 21 inches. Radish-red with a broad margin of silver.

Elmus. 22 inches. Rose-red with a border of ivory.

Johanna. 21 inches. Pure salmon-rose.

Kansas. 23 inches. Creamy white with yellow anthers.

Korneforus. 22 inches. Bright scarlet with no shading.

Lord Carnarvon. 24 inches. Soft rose-pink brushed on a creamy background. LATE.

Nova. 22 inches. Bright salmon-rose.

Queen of the North. 24 inches. Very bright rose-pink above a broad base of white. VERY LATE.

Sardonix. 22 inches. Lavender, faintly tinged rose.

MENDEL TULIPS

Brightling. 20 inches. Deep rose, flushed salmon.
Captain Smoolenaars. 19 inches. Bright rosy red.
Zenith. 21 inches. Clear silky rose.

SPECIES TULIPS, BOTANICAL TULIPS, TULIPAS

Australis. 12 inches. MID-MAY. Soft tan, tipped cinnamon. Flowers about the size of an eye-cup.

Biflora. 3 inches. LATE MARCH OR EARLY APRIL. White, star-shaped flowers of small individual size clustered two to three to a stem.

Chrysantha. 6 inches. EARLY MAY. Crimson-rose outside, soft primrose inside. Tiny flowers.

Clusiana. 10 inches. EARLY MAY. Outer petals cherry-rose, edged white, inner petals creamy white. Small blossoms.

Cornuta Stenopetala. 15 inches. EARLY MAY. Yellow, streaked red. Oddly shaped, with abnormally long, thin petals, twisted and furled, tapering to a point.

Dasystemon. 5 inches. LATE APRIL. Yellow, tipped white. Small, cluster-flowering.

Eichleri. 10 inches. LATE APRIL. Dazzling red with striking inside base of black. About the size of a demi-tasse cup.

Fosteriana. 12 inches. LATE APRIL. Brilliant scarlet-red. Large, flowing blossom.

Fosteriana, Red Emperor. 16 inches. LATE APRIL. Seedling of fosteriana. Most brilliant scarlet imaginable. Overwhelming in size and color.

Kaufmanniana. The Waterlily Tulip. 6 inches. LATE MARCH OR EARLY APRIL. Outer petals carmine, margined cream. Inside cream with yellow base. Opens out flat in daytime, closes at night.

Kaufmanniana Brilliant. 8 inches. EARLY APRIL. Bright carmine form of kaufmanniana.

Marjoletti. 12 inches. EARLY MAY. Creamy white with thin edge of carmine up side of petal.

Persica. 5 inches. MID-MAY. Outside yellow, tinged green. Inside deep yellow. Small, wide-open, fragrant flowers in clusters.

Praestans. 12 inches. LATE APRIL. Flashing orange-scarlet. Two to four blossoms per stem.

Sprengeri. 9 inches. LATE MAY. Outside maroon, shaded buff, inside deep red. Globular blossoms.

Sylvestris. Florentina Odorata. 14 inches. LATE APRIL. Bronzy yellow, changing to butter-yellow. Very fragrant.

Viridiflora Praecox. 18 inches. MID-MAY. Really a Cottage but listed with Species because of unusual color and form. Apple green, edged soft primrose. Narrow petals.

CHAPTER TWELVE

The Supply, Present and Future

THE fact that Holland is our main source of fall-planting bulbs, especially of tulips, was forcibly brought home to American gardeners when imports from that country were cut off during World War II. Fortunately, a small tulip-growing industry, with an annual crop of from five to ten per cent of that of Holland, existed in England. Fortunately, also, for the American consumer, the British restricted the sale of bulbs except for export and shipped practically the whole crop here. Had it not been for these imports from Britain, which reached a total of 34,000,000 in 1941 according to the figures of the U. S. Department of Commerce, there would have been a tulip famine here during World War II. It nearly came to that in 1944 when the British again permitted the domestic sale of their bulbs.

Although the majority of tulips of any respectable size sold in this country during the war came from Great Britain, some were also produced by American growers. Commercial tulip growing had existed here on a small scale before the war. In competition with imported bulbs the market was limited. The top sizes went chiefly to florists for early forcing. Since they matured earlier in the American climate, these bulbs could be brought into bloom sooner than the earliest arriving Dutch bulbs. In 1939, a year when approximately 110,000,000 tulips of eleven- and twelve-centimeter sizes were imported from Holland, fewer than one million American grown bulbs of equal sizes were sold. Besides these, an undetermined number of smaller sized bulbs went to fill the retail demand for inexpensive tulips.

Many people wondered why, in the tradition of American ingenuity, growers here could not seize the opportunity afforded by wartime exclusion of Dutch bulbs to expand and capture the market for the domestic product. Indeed, a number of beautifully illustrated magazine articles appeared implying that they had done just that. One went so far as to predict that most of our bulbs would henceforth be "mass-produced" at home. Facts do not bear out either the report or the prophecy.

It is true the war did stimulate dealers and growers to give intensive cultivation to all tulip plantings, including some that had hitherto been treated rather casually as having small commercial possibilities. Also, some new plantings were made where stock and space were both available. But obviously it was impossible during the war for American growers to expand their volume to even a major fraction of the former Dutch imports. Tulip bulbs, unlike rubber, cannot be made from synthetic products. Nor are they grown from seed like wheat.

There are only two ways growers can increase tulip acreage. One is by buying new planting stock. The other is by withholding from the market bulbs which would normally be sold and using them instead to enlarge their own plantings. The war made both courses impractical. Actually, American production tended to decrease. Bulbs could not be brought from Holland to augment supplies and, while a portion of the British imports were used for stock, most went into retail trade channels. Demand so topped supply that, far from holding back tulips to build up field stocks, growers sold their second, third and even their fourth and fifth sizes. This left dwindling reserves of progressively smaller bulbs.

If you were a buyer during the war, you may have had first-hand knowledge of the steady decline in quantity and quality of domestic tulips. You found shelves filled with fewer and poorer bulbs until, by the fall of 1944, you may have felt that "rubbish" was a flattering term for what you were offered. Yet these bulbs would have been jumbos compared with the possible product in autumn 1945, had not Dutch imports arrived then by the tens of millions.

You may have concluded from the poor quality of wartime domestic stock that all American bulbs are inferior to Dutch. If so, you are wrong. The Pacific Northwest has produced just as fine bulbs of certain varieties as has Holland. As a matter of fact, if you provide proper conditions, you can grow top-size bulbs in your own back yard. The percentage of twelve-centimeter ones in your crop will probably be so low, however, that they will be very costly in terms of your own time and efforts or in cash if you hire labor to do the work.

The problem of the domestic commercial grower, therefore, is not to produce merely *some* tulips comparable in quality to Dutch bulbs. His success depends on an annual harvest permitting withdrawal of enough salable bulbs to cover his costs and yield a profit, yet leaving stock for replanting sufficient to maintain his acreage. Many American growers are attempting to meet this challenge in the post-war period. They are renewing their war-exhausted stocks with importations from Holland, rightly concentrating on kinds most suitable for the early forcing market, but adding some garden varieties too. How successful they will be the future will tell, but American gardeners are bound to benefit with growers on two continents competing to supply them with ever finer bulbs.

The effect of the war on future tulip supplies from Holland was also a subject of much speculation here before the liberation. Many feared that physical damage or restrictive measures might seriously cripple that important feature of Dutch economy. Fortunately this did not occur. Bulb sales boomed during the years of German occupation. For the first time since the early 1930's, each season did not end with growers facing the problem of a price-depressing surplus. This was true even though the United States and England were cut off from the export market.

This condition resulted from the enormously increased demand for bulbs on the continent, coupled with the reduction of tulip acreage by the Dutch government in 1939 before the invasion. No further reductions were imposed by the Germans. Neither were there any increases. Meanwhile sales rose. Whatever ills beset Hitler's Europe, unemployment, especially in Germany, was not one of them. Everywhere workers were wanted for war plants and, for many, wages were higher than ever before. Goods which ordinarily might have been purchased with this money, such as new homes, automobiles, furniture, clothes, or even extra food, were not available but flowers were. Flowers have always been used by all classes in Europe to an extent not even approached in America. Bulbs particularly fitted the European florist's need during the war because they required less heat to be brought into bloom than other greenhouse products—and coal was scarce.

You may have read of bulbs being eaten in Holland for lack of food. These stories had a basis in fact, although the impression that a major portion of the bulb crop was thus consumed is erroneous. In the fall of 1944 Allied bombing, plus a railroad strike led by the Dutch resistance movement, prevented shipment of millions of bulbs packed and ready for export. Such bulbs as were edible of this surplus made a welcome addition to the food supply during the critical months which followed.

It was in the winter and spring of 1944–45, just before the liberation, that Holland underwent its worst period of food stringency. Crocuses then were ground into flour. Tulips, with the skins peeled, the root bases and embryo flowers within the bulbs cut out, were boiled with a little water and mashed. Hollanders report that thus prepared tulips tasted like sweet potatoes, but, regardless of taste, they helped keep people from actual starvation.

In general bulbs were grown during the war, as always, for ultimate flower production. Sales were high and so were receipts in guilders. Growers wished to convert their money into tangible property. While prices of bulbs for internal sale and export were rigidly controlled by the occupying power, the price of planting stock and of new seedlings was not. There was, therefore, lively bidding for bulbs of new varieties of tulips, daffodils and hyacinths. Speculation reminiscent of the tulipomania days of the seventeenth century took place. Bids of $200 to $300 per single bulb were ordinary. A price of $5,000 for half interest in one bulb was recorded.

As a result, the hybridizing end of the industry flourished. Growers who purchased new stocks may not recover their investment but American gardeners will benefit in two ways. First, the development and distribution of seedlings thus brought about will bring a steady stream of new varieties to the retail market. Secondly, there was a wholesale improvement in general growing stock. Not all the profits went into individual bulbs of costly new seedlings. Some went to replace acres of common varieties like Clara Butt and Inglescombe Yellow with stocks of superior varieties like Caroline Testout and Mrs. John T. Scheepers which, while they had existed before the war, were scarce and high priced. Varieties that were novelties in 1939 are now, in many cases, the plentiful ones. The pre-war common sorts, many of them, have gone to tulip Valhalla and many old favorites will be mourned, sometimes justly. But the steady introduction of such new varieties as the bright orange-scarlet Monte Cristo, the rose-blend Orange Ophelia, the soft yellow Treasure Island and the creamy Delbay will more than console us.

CHAPTER THIRTEEN

Those Delightful Daffodils

DAFFODILS gladden our eyes when the new leaves of trees and shrubs barely show green. They remain colorful until the branches are decked with full-grown verdure. April without them would be as dull as May without tulips.

Daffodils, or, to use their Latin name, narcissi, are members of the amaryllis family. They have been cultivated in Europe for as long as civilized man has lived there. Moderate in their demands, they are lavish with rewards. They can be grown, in different varieties, anywhere in the United States except in the driest desert, the muggiest swamp or on the highest snow-capped mountain. They tolerate a wide variation of soil provided it is well-drained and not too acid. All varieties, from the large trumpets with bulbs the size of oranges to the small species whose bulbs are no bigger than large peas, like a four-inch covering of earth.

Not long content with sending up two or three blossoms, each large new bulb you plant soon divides and multiplies until it produces a tight cluster of stems. How well the increase continues to flower depends on the character of the soil and on whether the foliage receives as much ripening sun as each variety may require. Narcissi planted in the garden should be taken up and divided every two or three years. Then they will not suffer from overcrowding and young bulbs can mature properly and multiply again. When they are naturalized in drifts, survival of the strongest offspring must be depended upon to provide bloom for the group.

Sometimes, despite our best intentions, the year slips by without our attending to the task of lifting and dividing. The results vary surprisingly. I recall one group of John Evelyn, planted in light, fertile soil. I let it go for two years after I first decided it needed separating. The second year—four years after I had set out an original fifteen bulbs—I reaped the undeserved reward of ninety-five large and lovely blossoms. When I dug up the clump, there were more than a hundred bulbs and offsets. Another clump of fifteen John Evelyn, however, planted at the same time but in heavier soil, yielded me after similar neglect just three stunted flowers and numerous green spears. I know if I had then dug up this second planting and lined out the bulbs in the open field for two years, they would have come back to flowering strength, but I confess that lack of time and space forced me to discard them in favor of new bulbs.

You will find that daffodil blossoms last longer when bulbs are planted in the partial shade of tall trees or buildings. These temper the sunshine which is sometimes hot and searing during the blooming season. This should not, of course, deprive ripening foliage of at least a half a day's strong sunlight.

There is another point regarding shade and daffodil bloom to keep in mind. Blossoms always turn toward the sun. The artful gardener knowing this makes them face the path from which he expects to view them. In full sun they will look east or southeast, so plant them north and west of the spot whence you wish to see them. If narcissi are in morning sun, be sure they are set west of the path. Backed by house or evergreen hedge they cannot help facing you. I know a rectangular garden bounded on three sides by hemlocks, on the fourth by a stone wall. Daffodils are planted in the rear of each boundary bed, fairly close to hemlocks and wall. Shade behind them forces blossoms to face towards the center of the garden.

Practically everyone likes daffodils but too few gardeners know the varieties individually. Many who select tulip, rose or peony by name are familiar with daffodils only as mixed plantings of cheerful white and yellow April blossoms. This is unfortunate, for narcissi have personalities which are no less unique because they are less blatant than those of tulips. The white triandrus hybrid Thalia, for example, has a wholly different character from the golden trumpet King Alfred. Even kinds of the same type possess the spice of variety. The small, late poeticus Recurvus, with sharply reflexed petals is very different from the tall Actaea with huge overlapping petals. Recurvus is charming naturalized by the dozen under an apple tree or by the thousand in an orchard. Actaea should be planted in the border with other exhibition narcissi.

If you make friends with daffodils individually, you will enter a new realm of gardening pleasure. You will experience fresh delight in the nuances of form and substance among the various kinds and in their slightly different shadings. You will no longer think of the daffodil as "yellow, nothing more," but appreciate the flaming red crown of Dick Wellband, the great height of the light primrose Fortune and the wonderful size and substance of the bright yellow Carlton. You will consider the daffodil one of the loveliest garden personalities Providence has bestowed upon us.

The next time your daffodils are in bloom, do not be content merely to view them from a distance. They are not plantings in a public park or specimens in a botanical garden but are yours to enjoy intimately. Walk among them, dwell upon this one and that. Occasionally lift up their heads to see the full expanse of the bloom and their detailed perfection of form.

Narcissi lend themselves to every kind of floriculture. To greenhouse growers, both amateur and professional, they are as standard as carnations. Outdoors they suit many garden styles but do not look well in open geometric beds which are viewed from all sides, since the blossoms face but one direction.

Different garden uses are suggested by variations in size of narcissi. They range from tiny varieties like Minimus, three inches tall, to such giants as Diotima, with a blossom six inches wide on a stem eighteen inches long. Rock garden pockets make ideal settings for the fascinating miniatures. The larger varieties are for bolder display.

Daffodils are lovely in masses. In spring when nature presents great stretches of bare earth, plantings cannot be too extensive. Along a brook, in open meadow, by the woods' edge or under tall trees whose open foliage admits filtered sunlight, they are charming. For best effect in such places each drift should be of a separate variety, its strength insured by spring and fall fertilizing.

It seems to me that white birches sprang into being just to provide ideal companionship for daffodils. If no birches grow on your property, but you have space, by all means plant a group of saplings. If you own acreage, have a forest of them! Beneath them plant drifts of daffodils, with colonies of blue Mertensia virginica, white trillium and lavender hepatica.

In such woodland plantings summer succession may or may not concern the gardener. It is perfectly satisfactory to omit it, leaving the spring plants to ripen slowly and appear again another year. Native ferns, however, may be planted to afford cool spots of green during the warm months. Where sufficient

sunlight penetrates, the native lilies, canadense, philadelphicum and superbum, may be selected for June and July color.
If there is enough moisture, the white Hosta subcordata, plan-
tain lily, will flourish. Hosta fortunei robusta glauca with its
steel blue foliage also thrives in shade.

Under birches and tall pines in one attractive woodland
area I know, daffodils, erythroniums, scillas and hepaticas are
interplanted with Myrrhis odorata, sweet cicely. This comes
up in May and completely covers the waning foliage of the
bulbous plants with feathery, fern-like leaves deliciously
scented with anise. If cut back sharply in June, sweet cicely
produces second growth which is fragrantly green through the
summer.

Narcissi so planted in the woods or on the north side of the
house get less ripening sunshine than if they grew in open
garden or meadow. It is therefore advisable to avoid sun-
dependent varieties like King Alfred and to select for such
sites those like Yellow Poppy, Alcida and Hera which seem to
require less sun in order to flower continuously. In Chapter
Twenty-five on Woodland Plantings, you will find a list of
others.

Daffodils are appealing when planted in thick, informal
stretches along a drive, by a garden wall or as an edging for
a boundary line of shrubs and evergreens. In such places a
mass planting of one variety or a succession of different kinds
is equally pleasing. And for companions there are blue grape
hyacinths, forget-me-not-flowered anchusa, Pulmonaria an-
gustifolia, pansies and primroses.

You can also use daffodils to bring early color to the perennial border. Here you may wish to hide the ripening spears by
plaiting them together and pinning them down or you can
conceal them and fill in subsequent gaps by interplantings
with annuals. Colonies of perennial columbines in front of the

early narcissi, shasta daisies and stokesias for the later ones will accomplish the same purpose.

Daffodils by themselves or combined with tulips may be planted in a bed reserved for spring bulbs and summer annuals. Then the narcissi are planted to the rear of the May-flowering tulips since the daffodils reach their full height while the tulips are still low. The tulips when full grown conceal the daffodil foliage.

The collector (and the new gardener should start out as a collector of daffodils) will want to acquire rarer kinds by ones, twos or threes. Cost of the newer kinds may dictate this procedure, although daffodils multiply so readily that the initial cost can legitimately be considered good investment. And there need be no hesitation about planting narcissi in small individual groups or even in placing a single outstanding specimen between larger clumps. An unusual variety can stand out effectively in this way.

Narcissi generally catalogued as species and some of the smaller hybrids are best planted in nooks where small flowers can be appreciated. Here they have special charm. I do not hold, however, with those who praise the rare, small species with the implication that there is something vulgar about large varieties. The little ones intrigue me and I would never be without them but the gorgeous hybrid giants bowl me over.

Many of the species come to us but recently grown from seed. They are small bulbs which readily dry out if kept unplanted for long. Therefore, they should be set out as early in September as possible in well-drained soil containing moisture-retentive humus. They like full sun, often baking sun, after they bloom, and on no account should they be shadowed by the heavy foliage of surrounding plants.

CHAPTER FOURTEEN

Narcissi by Name and Class

"Many idle and ignorant gardeners . . . doe call some of the
Daffodils, Narcissus, when, as all that know any Latine,
know that Narcissus is the Latine name and Daffodill the
English of one and the same thing . . ."

THESE words, written by the horticulturist John Parkinson
more than three hundred years ago, indicate that the gardening public was just as confused on this question then as now—
and authorities were just as stern! But perhaps amateurs of
today have more excuse for being perplexed about terms than
their "idle and ignorant" predecessors of three centuries before. A generation ago, writers and catalogue makers were
dividing this genus into the Magni-coronati type embracing
the large trumpets which they called in English True Daffodils and the Parvi-coronati type which included the small-
cupped poeticus varieties always listed as Narcissi. In between
were those with medium cups which were classed as Medi-
coronati and were also called Narcissi.

As hybridizers developed new variations, this division into
three classes proved inadequate. Eventually the daffodil committee of the English Royal Horticultural Society drew up a
classification which is now considered official in this country
as well as in Great Britain. In this arrangement, varieties of

the genus are grouped in eleven divisions. This classification, although lengthy, has been adequate until this time. Now new hybrids are clamoring for attention and further revision will soon be in order. Let us hope it will be shorter and simpler. One proposal may soon be adopted, that of omitting the leedsii division. Those in that group with large crowns will, if the plan goes through, be classed as white incomparabilis and those with small cups as white barrii.

Regardless of any subdivisions of the genus, it is true today as it was in Parkinson's time that a daffodil is always a narcissus and a narcissus is always a daffodil. Today gardeners complicate matters further by misuse of the term Jonquil. Some use it for the large trumpet narcissus, some for the white poet's daffodil. It applies to neither. Correctly, a jonquil is the little yellow species of narcissus, or daffodil, with rush-like foliage, or a hybrid of this type.

You may think the question of terminology and class tedious. But you should become familiar enough with terms so that you will cease to worry whether the bulbs you ordered as daffodils will turn out to be white with a flat eye because they arrived labeled narcissi. And you should know better than to order jonquils if you really want large crowned daffodils.

The end of the narcissus quarantine and resumption of imports from Holland has spelled good news for American gardeners. Growers here and abroad now compete to provide us with the best daffodils possible. The finer kinds, hitherto available only as high-priced novelties, are now appearing in catalogues at the same price levels as the older sorts. A number of new sweet-scented "pink" daffodils are on the way. Indeed, a long period of fine narcissus growing lies ahead.

I am continually asked by gardeners, who underestimate the capacity of their gardens for accommodating a larger range, to select a reasonably priced best dozen for them. From the trumpets I would select golden yellow Diotima for its great size and beauty of form, the primrose British Monarch, white Beersheba and bi-color President Lebrun. The yellow Carlton, Dick Wellband, whose red crown is backed by huge white petals, and Yellow Poppy, a shade-growing kind of medium size and perfect form, are my choices among the incomparabilis. The tall barrii Firetail would be included. From the leedsii I would select Tunis, whose crown is edged with pale copper, and Mrs. R. O. Backhouse, the famous "pink" daffodil whose cup really has a tone of apricot-pink. The white triandrus Thalia and the free-flowering jonquilla Golden Sceptre would also be in the collection, as would the poetaz Scarlet Gem and the poeticus Actaea. Of the doubles I would grow the orange-centered Feu de Joie. As improved varieties appear I would make changes, but this is my list of today and it numbers fifteen, since no collection of the finest daffodils could possibly be limited to twelve.

The following more extensive list of varieties is still far from comprehensive. Most daffodil enthusiasts grow no fewer than two hundred kinds. They may justly complain that many fine sorts are omitted from this selection. It has been limited to keep it within the range of an average gardener seeking to make a reasonably extensive acquaintance with the best:

1. Trumpet. Trumpet-shaped crown as long as or longer than perianth petals.

   a. Yellow

      Aerolite. 16 inches. Soft primrose perianth, chrome trumpet. Will naturalize in shade.

      British Monarch. 16 inches. Primrose with long crown heavily frilled at end.

      Diotima. 20 inches. Golden yellow. Huge expanding trumpet. Star-shaped perianth.

Golden Harvest. 18 inches. Golden yellow. **Large** trumpet and perianth. Very free-flowering.

King Alfred. 18 inches. Uniform golden yellow trumpet and perianth. Trumpet nicely frilled at end. Excellent for forcing or for garden.

Minimus. 3 inches. Deep yellow. Miniature trumpet daffodil of perfect proportions.

Minor. 6 inches. Bright yellow. A charming miniature trumpet, slightly larger than Minimus.

b. White

Beersheba. 16 inches. Pure white. Trumpet is long and graceful with attractively frilled edge. Best white.

Imperator. 14 inches. Snow white perianth, long creamy trumpet, frilled at edge. Largest white.

Lovenest. 18 inches. White perianth. Short trumpet opens yellow, passes to cream, then develops pink tone.

Roxane. 14 inches. Perianth white. Trumpet opens pale yellow, matures white, and is widely expanded and frilled at edge.

c. Bi-color

Oliver Cromwell. 18 inches. Sulphur yellow, informal perianth. Trumpet is deep primrose.

President Lebrun. 18 inches. Snow white perianth. Rich yellow trumpet of large size, fluted and frilled.

2. Incomparabilis. Crown greater than one-third but less than equal the length of the perianth petal.

a. With yellow perianth

Carlton. 14 inches. Bright yellow of huge proportions. Its immense, wide crown is heavily frilled at the end.

Damson. 16 inches. Light yellow perianth with informal and broadly overlapping petals. Long fluted crown with vivid red edge.

Dorine. 16 inches. Perianth light yellow and very broad. Shallow cup is bordered orange. VERY LATE.

El Dorado. 16 inches. Light primrose perianth. Deep
yellow crown is wide open and fluted to base.

Fortune. 24 inches. Bright yellow perianth is wide
and formal. Crown of same color is narrowly bordered red. Large blossom held erect on unusually
tall stem.

Havelock. 20 inches. Uniform bright yellow. Crown
is deep and broad.

Jalna. 18 inches. Deep primrose perianth and crown,
with cup broadly margined vivid red. EARLY AND
LONG LASTING.

Red Cross. 20 inches. Light yellow perianth with
large crown of chrome thinly bordered rose.

Scarlet Elegans. 16 inches. Deep golden yellow with
brilliant scarlet crown.

Yellow Poppy. 18 inches. Soft primrose with cup delicately margined apricot. Perianth petals are formally arranged and shallow crown is delicately
frilled at edge.

b. With white perianth

Agra. 16 inches. Creamy white perianth. Open crown
of orange-yellow, edged deep orange.

Dick Wellband. 22 inches. Snow white perianth of
huge size. Large, nearly flat crown of vivid scarlet.

Francisca Drake. 16 inches. Large white petals slightly
reflexed. Deep yellow cup, edged orange.

John Evelyn. 14 inches. Pure white overlapping perianth with lemon yellow crown densely frilled and
crested.

3. Barrii. Crown less than one-third length of perianth.

a. With yellow perianth

Afterglow. 18 inches. Creamy yellow with primrose
cup edged apricot-rose.

Marion. 16 inches. Deep yellow with orange-edged
cup.

Norman. 14 inches. Broad chrome perianth. Wide
primrose crown with vivid crimson edge.

Tredore. 14 inches. Broad perianth of primrose, wide crown of orange-red.

b. With white perianth

Adler. 14 inches. Snow white petals framing bright yellow cup thinly bordered orange-red.

Alcida. 14 inches. Creamy white perianth with lemon yellow crown tipped red.

Firetail. 18 inches. Snow white petals framing small, but fiery red cup.

Lady Diana Manners. 18 inches. Broad perianth with wide yellow cup margined deep red.

4. Leedsii. Crown and perianth of different dimensions.

a. Giant. In dimensions like incomparabilis

Daisy Schaeffer. 16 inches. Pure white petals broadly overlapping. Huge crown, opening primrose, changing to white at base.

Gertie Millar. 14 inches. Snow perianth. Ivory crown, frilled at edge and fluted to base, often measures three inches across.

Mrs. R. O. Backhouse. 14 inches. Creamy white, flaring perianth. Rather short trumpet opens buff, matures a soft apricot-pink. LATE.

Silver Star. 22 inches. Broad white petals. Crown opens chrome but turns creamy white.

Tunis. 14 inches. Milk-white perianth. Giant crown opens primrose, passes to ivory, then deepens to copper at its frilled, recurved brim.

b. Small-cupped. In dimension like barrii

Hera. 12 inches. Perianth white, fluted cup opening primrose changing to cream.

Mrs. Nette O'Melveny. 16 inches. Broad white petals, small cup of lemon yellow faintly tinged orange at brim.

White Lady. 18 inches. Milk white perianth, with small cup of yellow turning to ivory and deeply frilled at edge.

5. Triandrus Hybrids. Varieties whose ancestors include one of the various triandrus species. Generally all-white with short pointed petals recurved. Usually cluster-flowering.

Agnes Harvey. 14 inches. Snow white perianth and cup. Informal petals. Not generally cluster-flowering.

Elizabeth Prentice. 14 inches. All-white flower of erect habit. Large cup is slightly fluted.

Moonshine. 12 inches. Creamy white, drooping clusters of star-shaped flowers.

Queen of Spain. 14 inches. Lemon yellow with sharply reflexed petals.

Thalia. 18 inches. Pure white florets of large size with recurved petals.

6. Cyclamineus Hybrids. Varieties one of whose ancestors is the species, cyclamineus.

February Gold. 12 inches. Bright yellow with perianth petals recurved. EXTREMELY EARLY.

March Sunshine. 12 inches. Golden yellow with narrow reflexed petals. A LITTLE LATER THAN FEBRUARY GOLD BUT STILL VERY EARLY.

Turn A'Penny. 10 inches. A new hybrid, apparently with cyclamineus blood. Creamy yellow perianth with broadly overlapping petals. Small, lemon-yellow cup edged crimson.

7. Jonquilla and Jonquilla Hybrids. Usually all-yellow and frequently cluster-flowering.

Campernelle. 12 inches. Flat perianth and tiny cup of golden yellow. Fragrant.

Golden Sceptre. 16 inches. Large florets of deep yellow.

Simplex. Single Sweet Jonquil. 8 inches. Small blossom of pure gold. Very fragrant.

Trevithian. 16 inches. Deep, luminous, primrose florets.

8. Tazetta and Tazetta Hybrids. Cluster flowering. Tender Polyanthus.

Paperwhite Grandiflora. Fragrant clusters of small, pure

white florets. For indoor growing only in climates colder than Florida or Southern California.

Soleil d'Or. Clusters of florets with primrose perianths and orange cups. Sweet scented. Also for indoors.

Hardy Poetaz.

Glorious. 16 inches. White with yellow cups edged orange-red. Two to three florets of large individual size per stem.

Halvose. 14 inches. Pale primrose perianth with orange-yellow cup. Many florets per stem.

La Fiancée. 16 inches. Snow white perianth, lemon yellow cup. Thickly clustered.

Red Guard. 16 inches. Primrose perianth, deep red cup. Individual florets of large size.

Scarlet Gem. 16 inches. Petals of deep chrome, cups of vivid scarlet.

9. Poeticus.

Actaea. 18 inches. Snow white perianth with broadly overlapping petals. Flat eye of yellow with bright red rim.

Crenver. 18 inches. Formal perianth of pure white with red-rimmed eye.

Recurvus. Pheasant's Eye. 10 inches. Markedly recurved white petals, small, crimson-edged eye. VERY LATE.

10. Double.

Cheerfulness. 14 inches. Small white florets with creamy yellow centers blossoming in clusters.

Daphne. 16 inches. Pure white, gardenia-like, double flower.

Holland's Glory. 18 inches. Soft primrose, trumpet-shaped.

Insulinde. 14 inches. Sulphur yellow with center petals deep orange.

Irene Copeland. 14 inches. Alternating white and creamy white petals. Very full double.

Mary Copeland. 16 inches. Snowy white with center petals orange red.

Twink. 16 inches. Outer petals light yellow, inner petals orange-yellow.

Valencia. 14 inches. Deep yellow petals interspersed with creamy yellow. Very large, full double.

11. Various. Each a recognized species.

Bulbocodium conspicuus. Hoop-petticoat daffodil. 6 inches. Deep primrose. Starry perianth, composed of tiny, thin petals, frames a medium-sized cup.

Bulbocodium citrinus. 6 inches. Lemon yellow form of Hoop-petticoat daffodil.

Cyclamineus. 5 inches. Golden yellow. Tube-like crown. Thin perianth petals reflex straight back from cup.

Juncifolius. Golden yellow. 6 inches. Tiny flower with rush-like foliage.

Triandrus albus. Angel's Tears. 5 inches. Pure white. Small, pointed, recurved petals surrounding miniature cup.

Triandrus calathina. 8 inches. Creamy white with fluted cup. About twice the size of albus.

Triandrus pulchellus. 8 inches. Primrose perianth with creamy white cup.

CHAPTER FIFTEEN

The Return of the Hyacinth

Hʏᴀᴄɪɴᴛʜs—fragrant, colorful and indispensable—for thousands of years have brought delight to the heart of man. These major spring flowers bloom before daffodils are under way and offer a wide variety of color while May-flowering tulips are still in green bud. Since hyacinths include blue, their color span exceeds that of tulips, although the shades are always soft.

There was a time when hyacinths were a more important feature of outdoor planting than they are today but their popularity is returning. Gardeners are taking renewed satisfaction in these sturdy spikes of thickly clustered bells. They are discovering that practically every garden offers an opportunity to display them.

Hyacinths for a time were under a cloud. They were considered suitable only for conventional designs and the planting styles of this generation emphasized the informal. Now formal use of them in an adequate setting is again recognized as beautiful. The individual flower is thus revealed in its perfection, while the garden is filled with fragrance for weeks.

If you have sunny beds of geometric design by all means start the season with hyacinths. You must be absolutely formal, however, edging the beds evenly with a low line of box, clipped ivy or Teucrium chamaedrys. Design your own color pattern but follow it precisely. Select varieties which have the same blooming period. Place the bulbs exactly to scale and not more than eight inches apart from center to center. Then the foliage will provide sufficient ground cover. Cover each bulb with just four inches of soil so that all will flower together and at the same height. Plant only uniform, top size bulbs.

To free formal beds for summer plantings hyacinths after flowering are lifted and heeled in, with varieties kept separate. When leaves have ripened the bulbs are removed from the trench and stored until autumn. In October they are sorted. Only those of a size comparable to the ones originally planted are put back in the beds. The smaller ones are used in the cutting garden or for informal plantings. Additional new bulbs may have to be obtained to make up the quantity required for the next year's uniform display.

When I see fine formal plantings of hyacinths in my friends' gardens, I nearly burst with envy. Having no formal garden of my own I have never attempted a poor imitation by carving circles and squares out of the lawn and filling in with hyacinths. But I do plant them informally, quantities of them, for the beauty and fragrance they bring in spring. Though not often included in perennial beds, hyacinths provide there an early center of interest. Pansies, Anemone pulsatilla or blue and lavender shades of Phlox subulata look well planted in front of them while daffodils, early tulips and Anchusa myosotidiflora make excellent companions.

Borders along a picket fence or below a stone wall are fine sites for hyacinths. One of my friends has such a narrow border beside his house and below his library window. With a southeastern exposure and in the sunshine reflected from the wall, hyacinths blossom there every spring two weeks ahead of mine.

Many other situations are fine for hyacinths. A broad band bordering the peony bed is attractive. The light pink variety, Crown Princess Margaret, is lovely before the early ruby growth of peonies. Hyacinths also look well in a single line or in repeated colonies to the fore of low shrubbery. I know of one planting of the dark blue Duke of Westminster with groups of the early flowering daffodil Silver Star behind it. The arching stems of forsythia complete a lovely picture, since the bulbs are happy in the loose soil and receive plenty of sun during their ripening period.

On one property which has far too many trees for any kind of garden, not a summer flower is attempted, but in hyacinth time there is a gorgeous display. To the left of the drive lies a narrow strip shaded by tall oaks with shrubs underneath. Grass will not grow but there is an attractive border of early spring bulbs. The violet hyacinth, Grand Maître, hugs the curb, while behind it are great pools of the orange Single Early tulip, De Wet, and the golden trumpet daffodil, King Alfred. The hyacinths receive enough sun to carry on. The tulips and narcissi grow under difficulties, but with partial replacement every other year the display is maintained.

The culture of hyacinths is similar to that of other major spring-flowering bulbs. They like a four-inch covering of good loamy soil and a half-day of sun both for blooming and ripening. Hyacinths planted informally may be left in the ground for a long time. Mine stay from six to eight years. While I take pleasure in the full-bodied substance of the first year's flower, I also enjoy the many spikes of loosely clustered bells which the divided bulbs send up in succeeding seasons. Hyacinths seem to enjoy being left alone, calling to mind the old couplet:

> "To keep its grace, this lovely truss
> Must not be given too much fuss."

Today these bulbs are offered in different sizes and in a wealth of varieties suitable for both indoor and outdoor growing. All but the French and Dutch Roman kinds are hardy. The smaller bulbs send up thin spikes of loosely hung bells which some gardeners find more graceful than the full trusses produced by the top size bulbs. Certain kinds, like the pink variety, Gertrude, for example, have such thick inflorescence that they present a stuffy appearance. I think all the double-flowered hyacinths have this look.

The following varieties of single hyacinths are selected for outdoor beauty and growing vigor:

Arentine Arendsen. Pure white. Slender, tapering spike. EARLY.

Bleu Aimable. Lavender blue.

City of Haarlem. Primrose when forced, creamy yellow outdoors.

Crown Princess Margaret. Large, full spike of light rose bells.

Dr. Stresemann. Porcelain blue with dark purple stem showing through.

Duke of Westminster. Clear dark blue with white center on each floret.

Grand Maître. Bluish violet. Easy to force and very free-flowering outdoors.

Heraut. Shell pink, flushed rose. EARLY.

Ivanhoe. Dark blue. LATE.

Lady Darby. Soft rose.

La Grandesse. White waxy bells.

L'Innocence. Snow white. Flat topped truss.

Myosotis. Pale blue, shaded lilac. Loosely hung bells.

Oranjeboven. Salmon-orange. Medium-sized flower of unusual shade.

Prince Henry. Light primrose.

Royal Scarlet. Unusually deep rose for a hyacinth. Medium sized spike.

CHAPTER SIXTEEN

Early and Irrepressible

Every year before there are any other visible signs that winter will not last forever the earliest and most irrepressible of the spring bulbs blossom. While the major hosts of the flower kingdom linger in their safe retreats, the audacious snowdrops, chionodoxas, winter aconites, crocuses and squills push forth to scout the way. These little bulbs have been developing near sheets of ice and snow in that top layer of the earth's crust where winter's heaving and thawing work such havoc on larger but less stalwart plants. Despite frost warnings, out they come, daring winter to do its worst, an impudent challenge which is never turned down.

Every garden, no matter where it is, should have some of these small staunch harbingers to cheer the heart and stiffen the spine of the gardener as he watches their brave show from his warm house. The primrose flash of winter aconites, the fresh astonishing clusters of blue chionodoxas, and the tufts of purple crocuses, opening here and there in the garden, are an unfailing delight. Indeed, I know gardeners who every spring search among the leaves for the first snowdrops with all the glee of children hunting hidden Easter eggs.

These early gems can be more than heralds, lovely as they are in that role. If you have seen only individual flowers of the earliest spring bulbs, you have no idea how imposing they can be when planted in masses. If you have previously tucked a dozen or so squills and crocuses into odd corners, try colonizing them by the hundred or even thousand. They make a telling display. Freely planted, they proclaim with glorious drifts of beauty not that spring is on the way, but that it has already arrived.

GALANTHUS—SNOWDROPS

Earliest and most insistent of the advance guard of spring is the snowdrop, or galanthus, a member of the amaryllis family. Let winter show the slightest sign of weariness in January or February and these indomitable plants, whose sharp pincers have already thrust through icy ground, rush into bloom. They blossom while the robin from the safe vantage of the warm south still ponders his northern journey.

One year I had flowers from a single colony of Galanthus elwesii in January, February and March. It was a bitter old-time winter but in mid-January the weather relented enough for a few of the white bells to come boldly forth. More buds were about to open when the cold again descended with a sudden snow. The mercury never got above the low twenties until Lincoln's birthday, which ushered in a balmy week. The disappearing snow revealed snowdrops in full bud. They had spent the intervening weeks waiting until the white blanket melted down to their feet. A goodly number of them immediately flowered only to be greeted again by sleet and cold. Surely, I thought, this was the end of them for that season; there would be no further attempt. But with the first mild weather of March I was delighted to see the most profuse bloom of all.

Room for snowdrops can be found in almost any garden. If no other place is available, a tiny colony on either side of the front door steps will yield late winter delight. Snowdrops naturalize easily when planted under three inches of soil. One of the prettiest sights I ever saw was a gently sloping hill naturalized with snowdrops. There were trees enough to offer the right amount of shade, while their annual fall of leaves provided humus. Both shade and humus were also welcome to scillas, trilliums, dutchman's breeches and bloodroot naturalized there so that this hillside gladdened the eye each spring for the many years I knew it—and for all I know it still does.

The following varieties of snowdrops are recommended:

Byzantinus. White, large, extremely early. Rare.
Elwesii. White flowers, tinged green. The variety most commonly offered. Needs warm sun to naturalize.
Fosteri. White with deep green foliage. Large and tall. Rare.
Nivalis. White flowers. Later to bloom than Elwesii and smaller, it is better for naturalizing. Thrives in shade in soil containing humus.
Nivalis Flore Pleno. Double-flowered white form. Fairly rare.

CHIONODOXAS—GLORY OF THE SNOW

These lovely chionodoxas give the garden its first color. Familiar to most gardeners as four-inch clusters of bright blue blossoms with white centers, they are sometimes confused with Scilla sibirica. Squills are a deeper blue and hang their bells, while chionodoxas look up.

These members of the lily family usually come on the heels of snowdrops, although snowdrops by natural inclination would flower weeks ahead, if the cold relented soon enough. Chionodoxas come in time for the bloom of early shrubs and trees. Planted beneath forsythia and Magnolia stellata or with the species tulip, Kaufmanniana, they are a charming sight. They naturalize readily by seeding themselves wherever they are left undisturbed in humus-filled soil under light shade.

Plant chionodoxas by the hundred or the five hundred in a thin copse of white birch. They will reward you with yearly sheets of blue when the daffodil buds are beginning to show color. If you have a bank or woodland path include chionodoxas in your planting. If a large boulder juts out from some bank or slope, create a beautiful picture by planting masses of chionodoxas above it and down the sides of the bank where the stone emerges from the earth. A two-inch soil covering is sufficient for these bulbs.

It is said that chionodoxas do not naturalize under evergreens, but I once planted a large colony under a hemlock which crowned a little knoll. They not only thrived, but produced many seedlings. In a few years rivulets of vivid blue were running down the slope from the original planting.

The following varieties of chionodoxas are recommended:

Gigantea. Clear azure blue. A larger species than the familiar luciliae. About six inches tall.

Luciliae. Bright, azure blue with white centers. The variety chiefly grown.

Luciliae alba. White form of luciliae.

Luciliae rosea. Pink form. Buds open a good blush color, which fades to a very pale pink with maturity. Both the white and pink are as hardy as the blue, but not so effective when naturalized.

Sardensis. A deeper blue than the ordinary Luciliae, but slightly smaller.

ERANTHIS—WINTER ACONITE

The winter aconites are the earliest yellow flowers. They open up like buttercups, bright but not golden. They are framed by a deep green ruff. Thickly colonized, they convey a deceptive but welcome sense of warmth to the early spring air.

Winter aconites grow best in areas where they get early season sun on their blooms but protection from hot rays in summer. A good spot is by the south corner of the house under a tree whose lowest boughs are at least eight feet from the ground. It is all the better if the grass grows too sparsely to form thick sod, but thickly enough so that the gardener is not tempted to plant anything over the winter aconite.

The eranthis belongs to the ranunculus clan and grows from little tubers which look like enlarged and thoroughly desiccated raisins. They are best planted not later than August or early September, but as they usually come over from Holland with the tulips and daffodils they may not arrive before October. They should be planted promptly. To increase the percentage of yield, place the tubers in wet sand overnight or until they plump up. Give them a two-inch covering of soil. The best available varieties are the following:

Cilicica. Primrose flowers with deep green foliage tinged bronze. Large.
Hyemalis. Bright primrose backed by deep green ruff. The best known and most commonly grown winter aconite.
Tubergenii. Deep yellow hybrid of large size. Rare.

CROCUSES

The spring-flowering species and hybrids of the crocus are beloved by gardeners and are the familiar early members of the bulb kingdom. They may be seen scattered on suburban lawns in every community. The tender green leaves win the devotion of rabbits, while the succulent corms are too often a highly prized delicacy of squirrels.

You have probably grown a few crocuses in the lawn or beneath shrubs, or to the fore of the foundation planting. Have you ever tried massing them under a large tree? Plant a great patch of five hundred or a thousand corms of violet Gladstone, porcelain blue Enchantress or white Snowstorm under a lofty elm or beech. You will never forget the sight.

You will also enjoy crocuses in an informal border along the flagstone path or the shady side of the house. If you plant them in the lawn, be sure to skip the crocus areas for the first two mowings. You may omit this precaution only if you are willing to plant new bulbs every other year. You can naturalize them easily in the meadow or a lightly shaded wood, provided you carry out vigorous liquidation programs against rabbits and squirrels. You will find crocuses, like all of the early bulbs, at home in the rock garden and they are easy fun for the winter window gardener.

For any planting site a wide range of varieties is available. Hybrids of the original crocus vernus are sold as "Dutch Crocuses" and are grown commercially in bewildering array. They come in white and yellow and in many shades of blue, lavender, violet and purple. They possess such fascinating individuality that they should always be bought and grown by name. There are also many species collected and propagated as original types, which are truly delightful and even more suitable for woodland and rock garden. All kinds need but a two-inch soil covering.

Below is a selection of types and colors which deserve space in the garden:

CROCUS VERNUS (DUTCH CROCUS)

Enchantress. Porcelain blue with violet base.
Excelsior. Lavender blue. Enormous flower.
Mammoth Yellow. Golden yellow. Very free blooming.
Maximilian. Sky blue, shaded lavender. Small flower.
Mikado. White ground, striped grey and mauve.
Purpurea Grandiflora. Rich, deep, dark purple.
Gladstone. Large, wide open violet. Large, wide open blossom.
Snowstorm. Glistening white. Large blooms.
Striped Beauty. White ground with stripes of violet.

Biflorus. The Scotch Crocus. White background, striped lilac.
Wild looking, wide open flower. VERY EARLY. Blooms in
February or March.

Imperati. Buff, feathered lilac-purple. Inside soft lilac. Long
blossom.

Korolkowi. Sulphur yellow shaded tan. Starry flower.

Sieberi. Pale lilac with very bright orange anthers. VERY
EARLY.

Susianus. Cloth of Gold. Deep orange yellow. Medium sized
flower which opens out perfectly flat.

Tomasinianus. Wide open flower of soft lavender blue. EARLY.
Exceedingly prolific.

SCILLA SIBIRICA—SQUILLS

The scilla genus of the lily
family gives us many indispensable garden flowers, but
none is more welcome than the
early species, sibirica, known
as the blue squill. Its intense
blue appears as the crocuses
fade and after the earliest
daffodils and tulips have
begun to bloom. Its stems
grow four to six inches tall
and hold three or four open
bells which often do not fade
for weeks.

Early scillas look well beneath shrubs or trees, along
the woodland path or in the rock garden. They naturalize
easily under three inches of soil, and are desirable for lasting

woodland drifts of blue or for plantings with early yellow daffodils.

The relatively late flowering time of scilla sibirica among the early bulbs affords opportunity to combine it with other flowers. Try planting the type, coerulea, with Tulipa kaufmanniana. Or combine a group of the new variety, Spring Beauty, with kaufmanniana Brilliant. Naturalize drifts of sibirica with Narcissus incomparabilis, Carlton, and leedsii, Silver Star, for striking contrast.

The following are the best varieties for the amateur to grow:

Scilla Sibirica Alba. White form of the squill.
Scilla Sibirica Coerulea. Type form. The blue squill of commerce.
Scilla Sibirica Atrocoerulea. Darker blue and a little taller than the type.
Scilla Sibirica, Spring Beauty. Intense bright blue bells. Very large and taller than the type. Very free flowering.

CHAPTER SEVENTEEN

Satellites for Spring Stars

THE early harbingers are followed by a truly vast display of spring beauty from bulbs. Then come the hyacinths, daffodils and tulips to which you rightly give first consideration when planning your spring garden. But these are only a fraction of the flowers which bloom every year from bulbs planted in the fall. There are many other kinds, such as the dogtooth violets, snowflakes, fritillarias and alliums which are not only pleasing, but moderate in price and easy to grow.

Many of these additional bulbs, brodiaeas, calochorti and erythroniums, for example, are native to this country. Others, like muscari, scillas and Fritillaria meleagris, have been grown in Holland for years. Even today you will find these catalogued under the wholly insufficient title—which gives no hint of their loveliness—of Miscellaneous Bulbs.

Whatever their grouping or origin you will want these less well-known bulbs to complete your spring planting. Some you will find invaluable as companions for the major flowers in the mixed bulb border or in perennial beds. You are probably familiar with grape hyacinths planted in the foreground of daffodils. There are an infinite number of other possibilities. Try planting clumps of the late snowflake, Leucojum aestivum, between drifts of the yellow Narcissus incomparabilis, Carlton. For effective contrast set small groups of the old-fashioned, dark orange crown imperial, Fritillaria imperialis, at the edge of a birch copse with large colonies of Narcissus leedsii, Hera, or Narcissus triandrus, Thalia.

The rock garden provides an ideal place for many of these interesting spring bulbs. Here there are small pockets where it is easy and convenient to provide the special soil requirements needed by certain native kinds, such as the calochortus and Western fritillarias. A vine-covered slope or bank provides fine setting for grape hyacinths and scillas. Along a woodland path Spanish bluebells, Scilla campanulata, will colonize in thick patches under both deciduous and evergreen shade.

As varied as the ways in which spring-flowering bulbs can be planted is the list of the flowers themselves. To discuss adequately all of the different species and varieties which could be grown in the United States would tax the limits of a book, let alone those of a single chapter. I shall therefore limit this section to those bulbs which are generally available, reasonable in their cultural requirements, and for me necessary to the full enjoyment of spring.

For gardeners who think of their plants in terms of how easy or difficult a flower is to grow I would make three groupings. Almost certain of success, even in the poorest environment and with the maximum of neglect are the following: alliums, bulbocodiums, leucojums, muscari, Ornithogalum nutans, puschkinias and scillas. Easy to grow if some slight attention is paid to their culture are these: brodiaeas, calochorti, camassias, claytonias, dicentras, erythroniums, fritillarias, ixiolirion, zygadenus. Recommended for the gardener who will take trouble to grow flowers not commonly found in spring gardens are anemones, ixias, ranunculus and sparaxis.

All these are planted in the fall and will blossom the following spring or summer. Some can be held over for spring planting. Most are perfectly hardy but some, when planted north of Mason and Dixon's line, must have special protection. The discussion is alphabetical rather than according to importance or time of bloom.

ALLIUM

There are three kinds of alliums and gardeners should have positive feelings toward each. There are alliums which should be cordially hated because they are weeds. I mean the wild garlic or wild onion so rampant and so difficult to eradicate wherever it gets a foothold. Other alliums, scores of varieties, should be beloved for the colorful and often fragrant flowers they bear. A third group embraces the succulent onions, shallots and chives which add so much flavor to fine cooking which gardeners as well as others can enjoy.

The flowers of alliums are borne in clusters or umbels at the top of stems from five inches to four feet tall. On some varieties the florets hang down. On others they are held erect. Allium species are found in a wide range of color. Those commercially available include purple, blue, lilac-rose, yellow and white. The blooming season extends from May to August.

If you do not already grow alliums it is probably because you do not know them. You will find them robust in loamy soil in from half to full sun. Plant them under a three-inch covering of earth. In a few years you will probably have a dense colony ready for thinning. You can make a new planting from the increase. Use the shorter varieties for the rock garden and the taller ones for shady nooks and for cutting. Remember, in cultivating alliums, that the foliage when broken gives off a strong onion odor although undamaged it has no scent. For this reason you will want to use fern or other foliage to make your allium bouquet.

The following species are desirable:

Acuminatum. 12 inches. LATE MAY. Flower segments half white, half pink giving effect of pink flower. Large umbel with erect florets. Colonizes freely in sun or semi-shade.

Atro-purpureum. 40 inches. AUGUST. Wine purple. Large flower heads.

Azureum. 18 inches. EARLY MAY. Deep blue. Dense clusters.

Cernuum. 15 inches. JUNE. Loose umbel. Naturalizes vigorously in sun or light shade.

Flavum. 10 inches. LATE JUNE. Clear yellow. Loose cluster of pendant florets. Foliage stays green all summer.

Giganteum. 48 inches. JULY. Light violet. Large, globular blossoms. Foliage grows in low rosette.

Moly. 12 inches. EARLY JUNE. Bright yellow.

Neapolitanum. 15 inches. EARLY MAY. White. Needs light mulch north of New York.

Neapolitanum Grandiflorum. 18 inches. EARLY MAY. White. Larger form of neapolitanum.

Ostrowskianum. 10 inches. EARLY JUNE. Reddish violet.

Pulchellum. 12 inches. JULY. Soft lilac.

Purdomii. 5 inches. LATE JUNE. Bright lilac.

Rosenbachianum. 48 inches. JUNE. Bright violet-rose. Huge flower heads.

Stellatum. 15 inches. AUGUST–SEPTEMBER. Lilac-rose. Loose umbels.

ANEMONE

Over the northern portion of the country the fibrous-rooted anemones, japonica and pulsatilla, are often seen in gardens but the tuberous-rooted varieties are restricted to indoor growing. These are gay and bright, very popular as florists' blossoms. If you have a little greenhouse undoubtedly you do grow some of the vivid forms of Anemone coronaria. Even without the greenhouse you can still have these "lilies of the field" blossoming outside in the spring, if you are willing to go to a little trouble.

For outside blooming plant the small tubers under three inches of soil in late October or November. Cover them with a six- to eight-inch mulch of leaves or coarse peat moss as soon as frost enters the ground. When the season for heavy frosts is past, gradually remove this covering as the foliage comes through. Your friends will exclaim, "How did you ever get these to bloom out in the garden?" when they see the bright red and blue of the poppy-flowered sorts or the mixed colors of the double strains.

You can also grow anemones outdoors from bulbs planted in the fall in shallow cold frames. Mulch in the same way but do not put a covering sash over the frame. If you plant the tubers in the earth at the bottom of the frame the bloom will, of course, be restricted to this enclosure. To avoid this, plant the anemones in pots and sink these in the frame. Then just before blossoming move them to the garden beds plunging them deeply enough so that the pots will not show.

You can enjoy anemone bloom outdoors by planting in the spring instead of the fall, but the more difficult fall-planting results in better yield. If you set out your tubers in the spring, you may either buy them in the fall and store them over the winter, or purchase them from held-over commercial stocks. In either case a certain percentage of the tubers will have lost their vitality by spring but enough will come through to make a worthwhile and inexpensive show.

However and whenever planted, the anemone should be in good, loamy soil high in humus content. After the foliage ripens, the bulbs may be dug up and stored over the winter in the same manner as tender summer-flowering bulbs. Or they may be left in the ground provided you give them as much protective mulch as would be required by new tubers planted outside in the fall.

A number of species anemones exist which are hardy with light protection or when grown in very sheltered positions in the rock garden or on a sunny, southern slope. Most of these are too rare in this country to warrant mention but the wild, native wood anemone or windflower is an exception. This will naturalize for you if you can find a spot it likes in a lightly shaded area.

If you are a gardener who wants only bulbs which demand no special treatment or time-consuming care, forego anemones or buy them from the florist. If you like to fuss with uncommonly pretty flowers not usually found in gardens, you will find these varieties interesting and beautiful:

Blue Poppy. 12 inches. Bright blue. Large single blossoms.
De Caen. 12 to 14 inches. Mixed colors. French strain of poppy-flowered varieties.

His Excellency. 12 inches. Bright scarlet, white base with
black center. Large 3-inch blossom.

Quinquefolia. American Wood Anemone. 4 inches. White,
faintly tinged pink on petal reverse.

St. Brigid. 12 inches. Mixed colors. Double flowered strain.

The Bride. 12 inches. Pure white.

BRODIAEA

Brodiaeas, natives of the Pacific
states, are welcomed by the gardener who wishes to go a little beyond the ordinary run of spring
flowers. We are indebted to the
late Carl Purdy of Ukiah, California, for discovering many species of brodiaeas and making them
available. Bright blue, lavender,
red and yellow are colors repre-
sented in the brodiaea spectrum.

Plant brodiaeas promptly on arrival in late September or October.
They will thrive in sun although
some kinds naturalize in moderate
shade. They like loose gritty soil with enough humus to hold
a fair quantity of moisture. A covering of three inches is sufficient. Since the foliage is small and the flower stems lanky, they
look best planted closely and near the foliage of perennials.

I have grown a number of varieties from time to time, and
while they usually flower the first year I have learned not to
expect them to last forever. The following kinds I have found
attractive and reliable:

Bridgesii. 15 inches. LATE MAY. Reddish violet florets in cluster at top of stem.

Californica. 24 inches. LATE JUNE. Deep blue. Thick umbels.

Capitata. 8 inches. MID-MAY. Violet-blue. Dense clusters.

Coccinea. (Floral Firecracker) 18 inches. MID-MAY. Vivid red, capped green. Long tubular florets hanging in cluster at end of stem. Protruding white stamens suggest firecracker fuse.

Grandiflora. 12 inches. EARLY JUNE. Deep purple. Large cluster of trumpet-shaped florets with glossy petals. Naturalizes in clay.

Ixioides Splendens. (Golden Star) 10 inches. LATE MAY. Golden yellow with brown mid-vein. Loose umbels of starry florets.

Lactea. 10 inches. LATE MAY. Milky white with green mid-vein. Loose cluster of cup-shaped flowers.

Laxa. (Blue King) 10 inches. MID-MAY. Deep indigo blue. Long tubular flowers.

Uniflora Violacea. (Tritelia Uniflora Violacea) 6 inches. EARLY MAY. Violet-blue. Starry clusters of fragrant florets. Naturalizes with a little protection in sun or shade.

BULBOCODIUM—SPRING MEADOW SAFFRON

The meadow saffron, a little known, crocus-like flower, is one of the earliest and best of the spring bulbs. The only variety in cultivation is vernum, a lavender-pink. Your friends will inevitably mistake it for an early crocus and will wonder how it got to be so large and so pink. Bulbocodium is charming for the rock garden and excellent for naturalizing with chionodoxa and species crocus. It likes a three-inch covering of light soil and full sun or very little shade.

CALOCHORTUS—GLOBE TULIPS, STAR TULIPS, BUTTERFLY TULIPS

Mariposa

The bright-hued, dainty flowers of calochortus bring gaiety to the spring garden. They are western natives and many of them are more finds of Carl Purdy's. They will flourish in your garden for many seasons if planted under three inches of soil which is not heavy or soggy. With too much cultivating or too protracted a rainy spell in summer they may die out. If they do, they are well worth replacing.

Calochortus species are classed according to flower form as globe tulips, star tulips and butterfly tulips. Colors include lavender, yellow, pink and cream. Most have handsome brown eyes of varying size and intensity. All flower in late May.

GLOBE TULIPS

Will grow in light shade.

Albus. 18 inches. White satin lanterns swinging on slender stems.

Amabilis. 16 inches. Rich yellow with deep brown centers. Branching stems.

Amoenus. 8 inches. Soft pink.

STAR TULIPS

Will grow in light shade, shorter and suitable for rock garden.

Benthami. 5 inches. Bright yellow with black markings on base. Wide open flowers.

Maweanus Major. 6 inches. White with lavender hairs. Starry flowers.

Maweanus Purpurascens. 6 inches. Deep violet-purple.

Butterfly or Mariposa Tulips

Will grow in sun or very light shade.

Vesta. 18 inches. White flushed lilac or rose with broad center zone of deep brown.

Venustus Citrinus. 15 inches. Bright yellow with black eye. Wide flower often five inches across.

Venustus Eldorado. 18 inches. Varied color markings of white, claret, lilac and pink.

Venustus Oculatus. 18 inches. Vari-colored in tones of white or cream tinted purple.

CAMASSIA

The camassias should never be overlooked. They produce large effective flowers in graceful spikes of thirty to fifty individual florets. Camassias are effective in colonies of fifteen to twenty-five naturalized in woods where the soil is not too dry or along the banks of streams. They need a four-inch covering of soil. Blooming late in May, they lengthen the season for woodland flowers.

The following varieties are recommended:

Leichtlinii. 40 inches. Varying from light blue to gentian blue. Star-shaped florets.

Leichtlinii White. 40 inches. White and cream florets.

Quamash. 20 inches. Deep blue. Fine for naturalizing in open meadows.

CLAYTONIA—SPRING BEAUTY

The well-known little flower of the woods, spring beauty, Claytonia virginica, belongs here because it grows from a corm. It belongs in your garden because it is a picturesque symbol of early spring. Delicate white flowers tinted pink are clustered at the top of a five-inch stem. Spring beauty loves shade and woodland soil. Large plantings will thrive among colonies of snowdrops and the two rejoice in the shelter of ferns. The corms should be set three inches below the surface of the soil.

DICENTRA—SQUIRREL CORN, DUTCHMAN'S BREECHES

Two dicentras, close cousins of the bleeding heart, should be among the bulbs you plant in the fall. They are canadensis, the squirrel corn, and cucullaria, dutchman's breeches. Both grow from small tubers or clusters of tubers. Both produce plants under a foot tall with little racemes of white flowers in early April. Their fern-like foliage persists long after the flowers fade. They like shade and a woodland environment and should have a three-inch covering of soil.

The individual flowers of squirrel corn are heart shaped while the dutchman's breeches hang like miniature white pantaloons. Keep trying with both these plants until you succeed—it may be the first time—in establishing a small colony of each. They will reward you for your trouble. Besides, tiny as they are, the little racemes last well when cut, which is not true of many wild flowers.

Dicentra cucullaria

ERYTHRONIUM—DOGTOOTH VIOLET

You will understand the first part of the common name of the erythronium as soon as you see the bulbs. These are white and of a size and shape to suggest the tooth of a dog. Unlike real dog teeth, erythronium bulbs cannot be kept in little boys' pockets. They should be planted immediately, before they have any chance to dry out. They will probably come to you packed in peat moss to conserve their natural moisture.

Each year I get great satisfaction from the sight of these fascinating plants sending their spears up through the brown surface of wooded areas. I like to watch the leaves spread and take on the form and mottling characteristic of the species. I find the foliage as interesting as the flower which is truly charming. Some erythroniums are tiny with very short stems, others grow twelve to sixteen inches tall and with proportionately larger blossoms. But they all look fragile, like miniature porcelain lilies on stems so slender you wonder how they endure without damage the strongest winds of late March and April.

Plant erythroniums in any shaded spot where there is a moderate degree of moisture. Plant them by themselves or in front of daffodils or the tall shade-loving Fritillaria lanceolata. The dogtooth violets like a loamy soil which need not be deep, for they have a habit of burying themselves. If the soil is too light for too great a distance down without clay or pebbles to stop them, they will simply dig themselves out of sight. Start them just three inches under the surface. If your soil in shaded areas is too clayey, you can mix the top six inches with peat moss or humus to make it satisfactory for erythroniums.

The eastern species, Americanum, is the familiar adder's tongue. In moist woods and shady slopes it is found in colonies which I am sure number millions. This species is sometimes transplanted and brought into gardens, but it is likely to be more productive of foliage than flowers. Most of the erythroniums in commerce today are collected California species. These not only flower more fully but have a wide color range. The blooms open about the middle of April and generally last through the first week of May.

The following varieties are recommended:

Californicum. 10 inches. Cream. Leaves mottled dark green.

Californicum Bicolor. 10 inches. Outer petals white, inner petals chrome.

Californicum White Beauty. 10 inches. White tinted cream, maroon zone at base.

Grandiflorum. 12 inches. Buttercup yellow. Plain green foliage.

Hendersonii. 12 inches. Lavender with maroon-purple centers.

Revolutum Pink Beauty. 14 inches. Light pink. Large clusters of blossoms. Will naturalize in almost any soil including wet clay.

Revolutum Johnsonii. 12 inches. Clear rose-pink.

Revolutum Purdy's White. 10 inches. Pure white flowers of large size.

Revolutum Praecox. 12 inches. Cream. Deep green leaves mottled brown.

Tuolumnensis. 16 inches. Golden yellow. Large, plain green leaves.

FRITILLARIA—CROWN IMPERIAL, GUINEA-HEN LILY, MISSION BELL

This far-flung member of the lily family includes widely different species, only three of which concern most American gardeners—imperialis, the crown imperial of old-time gardens; meleagris, the guinea-hen lily, and lanceolata, the mission bell, typifying the native group. Of these the largest and showiest is the crown imperial with bulbs the size of large hyacinths. Imperialis sends up thick stems three feet

Fritillaria imperialis

long. At the top a cluster of bells hangs to form an umbel eight
inches across. The color of the imperialis of our childhood
memories was always deep brick red, but other shades are now
grown.

The crown imperial likes sweet, rich soil with a covering
of four inches in full or partial shade. It is nearly always
planted, as it should be, immediately on arrival since its strong
odor is no temptation to keep it overlong out of the ground.
No discussion of this plant would be complete without some
reference to this odor which is given off not only by the bulb,
but also by the plant, especially in its early stages. In the early
spring air it is not unpleasant, in fact, faintly tangy, like the
smell of a distant skunk scented on a cool summer night in
the Adirondack woods.

Modern varieties, of which the best are listed below, include not only the old red, but yellow and orange as well. The
following bloom in early May:

Aurore. Orange-red.
Crown Upon Crown. Two decks of red bells.
Lutea Maxima. Bright yellow.
Orange Brilliant. Vivid orange-red.
Red Star. Bright red.

The meleagris is one of the smaller-flowered species of this
genus. The checkered lily, or guinea-hen lily, rises on wiry
ten-inch stems from which long, narrow leaves branch off at
intervals. The flowers hang down like squarish bells composed of six pointed segments.

Plant Fritillaria meleagris bulbs in large colonies under
three inches of loamy soil which will not dry out or bake in
summer. You can grow it in sun or light shade. Candid advice consists in telling you to order more bulbs than you expect to plant and to plant more than you expect will perma-
nently establish themselves. Discard all bulbs which appear

to have completely dried out on their way from Holland and plant the others when you receive them. The majority will come through the first year. Those which flower for three successive years can be counted on to appear regularly thereafter each spring unless thoughtlessly rooted out.

Hollanders grow Fritillaria meleagris in named varieties. These are either white or some form of purple or reddish purple. The purple shades are generally offered in mixture, and the white variety separate. This is a satisfactory way to buy them.

The mission bells, native to our West, are similar to Fritillaria meleagris but are a little taller with the flower segments opening out a little more. They include a greater variety of colors. Individual culture varies with the species but they all require a three-inch covering of loamy or gritty, well-drained soil. Sometimes, even in satisfactory situations, they will cease flowering for a year or two while they will produce a flat leaf but no flower stem. Then, if all conditions are favorable, blossoming will be resumed.

The following species are worth trying:

Lanceolata. 18-24 inches. Mottled brown and green. Likes shade and well-drained woods soil.
Pluriflora. 8 inches. Deep rose. Wide open bells. Sun lover.
Pudica. 8 inches. Pure golden. Individual, long bells. Naturalizes robustly in full sun.
Recurva. 15 inches. Deep orange. Sharply recurved bells. Naturalizes in woods.

IXIA—AFRICAN CORN LILY

Where are the reds and rose tones among the early flowers which come before the hyacinths, daffodils and tulips? Among the snowdrops, crocuses and muscari we have whites and yellows and blues. Among the muscari an occasional orchid-pink may appear but real rose is lacking. In southern gardens where the ixia, or African corn lily, is grown this lack is not felt for these foot high spikes abound in bright tones of pink and carmine as well as blue and yellow. These shades, along with bronze, copper and green provide a festival of color in late winter.

North of the Carolinas ixias are chiefly greenhouse dwellers. Yet they can be grown outside too from bulbs planted in October with the same care prescribed for anemones. Ixias are even more tender than anemones, so they are more dependent upon a sunny, protected spot and a little heavier mulch of leaves to keep them warm. Since this cannot be removed until the season of frosts has passed, ixias will not flower in the same relative part of the season as they do in southern gardens but they may be brought into bloom with the late daffodils. Trial spots in the garden should be saved for ixias. They produce a startlingly gay and unusual display.

These varieties of ixias are recommended:

Afterglow. Orange and amber. Deep bronze center.
Azurea. Light blue with eye of maroon.
Bloom Erf. A new strain offered in mixed colors ranging from white through light to deep pink. Three feet tall with racemes of twenty to forty florets.
Bridesmaid. White with carmine eyes.
King of the Yellows. Golden yellow, purple center.

Mozart. Pure golden yellow.
Smiling Mary. Bright cerise.
Viridiflora. Green with black eyes.

IXIOLIRION—SIBERIAN BLUEBELL

This little-grown flower
from Asia produces a surprisingly large stalk and flower
from a very small bulb. The
species pallasi is the only one
offered. This sends up a spike
eighteen to twenty inches with
the last eight inches bearing a
cluster of intense blue flowers.
The whole has somewhat the
appearance of a very elon-
gated, but extremely light and
feathery hyacinth truss, ideal
for cutting. Ixiolirion flowers
at the end of May. It is hardy
and can be planted in the fall without any mulch, although it
insists on light, friable soil. A three-inch covering is advisable.

LEUCOJUM—SUMMER SNOWDROP OR
SNOWFLAKE

The summer snowdrops or snowflakes are reminiscent of
those earlier flowers, the snowdrops, with which they are usually compared. Leucojums also have white bells hanging from
the ends of the stems. Snowflake bells are larger, however,
and the petals have distinguishing green tips. The thick foliage consists of deep green spears somewhat like narcissus
leaves except that the color has no tone of blue.

The hardy and interesting leucojums, in an early and a late form, bloom about a month apart; one opening in March and the other blossoming with the daffodils at the end of April. The late species is larger and taller. Both grow contentedly in the rock garden, open woods or on a stream bank. The early species needs but a three-inch soil covering, while the later kind should be given four inches. These species are readily available:

Aestivum. Summer Snowflake. 12 inches. LATE APRIL. White, green-tipped bells in clusters of three to five.
Aestivum Gravetye. 18 inches. LATE APRIL. Much larger-flowered and taller form of aestivum.
Vernum. Spring Snowflake. 6-8 inches. LATE MARCH. White, green-tipped bells in clusters of three to four.

MUSCARI—GRAPE HYACINTHS

The tight little blue spikes of grape hyacinths have come to be almost as well known in our spring gardens as the daffodils with which they associate so attractively. While they like the sun, they thrive abundantly in almost any kind of open situation and in any kind of soil, unless it is very heavy and waterlogged. Furthermore, they often escape from gardens and take over the surrounding farms, as the millions of "bluebottles" to be seen every spring in the fields and meadows of eastern Pennsylvania and Maryland so charmingly attest.

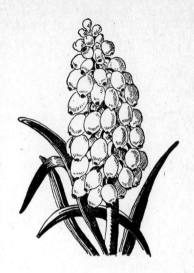

Muscari not only persist, but multiply. You may have had the experience of planting several hundred bulbs one year to find a few years later that you had several thousand. You will find this wonderful habit of increase adds to the usefulness of muscari as a naturalizer. Set the bulbs three inches apart, and under three inches of soil. You will have dense blue masses in a year or two. Then you can lift them, using the increase to start new colonies elsewhere.

Plant grape hyacinths in front of both white and yellow daffodils. Drift them with groups of blue Phlox subulata and perennial forget-me-nots to afford a contrasting variety of blues with the whites and yellows of the narcissi. An informal edge of muscari lends a finished touch to a border of Triumph tulips in any color range. A thick planting at the foot of low shrubs below your library window is something to look forward to every spring. Muscari also thrive in the rock garden or in the exposed areas of a bank. They make a pretty pattern naturalized in the light shade of an orchard or weaving a fine blue carpet beneath a single fruit tree.

While the deep blue and, to a lesser extent, the white forms are best known, there are others, interestingly varied in color and form. Perhaps you can find a spot for these:

Armeniacum. 8 inches. APRIL. Deep cobalt blue. Should be standard grape hyacinth for amateurs, although its foliage is rather strong and spreading for the rock garden.

Azureum (Hyacinthus Azureus). 8 inches. LATE MARCH THROUGH EARLY APRIL. Sky blue gem for the rock garden.

Botryoides Album. 7 inches. APRIL. White. Thin spike of closely knit bells. Combines well with purple Phlox subulata or purple species Iris, pumila.

Comosum. The Tassel Hyacinth. 8 inches. APRIL. Violet. Flowers borne in loose tassel at top of spike.

Conicum. 8 inches. LATE APRIL. Dark blue. Pointed cone.

Heldreichii. 8 inches. APRIL. Lilac-blue with ends of bells tipped white.

Neglectum. 8 inches. LATE APRIL. Deep blue. Fragrant. Pointed cone.

Neglectum Rosea. 8 inches. LATE APRIL. Rosy lavender.

Plumosum. The Feather Hyacinth. 9 inches. EARLY MAY. Violet-blue. Long spike of loose, feathery bells. Naturalizes easily.

Racemosum. The Starch Hyacinth. 8 inches. LATE APRIL. Deep blue with lower bells tipped white. Prolific grower.

ORNITHOGALUM NUTANS—SILVER BELLS

The ornithogalum is usually considered in only two of its species: highly, in the case of arabicum, an easily grown indoor bulb which sends up long spikes of starry white flowers with huge black eyes, and indifferently, in the case of umbellatum, the weedy star of Bethlehem, small of flower and mighty of spread. There is yet another variety, a very old one whose garden value has been overlooked although I predict this will not long be true. This is Ornithogalum nutans, or silver bells.

This species sends up a fifteen-inch spike ending in an eight-inch truss of fascinating, flaring, silver-green bells. Flowering in late April, it definitely completes any woodland planting of daffodils, trilliums and mertensia. Indeed, if you have that wooded area where "nothing will grow," this is for you. Ornithogalum nutans is charming rising among young fern shoots. Later the developed fronds nicely cover its foliage. Give the bulbs a three-inch covering of soil.

PUSCHKINIA SCILLOIDES—STRIPED SQUILL

The striped squill, Puschkinia scilloides, so much resembles the scillas that it is often sold as one. It produces slender stems six inches long. On these are loosely hung dainty light blue bells, each with a mid-vein of deep blue. Puschkinias add grace to the rock garden or to the sunny outskirts of the woodland. They are an interesting addition to any collection of small bulbs, and they thrive robustly when covered with three inches of light soil.

RANUNCULUS—DOUBLE BUTTERCUP

It seems to me that I recall ranunculus growing as commonly as nasturtiums along the borders of front yard flower beds in the days of my childhood. This conviction is probably only a

confusion of memory, since my early days were spent in eastern Pennsylvania, and I know ranunculus are not hardy enough in that region to be grown casually outdoors. Still, hardiness is variable and these may have been a particularly sturdy strain.

At all events the ranunculus varieties of today, in their colorful whites, yellows, oranges, rose tones and reds, though easy and popular greenhouse plants, are not very hardy. They may be grown outside from fall plantings in the open cold frame or in flower beds, provided the same protection is given them as was advised for anemones. Ranunculus are seldom offered in named varieties, but can be bought mixed or separately by color.

SCILLA—ENGLISH BLUEBELLS, WOOD HYACINTHS

The gardener who tries to stick to a budget and also make up his order from an alphabetical catalogue, must go back and do a lot of crossing out when he comes to scillas. These flowers are not minor in garden importance; they should form a substantial part of every spring garden however modest. In the preceding chapter we have discussed the species, sibirica, which rings down the curtain on Act I of the spring bulb drama, the part played by the early little bulbs. There are

other scillas, too; some are early but
the majority come upon the stage
with the tulips and late daffodils.

When I consider the late scillas I
think mostly of Scilla campanulata,
the wood hyacinth. These bulbs produce stems twelve to eighteen inches
high depending on the richness of
the soil. Surrounding the last six or
eight inches of the stalk is a loose truss
of large, open bells. Each hangs
gracefully on an individual stem
branching off the main stalk, the
whole making a spike handsome in
the bed and fine for cutting as well.

Tallest, showiest of the campanulatas is the variety Excelsior, a light,

Scilla campanulata

clear blue. I have used this by the thousands as a foreplanting with tulips. I once had a long bed in front of a hedge of
hemlocks in which some thirty varieties of late tulips were
planted in scallops of twenty-five each—a total of seven hundred fifty bulbs. In the indentations of the scallops I planted
some five hundred Scilla campanulata, Excelsior. With the
brilliant tulips and the soft green background of the hemlocks they made a thrilling May picture. After the tulips had
been lifted and replaced with new bulbs several times, the
scillas were dug for dividing. Not only were there five hundred Excelsior bulbs of good size to fill again the same space
from which they were lifted, but some five hundred more of
equal size were available for new colonies plus hundreds of
smaller bulbs for growing on.

Blue Queen, Rose Queen and Alba are other good varieties

of Scilla campanulata. Blue Queen is much the same color as
Excelsior but a little shorter with not quite so full a flower.
This variety is worth remembering because it will naturalize
under pines. Alba is enchanting as a foreplanting with red
tulips. Rose Queen is the best pink among scillas. In fact, it
is the best pink among all the minor spring bulbs.

As their name indicates all the wood hyacinths flourish in
the shade. Although I should not recommend more than seventy-five percent shade as a general rule, I have planted them
under such dense growth that they could hardly have had any
ripening sun at all. Still I had blooms for years. This shade-
enduring quality, plus the long blooming season and great
substance of the individual flower, makes Scilla campanulata
of unparalleled value for difficult areas. White and blue drifts
of them are beautiful among ferns and with the feathery foliage of the fringed bleeding heart.

Scilla campanulatas like sun too; no amount is too strong
for them. They will flourish in the open meadow or in the
sunny rock garden. Their height suggests planting on a low
plane of the rock garden where fairly large plants look well.
The richer the soil the larger the campanulatas will grow and
the more they will multiply. They give rich and undeserved
rewards to neglectful gardeners who plant them in none too
fertile or in poorly drained soil. I have found a three-inch covering of soil satisfactory for this species as for all scillas.

So devoted will you become to campanulatas that you may
feel tempted not to seek further among the scilla species for
additional garden beauty. But there are other attractive kinds
to know and grow. Some are smaller gems, interesting in form
and flower. Others add variety to the open border. Scilla
nutans, the storied English bluebell, is almost as large and
robust as campanulata and its blue is a little deeper. Its pendant bells are more recurved at the tips, giving the truss a

feathery appearance. You may want to use this variety for interplantings or in drifts as you do its larger cousin. It, too, thrives equally well in sun or shade.

If you have the collector's urge, all the following members of this genus will make you happy:

Autumnalis. 8 inches. AUGUST. Lilac-rose. Loose raceme of starry bells.

Bifolia. 5 inches. EARLY APRIL. Light, bright blue. Starry bells.

Campanulata Alba. 12 inches. MAY. Pure white.

Campanulata Blue Queen. 12 inches. MAY. Porcelain blue.

Campanulata Coerulea. Spanish Bluebell. Wood Hyacinth. 12 inches. MAY. Delft blue.

Campanulata Excelsior. 14-18 inches. MAY. Delft blue. Large truss.

Campanulata Rose Queen. 12-16 inches. MAY. Soft rose.

Italica. 9 inches. APRIL. Lavender-blue.

Nutans Alba. 10 inches. MAY. Pure white.

Nutans Coerulea. English Bluebell. 10-12 inches. MAY. Porcelain blue.

Nutans Rosea. 10 inches. MAY. Light rose.

Nutans Rubra. 10 inches. MAY. Reddish lilac.

Peruviana. The Cuban Lily. 12 inches. MAY. Bright blue. Large, thinly spaced bells. Not hardy north of New York and even where hardy may blossom only in alternate years.

Peruviana Alba. 12 inches. MAY. White form of cuban lily.

Peruviana Lutea. 12 inches. MAY. Very rare yellow form of cuban lily.

SPARAXIS

Sparaxis are colorful South African plants similar to the ixias from the same land. They grow taller than ixias by six inches, averaging two feet. They are suitable greenhouse plants but worth trying outdoors from fall planted bulbs if you are willing to gamble and take the necessary trouble. Given the same culture as ixias, they should flower in late

April or early May. They also may be planted in the spring but bulbs saved over the winter, like those of anemones, ranunculus and ixias tend to lose vitality. Sparaxis are usually offered mixed and are best bought that way for outdoor experiment, although the following three striking varieties are worth planting separately if you are fairly confident of success:

Fire King. Orange-scarlet, black centers.
Monica. Purple, yellow centers.
Salmon Queen. Light salmon, primrose centers.

ZYGADENUS

The zygadenus is a plant somewhat like the camassia which also blooms in May. It produces an eighteen- to twenty-four-inch spike. Thinly and irregularly spaced along this are the wide-open flowers. Zygadenus likes moist soil in full sun or light shade. It should be planted under four inches of soil. The species freemonti, a light yellow, is a valuable and interesting plant for late spring bloom.

CHAPTER EIGHTEEN

Iris from Bulb to Bowl

MANY of the loveliest irises grow from bulbs. These are becoming increasingly popular in American gardens. Where plantings of the bearded or German iris, the flat Japanese, the grassy leaved Siberian and other rhizomatous kinds flourish, the bulbous types add variety and charm.

Foremost among them are Dutch, Spanish and English kinds comprising the Xiphium group. Like the German iris these bear standards and falls, but the standards are shorter and the fall petals, before turning down, part to form a lip with a characteristic spot of yellow at the base.

DUTCH IRIS—IRIS XIPHIUM HYBRIDUM

The Dutch iris are hybrids developed by Holland growers from the Spanish. They are larger, more robust, and flower earlier, as a rule, than their progenitors. As they are most satisfactory for both indoor and outdoor growing, the majority of hardy iris bulbs now grown belongs to this group. The beautiful and familiar blue Wedgwood, forced by the millions, is sometimes classed as a Dutch iris, although it really belongs to the tender tingitana species.

Dutch irises open their crisp blossoms in the garden at the close of the May-flowering tulip season. Some varieties are all white, yellow, lavender or blue. Others have standards of one color and falls of another. Usually two blossoms develop on each stem and open in succession. With stems twenty to thirty inches long, Dutch iris is unrivaled for cutting. Taken in the bud stage, blooms will open in water and stay fresh for three to five days. Flowering as it does after the tulips and before the bearded iris reaches its height, this bulbous iris is most welcome and beautiful for arrangements, particularly the kind which suggest plant growth. Placed at the edge of a low flat container it gives the effect of a waterside planting in the garden.

American gardeners were commencing to plant these bulbs in quantity in the early nineteen-twenties when the quarantine cut them off. Deprived by this restriction, we had to do without them for a few years until Western growers imported and grew sufficient stocks for us to buy them here at higher but still moderate prices. With the quarantine now liberalized we can look forward to a more plentiful supply and at relatively lower cost.

I have found Dutch iris hardy without any mulch as far north as Massachusetts. Some gardeners stress late planting to inhibit the top growth which these bulbs send up in the late autumn and early winter. Yet one winter during which very severe cold alternated with mild spells, the leaves of my Dutch iris came up twice to about eight inches. Apparently they froze off each time but no damage to plant or flowers was noticeable the following spring.

This bulbous iris requires plenty of sun and a four-inch covering of nourishing, loamy soil. But no matter how favorable their garden situation, they do not last indefinitely. Three years is about as long as you can expect any one planting to continue flowering and two years is a good average. Yet so attractive are they for garden and table decoration that at their low cost they are worth replacing as often as necessary.

If you have any space set aside for flowers for cutting, plant generous amounts of this bright iris in your favorite colors or in mixture. Or use it in your perennial borders. Groups of white and blue Dutch iris look well between clumps of oriental poppies. The yellow varieties combine pleasantly with blue columbines and baptisias. Since the bulbs are small and the stems and foliage narrow, they require little space. You can easily plant twenty-five bulbs in three square feet. In contrast to the many months the rhizomatous iris stays green, the onion-like foliage of bulbous iris ripens very quickly. A nearby planting of babysbreath or flax will cover the area left by the disappearing leaves.

These varieties of Dutch iris will delight you:

A. Bloemard. Dark blue. EARLY.
Frans Hals. Light blue standards, yellow falls.
Golden Glory. Bright yellow.
Huchtenburg. Standards white, shaded blue; falls yellow with orange stripe.
Imperator. Clear, deep blue. Large.
Jacob de Wit. Light blue standards, dark blue falls.
Leonardo da Vinci. White standards, yellow falls.
Poggenbeek. Dark blue.
Therese Schwartz. Standards white, edged lavender-blue; falls lavender-blue.
White Excelsior. Pure white.
Yellow Queen. Pure yellow.

SPANISH IRIS—IRIS XIPHIUM

Spanish iris is the same height but flowers a bit later than the Dutch, thus prolonging the season of bulbous iris bloom

Tones of bronze on many varieties add attractiveness to shades of white, yellow, blue and purple. Culture is the same as for Dutch iris except that being a trifle less hardy the Spanish require a light mulch when planted north of Maryland.

These are recommended varieties:

Bronze King. Purple, edged bronze.
Cajanus. Canary yellow with orange yellow blotch on falls.
Excelsior. Light blue with orange blotch.
Golden Yellow. Deep yellow. Large.
Hercules. Bronze standards, lavender falls.
King of the Whites. Pure white.
Prince of Orange. Orange yellow, spotted bronze.
Reconnaissance. Dark bronze.
Solfataire. Deep blue. Large.

ENGLISH IRIS—IRIS XIPHIOIDES

The English iris is the largest flowered and also the least hardy of the three main bulbous groups. It is also probably the most beautiful, suggesting Japanese iris in its velvety texture. No yellows appear but there are rich clarets, purples, lavenders, blues and whites. In the latitude of New York, the English iris flowers in the first fortnight of June, a week or two after the Spanish and three weeks later than the Dutch. Although it might not survive a cold winter without protection, with a four-inch mulch of leaves and a sunny exposure, it lives and blooms beautifully.

The following kinds of English iris will add June beauty to your garden:

Baron von Humboldt. Dark mauve with carmine spots.
Beethoven. Maroon-purple.
Duchess of York. Bluish violet, white center.
Enchantress. Porcelain blue.
Mont Blanc. Pure white.

Othello. Blue-black.
Prince Albert. Purple standards, light blue falls spotted purple.
Ruby. Reddish purple feathered white.

IRIS RETICULATA

Other species of iris grow from bulbs. Most of them are of too uncertain hardiness and too great rarity to recommend except to collectors who enjoy the pursuit of the unattainable. One for every gardener to try, however, is Iris reticulata. Blossoming with the earliest crocuses, this is a pearl for the rock garden or sunny spot in the informal border. The large blooms are bright purple with yellow markings and delicate fragrance. The flower stem grows to eight inches while the sharp, pointed leaves rise five inches above it. Besides the type there are a number of varieties of reticulata in cultivation. Of these, Cantab, a light blue with orange markings and Krelagei, a bright violet with a bronze and orange line, are worth adding to a collection.

MORAEA

The moraeas are South African relatives of the iris. They are a large genus of many species whose flowers last but a day, but others appear successively throughout the season. Most moraeas are only suited to the greenhouse but one species, glaucopis, the "Peacock Iris" is hardy enough to be recommended for American gardens. It is a fragile-looking white flower the size of a quarter with a dark blue spot at the base of the petals. Planted in the fall under four inches of sandy soil and covered with a light mulch, it blooms the following May.

CHAPTER NINETEEN

The Lovely Lilies

No FLOWERS in the garden are more exciting than lilies, even if you grow only a dozen candidums or regales. When the long buds open in beauty and fragrance, you experience a great delight, and perhaps some wonder, at their sudden loveliness. You may also feel a justifiable pride in producing something so beautiful.

The sense of accomplishment which lilies in full flower bring to us, comes not, I think, from any recollection of difficult culture but from the general quality of rarity lilies possess. Whether there are a hundred in your border or only two or three, they stand out as something special. Other flowers are beautiful, but lilies are rare.

Perfectly hardy and seemingly untroubled by disease in their native habitats, when brought into the garden they require more care than such bulbs as tulips and daffodils. What a testimony it is to their age-long appeal that they have won the necessary extra attention from gardeners for at least 3,500 years! Lilies were admired in the gardens of King Minos of Crete. The Romans grew them for garland flowers and they have been tended by Western European gardeners from the Middle Ages to the present day.

The physical structure of lily bulbs indicates their need for careful handling. When you examine them, you will notice that, although they differ markedly in form and shape according to their several species, they are all unprotected by any hard skin. It is not surprising that bulbs with such fleshy scales lose moisture, bruise easily, and are susceptible to penetration by fungus spores. When your lily bulbs arrive do not delay planting a day longer than necessary. Break off and destroy any outer scales which appear damaged or decayed.

With lilies you will find it pays to follow cultural instructions more exactly than in the case of other fall-planting bulbs. They are less tolerant of improper soil conditions and incorrect planting depths. They must have plenty of moisture, yet require excellent drainage. In sandy soil they dry out. If this handicap confronts you, add peat moss, humus or compost. These moisture-retentive substances tend to promote soil acidity, a condition which lilies seem to prefer. Clayey soil must likewise be improved by the addition of hard coal ashes. The superphosphate-Bovung mixture is a good fertilizer for lilies.

Rooting habits of different species play a role in their culture. Many familiar kinds including auratums, regales and speciosums produce, besides the usual roots growing from the base of the bulb, additional roots which branch off from the stems about six inches from the top of the bulb. These varieties need to be planted with enough soil coverage so that no stem roots are exposed. Varieties like candidums and testaceums, on the other hand, which make only base roots, should never be covered by more than three inches of soil.

When planting, to facilitate drainage, tilt the bulbs slightly. If they are delivered to you with the old basal roots still on, protect these, working them, as you plant, into the loose earth below the bulbs. Many gardeners are particularly careful to provide lily bulbs with a cushion of sand. This is unnecessary if the soil drainage is good. If it is poor, the sand will be of little help.

Winter mulching is a question you may decide for yourself. The theory is sound. When the ground freezes, cover it to keep the frost in. Then lilies will not suffer from the heaving which accompanies alternate freezing and thawing and early spring growth with its possible subsequent damage from late frosts will be retarded. I have never covered lilies with a special winter mulch. In the latitude of New York it would have to be a heavy covering which would keep the ground solid during some of our winter thaws. And once the earth thaws, a mulch acts in reverse. It keeps the earth warmer than it should be and so promotes the early growth it was intended to discourage.

Regardless of winter mulching, all stem-rooting lilies need protection from the summer sun at the point where the stalks rise from the earth and the stem roots grow down. This shade at the earth's surface is necessary no matter how much the rest of the plant loves the sun. Where lilies are growing among annuals or perennials, these plants usually provide sufficient shade for the lily roots. When colonies of stem-rooting lilies are planted in front of evergreens, a light mulch of leaves, peat moss or grass cuttings is advisable.

Hardy as they are, lilies in cultivation are subject to certain diseases. They may acquire these after having flourished for a year or two in your garden as apparently healthy and vigorous plants. The most serious ill is mosaic, a virus disease which is carried by melon aphids. These insects feed on infected lilies or other infected hosts such as milkweed, bindweed or periwinkle. Then they transfer the disease to healthy plants. Mosaic virus lives in all parts of the plant including the bulb. It does not live in the soil or in dead plant tissue nor is it transmitted through the seed. A lily infected by mosaic will usually wither and die within two years. Lilium tigrinum is an exception. Although highly vulnerable to infection by mosaic, this lily survives even when infected and continues to produce plants and flowers. These may serve as a center for the spread of mosaic to other lilies.

Some lily species seem to acquire mosaic more readily than others, perhaps because their leaves are more appealing to the aphid carriers. Auratums and speciosums are readily infected while the late-blooming formosanum is not only sure to become a virus victim if any mosaic is present, but will speedily succumb to its effect. Among lilies not immune to mosaic, but slow to become infected are candidum, hansoni, henryii, martagon, regale, tenuifolium and their hybrids.

There is as yet no cure for this malady once a plant has become infected. Dusting the bulbs with disinfectant before planting will no more eliminate the virus if present, or guard against its later infection from aphids than a strong soap bath will ward off appendicitis. Eradication is the only control—more easily practiced by the commercial grower than the small gardener. Mosaic can be recognized by a mottling of the green in the leaves of plants afflicted by it. This is most noticeable early in the season but even then it is difficult for the inexperienced eye to identify, so do not go among your lilies and cast out all with variable green leaves, however promising their buds, on the off-chance they might have mosaic.

As the virus is not transmitted by seed, lily seedlings start out disease free. Some experts therefore recommend that amateurs grow all their bulbs from seed. While raising some of the easier sorts this way is a rewarding garden enterprise, its universal practice as a means of producing lilies for gardens is out of the question. At least ninety percent of those who love lilies and intend to grow them are far too busy to grow them from seed. Besides, the perfectly healthy seedlings you raise or buy may become infected by aphids which have fed on diseased lilies or other plants in your own or your neighbors' gardens.

Botrytis blight is the second serious ailment of lilies. This fungous disease attacks foliage and causes a progressive withering of leaves from the lower ones up. Sometimes it destroys the entire plant. It does not attack the bulb directly but when foliage is destroyed by botrytis, the bulb weakens since it is deprived of nourishment from the ripening of healthy leaf tissue. Although not a fatal disease like mosaic, botrytis is serious for growers, especially those dealing with the popular Lilium candidum, the most important sufferer from this malady.

But something can be done about botrytis. The foliage of plants can be sprayed with Bordeaux mixture. This has to be done after every rain, especially in the moist early spring, to keep leaves coated with a film which prevents germination of spores. While advisable for the large grower, such constant spraying would make the growing of candidums, beautiful as they are, too much of a chore for the home gardener. Fortunately botrytis can be checked or prevented if foliage can be kept reasonably dry in the early spring. Since moisture is necessary for the spread of the spores, you can plant candidum and testaceum lilies where morning sun reaches down to the base of their stalks and you can keep the soil surface around plants free of all dew-catching debris, mulch or low foliage. Chemical treatment of bulbs before planting is a worthless measure.

Prompt diagnosis of mosaic and speedy elimination of infected bulbs by commercial growers now keep most virus-infected bulbs from entering the market and getting into our gardens. Furthermore, growers are constantly experimenting to develop disease-free and resistant strains of lily species and hybrids. Bulbs of these new seedlings are now being offered.

Since they are still scarce, large bulbs of these clones are expensive, but worth trying in small quantities. An experimental attitude is warranted. While you may expect the bulbs of these new stocks to be disease *free* as advertised, you will need the proof of experience before knowing how disease resistant they will be in your garden.

Meanwhile, it is best to grow lilies freely for their beauty and without too much thought of their ills. As a matter of fact, disease is not the most frequent cause of the disappearance of lilies from the garden. Poor soil and drainage, the cutting down of foliage before it ripens and failure to shade stem roots are the usual causes of loss. If cultural preferences are considered, you will keep your lilies a long time—as you probably know from the colonies of regales, candidums, henryi and testaceums you or your friends have had for years.

It is also important to mark well the spot where lilies are planted. Those flowering after the middle of June usually do not appear above ground until the Single Early tulips have bloomed. The tight-fisted cluster of tiny leaves which then thrusts upward encloses all the flower buds. If you cultivate indiscriminately while these are breaking through the top two inches of soil you may destroy some or all of your lilies. So keep hoe and rake away from the lily areas unless plants are so plainly marked that you can safely work among them.

Time of planting should also be considered. Lilies are properly included among fall-planting bulbs because they mature in the autumn and the bulbs are ready for digging and shipping. Candidums should always be planted early so they may make their full growth. You will find some lilies offered for sale both in fall and spring. My advice is to secure and plant all that are obtainable in autumn. However, when it comes to transplanting your own seedlings or setting out bulbs secured directly from a nursery where they have wintered in the field

or been heeled in in a cold frame, spring planting will probably do just as well. Many lily bulbs, however, arrive so late
in the fall that gardeners find it inconvenient to plant them
then. They prefer to buy their bulbs from dealers' stocks held
over the winter for spring sale. Although they will probably
flower, these bulbs have neither the health nor vitality they
had before storage. Still, if you have neglected to plant lily
bulbs in the fall, it is better to plant them in the spring than
to forgo their beauty entirely.

Where to plant lilies is an easy problem. They do not look
well marching single file up the walk from the street to front
door, but are effective in nearly any other position. A large
colony set in the curve of a rhododendron border is a gorgeous
sight and they are a necessity in the formal garden or perennial border. If you have no garden, save space for lilies in the
strip primarily reserved for spring bulbs. Lilies may also be
planted in the corner of a front yard enclosed by a picket
fence, in the center of a pool planting, in a bed in front of a
wall covered by climbing roses, in space between large box-
woods or in places where hemlocks or yews furnish a background. Varieties you select for any location depend on when
you wish to see them in bloom since there is a lily for each of
the summer months.

Most lilies like plenty of sun with shade protection for the
base of stem-rooting kinds. There are some exceptions. Hansonii and henryi flower better in light shade, although both
are a little tall for the woods. The well-named Lilium giganteum from the Himalayas likes to send up its ten-foot stalk
under the protection of a tall, high-branched tree. The native
canadense and philadelphicum grow well in full sun or in
that dappled shade which the native superbum prefers. All
three, planted among ferns, enhance the woodland path wherever foliage is not too dense. If your woodland has open clear-

ings or bays, large colonies of auratums and speciosums will bring beauty there.

Most sun-loving varieties do not object to the third- to half-day's shade afforded by a wall or evergreen hedge. They grow taller there and the flowers last a little longer. Since they tend to reach out for the sun, their long stems usually need staking in such locations.

Lilies in general are too large for the rock garden. Sometimes the umbellatums and the elegans varieties are used but they look bulky in this environment and their predominating brick-orange color does not look well with plants usually blooming there in May and June. Two lilies, however, are splendid for planting in low level pockets between rocks. Lilium pumilum or tenuifolium with small coral flowers and feathery foliage has the daintiness and grace rock garden plants should possess. The vivid scarlet Lilium concolor, blooming a little later, also looks well.

Your campaigns against bulb-eating rodents will be most welcome to lilies wherever they are planted. Animals fond of a meal of tulips and crocuses find lily bulbs equally tasty. Deeply planted bulbs are not likely to be molested so long as other food is handier. Bulbs in rock garden pockets, however, are of convenient access to chipmunks and mice, so the fewer of these little predatory creatures you entertain, the better.

As your lilies begin to flower, you may wonder whether you should gather some for the house. How can you resist? Bowls of long-stemmed regale lilies cut when the lowest buds are just opening lend beauty and fragrance to living room and porch. Auratums fill the air with a sweet, spicy scent. Speciosum rubrums add a bright touch of color. And indoors all bloom for a long time as buds unfold slowly up the stem.

But, you ask, does cutting flowers injure bulbs? Indeed it

does, and very severely. To be effective, lilies must be cut with long stems. Since on most varieties leaves grow right up to the flowers, cutting is bound to deprive bulbs of strength. This does not kill them, but it does weaken them so that plants are smaller the following year. If you want to cut lilies and also have exhibition stalks and blooms next year, you will have to reinforce your planting with new bulbs. If you have seedlings coming along this will cost little, otherwise you will have to buy new bulbs to replace those weakened by cutting. Still, the pleasure of bringing lilies indoors is very great and knowing it is a luxury makes us revel in it the more.

CHAPTER TWENTY

Lily Species and Hybrids

L<small>ILIES</small> for today's garden are many and varied. Most of them are species but there are beautiful hybrids, too. You may have noticed named varieties in catalogues. You may also have seen lilies offered under a variety name with the word *hybrids* written after it, such as George Creelman *hybrids* or Theodore Havemeyer *hybrids*. These are really seedlings of the varieties whose names they bear. They deserve some explanation as does the whole question of lily hybrids.

As we saw in Chapter Two, bulbs of hybrid varieties are not "true" when produced from seed. No matter how many million bulbs of one variety there are in cultivation, they are all part of a single clone with but one parent raised from seed and they must be propagated asexually, that is, by bulb multiplication. It is different with species. Seeds of the species, Lilium regale, will produce more regales but each seed of a hybrid, like Theodore Havemeyer, will produce a different variety, resembling its parent but not identical.

Now, it can easily be seen that if a stock of lily bulbs is infected by mosaic, it can be completely wiped out, as the small bulbs, scales and bulbils by which propagation is carried on will all inherit the virus. If a grower should thus lose his entire field of regales he could start again from seed—in the same soil if he wished, since mosaic does not live in the soil. A species can live on so long as seeds of the species exist.

When stock of a hybrid is destroyed by mosaic, it disappears since it cannot be replaced by seed. In this way, many fine hybrids of the past, such as Parkmani and Hoveyi, were lost. The recent, splendid George Creelman seems to have met the same fate—at least so far as plentiful, commercial stock is concerned. However, growers have taken seed of the Creelman hybrids and now offer the best of the seedling progeny, each a separate variety or "hybrid" in its own right.

Not all hybrids have, by any means, succumbed to mosaic. Many are still grown in commercial quantities. For example, Lilium testaceum, an accidental cross between candidum and chalcedonicum, has delighted gardeners for over one hundred years.

The question of hybrids is important to the gardener, for here lies the future of lilies. The past fifty years have witnessed the discovery and introduction to our gardens of many wonderful species from China, Japan, Korea and elsewhere. During the next few decades, if mosaic is controlled and conquered, we can look forward to the production and maintenance of even more beautiful lilies hybridized from these species. Ten or twenty years from now we may be buying new and ever improved varieties of lilies as we now do of gladioli and tulips. It is an exciting prospect.

Lilies are classified by the botanist according to shape of leaf and flower. A convenient way for the gardener to consider them is by time of bloom. That is how the varieties listed below are grouped for the approximate latitude of New York. This collection of lilies which will bring flowers into your garden all summer long in a wide range of color and variety includes only a small portion of the many you can grow. All are hardy, available and easily grown. If a few, as noted, are vulnerable to mosaic they are worth growing in spite of it.

LILIES FOR LATE MAY TO MID-JUNE

CANDIDUM. THE MADONNA LILY. 4-6 FEET. BASE-ROOTING

It is safe to predict that the madonna lily, which has given us its beauty since 1500 B.C. will continue in favor for a long time. Its white is pure but vibrant. It does not suggest the white of the sepulchre as does the potted longiflorum. Bright golden anthers contrast beautifully with the snowy petals.

The buds of candidums, like clusters of white candles, are carried erect at the top of the stalk. There are five to twelve depending on the size of the bulbs. They open out horizontally into broad, fragrant, funnel-shaped flowers.

Madonnas have the unique characteristic of making a fall rosette of leaves which persists over the winter. For this reason bulbs should be planted early, in August or early September, and at a shallow depth, to facilitate this growth. A covering of two inches is sufficient, although if the soil is very light three will not be too much. This covering is measured from the top of the bulb, not from the tip of any sprouts which may have started before you were able to plant. If the sprouts are very long before you manage to get the bulbs into the ground, it is perfectly all right for them to protrude above the soil so long as you are careful not to injure them in planting. Candidums are lime *tolerant;* they do not *prefer* alkaline soil.

Blooming as they do in mid-June, candidums share their beauty with a host of other plants. In large colonies or borders they look well in front of evergreens, rambler roses, vines and shrubs. In the garden they enhance the charm of nearby perennials. Everyone knows the beauty of madonnas and delphiniums. So often are these seen together that gardeners desiring variety often try testaceum or regale lilies with their delphiniums, but only madonnas catch the exact blooming peak of these blue spires. If the combination of these two flowers seems common, you can try for perfection, which is always uncommon.

Madonnas spread their white sunshine attractively among annual larkspurs, behind coralbells, with campanulas and the late foxgloves. One of the most compelling plantings I ever saw was a colony of candidums associated with the claret-magenta flowers of mullein pink, Lychnis coronaria.

The longevity of madonnas depends on starting with healthy bulbs and fulfilling their cultural requirements. For a number of years I have traveled in early June along country roads in Eastern Pennsylvania. There my envious and admiring eyes frequently light upon large clumps of many-flowered candidums in farm yard corners where they have apparently been undisturbed for years. Their long contentment in these places suggests that the less cultivating we do among our madonnas the better.

A number of strains of candidums have been found in various parts of Europe, some with sufficient differences to be accounted separate varieties. Among these is salonikae which has paler yellow anthers and more open flowers than the type, and is earlier blooming by five days. Growers are experimenting with this and other strains of candidums to develop madonnas even more free-flowering and enduring than those we now know.

HANSONII. HANSON'S LILY. 4-6 FEET. STEM-ROOTING

The many flowers of this lily, which open with the candidums, are pendant and the petals recurved. The color is a warm yellow, fading in the full sun. The petals are heavily spotted brown except at the tips. Hansonii is a sturdy, long-lived lily, highly disease-resistant. Bulbs should be covered with five to six inches of soil.

Perhaps you have a tree near the corner of your garden which has grown a little large and casts a great deal more shade than you counted on when the garden was laid out. Beneath its boughs is an excellent spot for a colony of hansoni lilies. With plumbago and hostas they will solve the problem of what to grow in this area.

PHILADELPHICUM. THE WOOD LILY. 3 FEET. STEM-ROOTING

This plant is native from Canada to North Carolina. It bears three to five orange-red, maroon-spotted flowers. The leaves, like those of hansonii, grow in whorls spaced up the stem. Although stem-rooting, the stoloniferous bulbs are not large and need be covered with only four to five inches of soil. Philadelphicum is not a garden lily, but will naturalize in dry, sandy soil in meadow or thin woodland.

PUMILUM (TENUIFOLIUM). THE CORAL LILY. 1½-2 FEET. STEM-ROOTING

The small, pendant and recurved, coral-red flowers of this lily have great charm. Blossoming in June, just ahead of candidum, it produces abundant, fern-like foliage below the flower stems. The bulbs of pumilum, or tenuifolium as it is more generally known, require a four or five inch covering of earth. This lily is attractive among perennials or in rock gardens, also in beds by itself beneath library or dining-room windows.

UMBELLATUM. 3 FEET. STEM-ROOTING

This is one of the earliest lilies to flower, often opening before the end of May. It is grown in a number of varieties, all of which are erect-flowered. The majority are brick-orange or scarlet, although some have been produced which are yellow with scarlet markings. Most of the available bulbs of this group are umbellatum erectum and grandiflorum, both red-orange. Bulbs should be covered with five to six inches of earth and will grow in a wide variety of soils. The color of umbellatums limits their garden use, since so much salmon and apricot appears on the blossoms of trees and flowers at this season. A colony naturalized in open meadow grass, by a fence corner, or along a field stream is pleasing and cheerful.

LILIES FOR MID-JUNE TO JULY

AMABILE. 5-6 FEET. STEM-ROOTING

This variety from Korea bears from five to nine nodding, recurved, deep red blossoms branching out from the top of tall stalks. Bulbs are easily grown and should be planted with about a five-inch covering of soil. Amabile does well in either sun or light shade. In one garden, recently, I saw a handsome group of them topping a white fence in the lee of a large lilac.

CONCOLOR. 1½-2 FEET. STEM-ROOTING

Small, starry, bright scarlet flowers are held erect by this plant. It has rather long, pointed and slender leaves. Bulbs are not large and need but four inches of covering. Concolor is small enough for the rock garden. It grows readily from seed.

CROCEUM. THE ORANGEMAN'S LILY. 3 FEET. STEM-ROOTING

This is another lily with erect flowers. These are held in umbels, cup-shaped, brilliant orange in color, six to ten in number. Bulbs are adaptable to different soils and should be covered five inches deep. Hardy, disease-resistant croceum will make a bright spot of color wherever colonized.

Martagon. The Turkscap Lily. 3-5 Feet. Base-rooting

This hardy variety is native to a large part of Europe and Asia. Its flowers are pendant and so sharply reflexed that its name is used to indicate the group of all lilies of similar flower form. The wild martagon is rosy lilac, but it is grown in many forms and shadings. It has long been in cultivation. Bulbs should be covered with three inches of soil. Martagons thrive in partial or medium shade.

Martagon Album. The White Turkscap. 5-7 Feet. Base-rooting

This is by far the most beautiful variety of Lilium martagon. Taller than the type, it develops large clusters of beautifully recurved white blossoms. It thrives in light shade, although I have never found it lasting in woodland plantings. It is charming with dark evergreen foliage as a background.

Pardalinum Giganteum. The Sunset Lily. 5-7 Feet. Base-rooting

This variety is a showy hybrid of Lilium pardalinum, a native of the West Coast. The petals are golden yellow, heavily spotted maroon and bright scarlet on their sharply reflexed tips. It accommodates itself easily to most gardens when planted under four inches of soil. Use it for vivid color in late June.

Regale. The Regal Lily. 4-7 Feet. Stem-rooting

Well-named, this is truly the queen of lilies in American gardens, beautiful and stately, and of easy culture too. It often produces eighteen or twenty flowers from large bulbs. The trumpet-shaped flowers are held horizontally. Before they open the long buds take on a beautiful wine color. Then the petals turn back to reveal a fragrant white blossom with yellow throat and handsomely poised orange anthers. As it takes one to two weeks for this variety to complete its blooming, buds and flowers are seen for a long time in pleasing combination.

The regal lily has won its place because of its beauty and rugged constitution. Although not a shade grower, it is adaptable to a wide variety of garden situations, soils and climates. Its thin, tensile stems stand up to wind and rain. It multiplies and colonizes itself, when given the chance, and resists infection from both botrytis and mosaic. Bulbs should be given a six-inch covering of soil. They thrive in rich, loamy soil with high humus content, but they will tolerate a good deal of clay so long as drainage is fair.

If you are a busy or casual gardener unable, you think, to take time or trouble for lilies, grow regales. Plant them in groups at terrace corners, in repeated clumps along arborvitae, hemlock or yew hedges, in masses at the rear of beds of annuals. Set them between your peonies. Place them generously among other perennials. Let them accompany the later bloom of delphiniums. Plant them between the summer phlox with clouds of babysbreath, Gypsophila Bristol Fairy, in front. The thin, dark leaves of regales, which cling to the wiry stems, stay green a long time after flowering, giving the plant a not unattractive appearance as it ripens. A long undulating border of regales, in front of a wall or fence covered with pink roses, and with deep blue petunias at their feet, makes a display of astonishing loveliness.

Regale bulbs are plentiful, but these lilies can also be grown easily from seed. Raising them successfully from seed brings a pleasant feeling of accomplishment as well as a large and inexpensive supply of lilies. It is not a difficult process for the average gardener who has a sunny window available and owns a wooden flat or can procure one from a florist.

Mid-winter is the best time to start the seed. Scatter pebbles or pieces of broken flower pot over the bottom of the flat for drainage. Then fill with soil to within one-half inch of the top. Potting soil bought from a local florist is good, or you can prepare your own mixture of one-third sifted top soil, one-third sand and one-third leaf mold or Hyperhumus.

Space the seeds about a half-inch apart in rows one inch apart. The rows can be made with a pencil drawn along deeply enough so that seed will be about one-quarter inch under the surface when the soil is leveled again. Water thoroughly with a fine spray after sowing.

Place a pane of glass over the flat, but leave a one-inch opening at the end for ventilation. Then set the flat on the window ledge but cover it with a sheet of paper until germination takes place. This should occur in two to four weeks. Then provide a few hours of light, but not direct sun, daily until the tiny sprouts turn green. After this, remove the covering entirely.

The flat should remain indoors for about two months with the soil kept moist but not soggy. At the end of this time it can be moved to the cold frame. The sash cover of the frame should be removed but slats placed so as to filter strong sunlight.

As soon as plants are strong enough to be lifted they may be transplanted from flat to cold frame soil. This should be of the same consistency as that in which the seed was sown but further enriched by approximately two pounds of the superphosphate-Bovung mixture per flat of seedlings. The plants should be spaced four inches apart each way.

After you set the seedlings in the bottom of the cold frame, remove the slat covering, but mulch the rows with three inches of leaf mold. Water during periods of drought. During the first summer the lilies will make foliage growth but, of course, no flowers. After the foliage ripens, transplant the bulbs to a loamy spot in the garden which may serve as a nursery, although, if you have the room, it is better to leave them in the cold frame over the winter. In either case, give them a heavy mulch of leaves, and if they are in the frame, keep the sash cover off over the winter.

The following May, after all danger of frost has passed, remove the winter mulch, but leave enough at the base of the plants to protect the young stem roots. A few buds may appear this second summer, but for best development of the bulbs, pinch them off before they open. After the foliage has ripened the second fall, transplant the bulbs to their permanent location in the garden.

TESTACEUM. THE NANKEEN LILY. 5-7 FEET. BASE-ROOTING

This lily has no peer for beauty. It is a hybrid of candidum thought to have originated in Europe about 1836. Its foliage and stem resemble the candidum, but the trumpet-shaped flowers are pendant and the petals more recurved. It is difficult to describe the Nankeen lily. Its soft, pure color is composed of buff, flesh and taupe, but you must see it to appreciate it. The bulbs are at home in the garden and need but a shallow covering of two or three inches. They will flourish in almost any soil.

Testaceums are not fast growers. Therefore bulbs are fairly scarce and comparatively expensive, so that you will buy them by the piece and dozen where you buy other lilies by the dozen or hundred. But plant a few somewhere. They combine beautifully with larkspur or delphinium as they flower soon after the madonnas. Their buff beauty is charming when seen with the white phlox, Miss Lingard.

LILIES FOR JULY

Auratum. The Gold-banded Lily of Japan. 4-7 Feet. Stem-rooting

Even those grudging of admiration and slow to praise exclaim when they see an auratum lily, "Isn't it gorgeous!" Others more appreciative are rendered speechless. The enormous blossoms, carried horizontally, look especially large because they are bowl-shaped with wide-spread petals—a type of inflorescence characteristic of no other garden lily. Flowers are pure white, maroon-spotted, with a broad center stripe of gold on each petal. Long, maroon anthers dangle richly from within. The blossoms emit a cinnamon-like fragrance which is captivating but not heavy.

Auratums normally produce many flowers per bulb. Sometimes they also produce a type of abnormal plant growth, occasionally found among lilies, called fasciation. A huge, thick stem, which seems to be several stems in one, will arise bearing not dozens but scores of flowers. I once saw one with ninety-six, more a freak than a beauty.

The gold-banded lily was found growing wild on the slopes of Japanese volcanoes. Millions of bulbs were gathered for garden and nursery cultivation. While collected bulbs are disease free, the lily when domesticated has been found highly susceptible to mosaic. Deservedly popular, it is universally grown and just as universally dies out in the average garden. Nevertheless, when not infected by virus it is hardy, adaptable and long-lived. To me it is worth replacing as often as necessary. I should not want to be without it.

Auratum bulbs like gravelly, well-drained soil which is generously supplied with leaf mold or other humus. Bulbs require a soil covering of at least six inches. While the upper part of the plant should receive a good half-day's sun, the heavy stem roots need protection from its rays.

This lily is easily lost in garden beds. It is more content and shows off best when planted alone. Colonies of it are sensationally beautiful in front of the verdure of rhododendron, azalea and andromeda. On the small place the curves of the shrubbery border will accommodate it in clumps of twos and threes.

Auratum lilies have been found and cultivated in a number of forms. From time to time variants have been brought forward as hardier and more disease-resistant than the type. For some years many dealers concentrated on one of these, platyphyllum, in the hope that it would prove less susceptible to virus. While this variety yields large flowers and stalks, so far as I have been able to discover from personal experience and the reports of others, it does not last longer.

Many growers here and abroad have raised auratums from seed. During the war, with the Japanese supply cut off, they found a ready market for all the seedlings which could be produced and the bulbs were sold as soon as they reached flowering size, occasionally even before. Recently, a number of named auratum seedlings have been introduced as a new hybrid strain. Some of these varieties are strikingly beautiful and offer great promise for future development. For the average gardener, however, the present high price of these rare bulbs, in view of their unknown staying power, is even more remarkable than their beauty. When a mosaic-resistant hybrid comes along which is capable of scale propagation—or when the disease itself is conquered—then we may expect a yearly feast of auratum bloom from an original planting.

CANADENSE. THE MEADOW OR CANADA LILY. 3-6 FEET. STEM-ROOTING

This native variety grows wild over a wide area of the United States and Canada. It produces from five to twelve or more gracefully pendant, bell-shaped flowers, ranging in color from chrome yellow through shades of orange to red-orange. All are brown-spotted. Leaves are usually arranged in whorls.

The canada lily found in nature grows in moist, lime-free, humus-filled soil in meadows or at woodland edges. It will thrive in a similar environment when domesticated. Bulbs should be given a four-inch covering of soil. Canadense is a wonderful lily to naturalize in thin, moist woodland. It is also handsome and happy in the garden if soil is not limy, and if it contains plenty of humus. It requires shade for the lower part of its stalk. Canadense is much admired and frequently grown as a garden lily in England.

The supply comes chiefly from collected bulbs. These are generally sold mixed, although canadense flavum, a yellow, and canadense coccineum, a red, are sold separately. Collected bulbs have never been found to be virus-infected.

CENTIFOLIUM HYBRIDS. 5-7 FEET. STEM-ROOTING

Lilium regale, with sargentiae as prince consort, has been mother and grandmother to many a noble hybrid most of which, however husky and handsome, have succumbed to mosaic while the doughty dowager lives on. Princeps, one of the most striking descendants, has thus disappeared, but not without leaving seedling progeny. Some of these, from inter-marriage with the centifolium clan, have produced a strain which is sold as Centifolium Hybrids, or sometimes under the name of Centigale.

These individual seedlings resemble regale, but they are taller and the large flowers bloom a little later. The buds have the regale color, but when they open, the fragrant trumpets sometimes have yellow throats, sometimes green. Occasionally flowers are all white. The petal reverse is sometimes brown, maroon or rose and white. These seedlings come to you disease-free and given the same culture and garden use as the regal lily they are highly satisfactory.

GIGANTEUM. THE HIMALAYAN LILY. 8-12 FEET. BASE-ROOTING

This goliath sends up a mighty stalk two inches thick from a basal rosette of large, heart-shaped leaves. Its top is crowned with twelve to twenty long, tubular trumpets, fragrant and white. It must be grown in shade, in moist, loamy soil well-mixed with leaf mold. Despite their size, the bulbs should be covered with only two inches of earth. This lily makes early spring growth which sometimes needs protection from late frosts. Only large mother bulbs will flower. The offspring require a year or two of growth before reaching flowering size. Truly gigantic, this lily is beautiful in a spectacular way. The bulbs are rare and expensive enough to be bought by the piece but well worth growing as something striking, fascinating and a little stupendous.

GREEN MOUNTAIN HYBRIDS. 5-6 FEET. STEM-ROOTING

This is another fine seedling strain of regale descendants crossed with other species. The flowers are numerous, tall and handsome and come into bloom a week or so later than regales. The trumpets are fragrant and with interesting variations in the color intensity of the throat and in the markings on the reverse of the petals. These fine hybrids should be given the same culture and garden usage as the regale lily.

HENRYI. HENRY'S LILY. 5-8 FEET. STEM-ROOTING

This robust plant bears many pendant, bell-shaped flowers branching out from the top of a tall stem. The blossoms are orange-tan with a greenish center stripe and reflexed petal tips. The color has a tendency to fade in the full sun so that the lily is prettier when grown in partial shade.

Henryi is exceedingly adaptable and robust in the garden. Highly resistant to disease, it displays its orange-tan flowers yearly in late July to gardeners who sometimes longingly wish they were soft pink. The bulbs are not particular about soil so long as it is not too heavy and there are six inches of it above them.

A pretty pale yellow form of this lily has been introduced, citrinum, but its bulbs have lately not been available. Henryi, however, has lent its rugged constitution to numerous hybrids, some very beautiful, and it is still being used to produce additional crosses. Meanwhile, the species itself looks very well in the garden between white phlox and blue platycodon.

SHUKSAN. 4-6 FEET. BASE-ROOTING

This variety is the finest of the group known as the Bellingham Hybrids which are crosses of the native pardalinum with other species. Shuksan has many pendant, reflexed, bell-shaped blossoms hung from a rather tall stalk. The petals are bright yellow with dark reddish spots. This lily thrives in the garden under four inches of soil. It offers bright color in July.

SUPERBUM. THE AMERICAN TURKSCAP. 3-7 FEET. STEM-ROOTING

This native lily grows abundantly along the Atlantic coast and westward as far as Missouri. The flowers have the pendant, highly reflexed martagon form and are heavily spotted toward the center. They vary in color from yellow-orange to red-orange. Plants grow from three to seven feet high and occasionally to eight. They bear five to twenty-five blossoms.

Superbum grows wild in moist lowlands where the earth is rich in humus. It is usually found in open places shaded by tall grasses or low shrubs, but it will naturalize in thin woodland if the soil is rich in leaf mold. The bulb should have a four-inch covering. Like canadense and philadelphicum the supply of this lily comes from virus-free collected bulbs.

THEODORE HAVEMEYER. 4-6 FEET. STEM-ROOTING

Probably no more beautiful hybrid has ever been produced than this lovely cross between Lilium henryi and sulphureum. The long-petaled flowers open almost as broadly as auratums and measure six to eight inches across. They are warm ivory suffused with apricot with a center stripe of green on the reverse of the petals. Bulbs should be planted with a six-inch covering and will long endure in the garden. Blooming late in July, this lily is enchanting among phlox, platycodon, azaleamums and nicotiana. Seedlings are sold as Havemeyer hybrids. These are healthy and similar to their parent though in varied and unusual shades. They should be given the same culture and garden arrangement.

LILIES FOR AUGUST

SPECIOSUM. THE SPOTTED LILY. 4-6 FEET. STEM-ROOTING

This favorite summer lily is widely grown in both its red and white forms. The petals of its many large flowers are sharply reflexed and ruffled, displaying raised, distinctive papillae. Rich maroon anthers are extended on long filaments.

The red speciosum, or rubrum, is prevalent in two forms,

magnificum and melpomene. The rubrums shipped from Japan were largely magnificums. These have much crimson on the petals. In melpomene, the kind grown by most Dutch nurserymen, the crimson is chiefly supplied by the red papillae. While smaller and less colorful than magnificum, this variety seems more resistant to virus.

The petals of speciosum album are pure white, while the papillae, standing out, seem even whiter if such a thing can be imagined. The maroon anthers contrast beautifully. This variety is highly susceptible to mosaic, although American raised seedlings and Holland grown stocks are fairly free of it.

No lily lends itself to cultivation more easily, or adds more charm to the garden than the speciosum in both its white and red forms. When uninfected by virus it produces colonies which last for years in good garden soil well supplied with humus. Bulbs should have a covering of five or six inches depending on the size planted.

Speciosums are effective when grown in groups near evergreens or between shrubs. They are equally pleasing among the early August perennials and annuals. A large planting of rubrums near white nicotiana presents a combination of beauty and fragrance, while the same form is attractive planted to the rear of a group of the shasta daisy, Silver Star.

TIGRINUM. THE TIGER LILY. 4-6 FEET. STEM-ROOTING

There is something suggestive of the old-fashioned garden in this familiar lily. Its nodding, orange-red flowers have reflexed petals which are densely covered with purple-black spots. Its long woolly stems are well supplied with dark green leaves bearing large brown-black bulbils in the axils.

So enduring is tigrinum that it is often mistaken for a native lily in places where it has escaped from gardens and established itself in fields. It will grow almost anywhere there is sunshine. Bulbs should be covered with six inches of soil. Tigrinum is susceptible to mosaic but lives with it and continues to flower. It may thus become a virus host from which the aphids can transmit the disease to other lilies. If planted one hundred yards or more away from other stock, the danger appears to be eliminated, since that distance is too far for the aphid carrier to travel.

Tigrinum splendens is the best variety in color and size. A clump in a field corner by a rail fence where meadow grass is allowed to grow around it makes a bright August picture.

LILIES FOR SEPTEMBER

FORMOSANUM. THE FORMOSAN LILY. 4-7 FEET. STEM-ROOTING

The lily season ends with one of its most charming varieties. The tall, slender stems of formosanum bear long, tubular white trumpets prettily recurved at the tips. The flowers suggest the regales in fragrance and color. Sometimes brown or maroon markings appear on the reverse of the petals. Long grassy leaves grow thickly along the lower part of the stalk, more thinly up near the blossoms.

Formosanums grow in any loamy, lime-free garden soil. The tops like sun but the lower part of the stalk needs the protection of shade. The bulbs should have a five- or six-inch covering of earth. Mosaic readily infects this lily, causing its disappearance, but as it seeds itself easily, you can raise your own virus-free bulbs or buy them from the large stocks commercially grown from seed. If you grow your own seedlings, you can have first blooms in the fall from seed sown as soon as spring weather permits. The few flowers which appear the first August or September will, a year later, be succeeded by a mass of blossoms.

It is the taller, late-flowering form, sometimes known as Wilson's variety, of formosanum which is the more desirable for the garden. There is an earlier kind, Price's variety, formosanum pricei. Although it has similar flowers, the early variety, which blooms in July, is so short it seems stunted, seldom growing more than two feet. Some gardeners, however, report that this early variety has produced, for them, three-foot stems. Even at this height it should yield garden room to superior lilies which flower then. The later variety will start flowering in August, but many plants in a group will have blossoms well into the middle of September. I have seen hundreds of formosanums flowering as late as September twenty-fifth.

Because it bestows lily grandeur so late in the season the formosanum is exceedingly welcome. It is particularly charming among celosias which are just taking on color then. It is also effective when planted to the rear of zinnias or of aster, Blue Gem.

CHAPTER TWENTY-ONE

Spring Planting for Summer Bloom

Bᴜʟʙs play their part in bringing us the beauty of summer flowers. If in spring they are the whole show, in summer they are still indispensable. They add then to the floral pageant, sharing the stage with annuals and perennials.

When we think of summer-flowering bulbs we usually think of those planted in the cool of April and May, although hardy lilies, preferably set out the previous autumn, also add glory to each of the warm months. Those which come to mind as typical summer flowers from bulbs are the gladioli, dahlias and cannas, considered here; or the begonias, montbretias, tuberoses and others discussed in the next chapter. Sometimes these are all classed as tender bulbs because most of them must be lifted each fall and stored over the winter in frost-free cellars or sheds. Not all need be so treated, however, so it seems more accurate as well as more convenient to designate them simply as spring-planting bulbs.

The loveliness of their flowers is sufficient reason for growing any of these bulbs. Added to this is sureness of bloom and simplicity of culture. Take care to provide loose, well-drained, humus-filled soil. Set out the bulbs in April or May with due regard for the sun-or-shade-preference of each genus. Then you will be cutting flowers in June, July or August. And, except for gladioli, you will not need to include pest control as part of your program.

You may use spring-planting bulbs in many different ways. Gladioli, montbretias, Peruvian daffodils and many others are incomparable as cut flowers. The same bulbs also lend character to borders. Certain kinds you may wish to grow for special reasons, such as tuberoses for their nostalgic fragrance or tuberous begonias for their shade-loving qualities. Wherever you place them, summer bulbs are certain to provide color and gaiety for garden display and indoor decoration.

GLADIOLI

Foremost of the spring-planting bulbous flowers is the gladiolus or sword lily. Its popularity is well-deserved because it is beautiful, easy to grow, and available in hundreds of moderately priced varieties in a wide color range. The gladiolus illustrates to an unusual degree the democracy of bulbs, for it produces just as fine exhibition blooms in the ordinary back yard as in the carefully tended gardens of large estates; it will flourish just as well for the beginner, if he follows cultural directions, as for the seasoned expert.

Many hobbyists, in fact, who grow thousands of bulbs annually will plant none but gladioli. Every winter the storage bins of these specialists groan with corms—for botanically speaking, gladioli grow from corms, not bulbs. Such concentration may be deplored by you and me, but the devotees of this flower seem perfectly happy in their addiction and oblivious to lack of bloom from other plants.

Despite its present universality the gladiolus in its modern form is of fairly recent appearance. Species of this flower were known to the Greeks and Romans, but most modern varieties are hybrid descendants of crosses developed by nineteenth century European horticulturists from the South African species, saundersii. Near the end of the century a large stock of these hybrids was brought to this country where they became the property of John Lewis Childs of New York. This race was then further improved and renamed childsii. These bulbs, together with a strain of advanced saundersii seedlings simultaneously developed in France, constitute the parent stock of modern varieties.

The hybrids we grow today are extremely tolerant of soil variations. If you are troubled by clay too heavy for most flowers you can look for success with gladioli so long as you do not plant them in depressions which retain water in rainy seasons. You can add a foot or more to the spike by planting the corms in rich, sandy loam to which has been added the superphosphate-Bovung mixture or other fertilizer. If you use manure, keep it from coming into direct contact with the corms. If you want exhibition blooms, give the bulbs an application of fertilizer every three weeks, starting when the shoots are six inches tall. Work this nourishment into the earth at least six inches away from the base of the stalk.

The corms must be set deeply enough for anchorage. In moderately heavy soils a three-inch covering is sufficient to obviate the need for staking in all but the most wind-swept areas. In very light soils four or five inches is advisable. If fertilizing during growth is practiced, the resulting four- to five-foot spikes, heavily laden with large florets, are almost certain to need support unless the planting is especially well protected from strong winds.

You will notice that the leaves remain attractively green for weeks after the flowers have matured. Then they ripen and turn yellow. Dig the bulbs before this yellowing process is complete and while the foliage still shows some green. This early lifting is good because gladiolus corms do not like the cold wetness of soil in late autumn. It also prevents the tiny cormels formed between the old and new corms from ripening and falling off as you dig.

As the bulbs are lifted, allow them to dry out briefly in the sun. An hour or two suffices, or just time enough for the earth to dry and shake off easily. Cut off and destroy the stalks right down to the corms. Observe the formation of new corms above the shriveled remains of the old ones you planted. In between you will see tiny cormlets, or cormels, clinging to the base of the new growth.

Give the bulbs a ten-day drying period in a cool, dark place before separating them. Then gently pull them apart. Discard the withered parent corms. Store the new ones over the winter in a cool temperature—just above freezing is best. If you wish to increase your stock, save, also, the little cormels for planting out in the spring. They will reach flowering size in about two years.

Gladiolus corms which are one and one-half to two inches across with high, convex crowns have reached their maximum flowering potential. To secure the best blossoms, look for these when you buy. When you lift them in the fall, you may find that this best size has produced new corms which are even larger in diameter but with shallow and perhaps hollow crowns. Extra large, concave bulbs generally produce weaker growths and are more subject to disease. Therefore, do not be deceived by size. This is another reason for saving your little cormels. When all your corms of any variety have reached the large, flat stage discard them and depend for fresh stock upon the oncoming cormels.

You need worry little about diseases of gladioli if you ob-serve general garden sanitation, buy sound bulbs and examine all corms carefully before planting, discarding any with large scabs on the surface. One pest, however, you will have to take into account if you want assurance of success with gladioli. It is the extremely destructive gladiolus thrip, an insect one-sixteenth of an inch long. In hot weather, thrips come out in hordes from within the folds of the foliage to feast on the leaves and flower petals. Speckled leaves turning whitish and withered florets are outward signs of ruin from thrips.

The best time to start thrip control is before planting. Since the insects winter over on the corms, it is wise to remove the husks and, before setting out the corms, soak them in an insecticide solution for four to six hours. A satisfactory preparation, easily made for the home garden, is a mixture of four teaspoonfuls of Lysol per gallon of water.

If your bulbs have been planted without treatment, you can still ward off thrips by spraying every week or ten days from the time stalks are six inches high. A nicotine spray is excellent or one of the various commercial rotenone compounds. A mixture of one ounce of tartar emetic and two ounces of brown sugar with a gallon of water is an older spray which has proved effective.

Thrip control is helped by cutting off and destroying foliage when you lift the corms. This practice prevents insects from traveling down to the bulbs. As further precaution, you may store the corms for a short period in paper bags with one ounce of naphthalene flakes per hundred bulbs. Corms and flakes should be left together no longer than three weeks. Then store the corms for the winter.

If you are the kind of gardener who will not bother with bulbs you must disinfect or spray, you can still have gorgeous gladiolus blossoms unravaged by thrips by taking advantage of the fact that these wretched insects love heat and detest cold. Plant your gladioli in April so they will grow and bloom before that really hot weather arrives in which thrips do their worst work. And when you store your bulbs, place them where the thermometer hovers between thirty-two and thirty-five degrees. Few if any thrips will then survive.

My own gladioli, grown for fun, are mostly set out early and untreated. Those saved for later plantings are first immersed in the Lysol solution, but not sprayed thereafter. With this system I have enjoyed beautiful blossoms little troubled by thrips.

From April-planted gladioli you can gather blossoms in late June or early July. By successive plantings every two weeks until July fourth you can have fresh flowers through the summer and to the end of September. So valuable are gladioli for bouquets, you may wish to plant some only for cutting in rows between vegetables or in rectangular beds by themselves. Since the florets open progressively up the spike, cut the stems when the lowest buds are just starting to unfold. Then you will have a long period of indoor bloom.

These colorful flowers should also be grown where their full bloom can be enjoyed outdoors. They are gay in ribbon plantings along hedges or walls. They are useful to brighten areas in the flower beds where perennials are resting from their June bloom. The new soft tones of Pink Paragon and Rosy Morn as well as the old favorite, Picardy, are particularly harmonious in the garden.

If planted early in May, the violet-blue Mrs. Van Konynenburg will flower with phlox Columbia or Olympia, while the white Margaret Beaton with its scarlet center makes a striking companion for the brilliant phlox Charles Curtis. Anywhere the purple Pelegrina, yellow Gate of Heaven and white Vredenburg make a combination of gladioli to fill you with delight. Where there is a background of shrubbery, long borders of the white Maid of Orleans alternated with the deep red American Commander make a vivid display.

Occasionally you will find gladioli catalogued according to

size and shape of florets. More often, however, they are simply sold by name and color, although hybrids of the species primulinus are usually so designated. These have small, more widely spaced florets and present a lighter, more graceful appearance than the heavier exhibition sorts. Primulinus gladioli are particularly charming for arrangements either alone or combined with other flowers.

The named varieties of gladioli in commerce seem as numerous as the sands of the sea. So easily are new varieties raised from seed that hundreds are sold by local growers who produce too few bulbs for them to get into general trade. Some of these are excellent and if you live near enough to such a grower to inspect his blooms, you may decide he has finer kinds than you see at shows or find in catalogues. And you may be right!

The following varieties are a personal selection of generally available kinds. I think these are best in their respective color groups and will long find favor.

WHITE AND CREAM

Maid of Orleans. Evenly spaced milk-white florets.
Shirley Temple. Soft creamy white with yellow center.
Snow Princess. Huge, pure white florets on tall stem.
Vredenburg. Snow white, large spike.

YELLOW

Gate of Heaven. Ruffled petals of clear yellow.
Miss Bloomington. Deep chrome.
Mother Kadel. Beautiful soft primrose.

ROSE AND SALMON

Aladdin. Bright, reddish salmon with well-spaced florets.
Corona. Soft white, delicately shaded flesh with a picotee edge of rose.

Debonair. La France pink with creamy blotch on throat.
Magnolia. Beautiful soft peach.
Phyllis McQuiston. Deep pink.
Picardy. Favorite shrimp pink.
Pink Paragon. A truly remarkable soft, pure pink.
Rosy Morn. Soft coral, white center.

BUFF AND ORANGE

Barcarolle. Ruffled florets of salmon-orange.
Duna. Rosy buff.
Wasaga. Primulinus hybrid. Primrose-buff.

"SMOKY"

Bagdad. Old rose overlaid with grayish purple.
High Finance. Rosy orange overlaid with ashy gray.

RED

American Commander. Large, blood red.
Beacon. Scarlet with cream throat.
Commander Koehl. Deep red.
Dr. F. E. Bennett. Fiery scarlet.
Vagabond Prince. Rich ruby.

LILAC, VIOLET AND PURPLE

Blue Beauty. Lilac-blue shading to violet.
Charles Dickens. Violet with markings of deep purple.
Mrs. Van Konynenburg. A clear, violet-blue.
Pelegrina. Uniform inky blue-purple.

DAHLIAS

Dahlias, free-flowering natives of Mexico and Central America, are abundant and easy to grow. They boast a wide variety of color, and range in size from the large, formal, ball or decorative types growing on four- to five-foot plants to the small miniatures or pompons whose low stalks seldom exceed three feet. Dahlia enthusiasts who think these flowers are the most important of the year count their numbers by the thousands. Truly the dahlia is a handsome flower; it will reward proper culture with lavish bloom, and in some of its many forms is well worth planting for its summer flowers.

Dahlias grow, not from bulbs but from tuberous roots. When you lift the old stalk in the fall, you will discover a clump of these roots, each connected by a short neck with the base of the old plant stem. On the neck is the eye from which the new plant grows. Before planting divide the clump, taking care to preserve the eye attached to each root. Dahlias you buy are generally divided when you get them.

Plant the root divisions in an open, sunny location. Dahlias are heavy feeders, so enrich the soil before planting with the superphosphate-Bovung mixture or with a combination of bone meal and any dehydrated manure. Once a month during the growing season work a top dressing of fertilizer into the soil but not into contact with the plant.

Set the tuberous roots at the bottom of holes eight inches deep. Place the large types at least three feet apart each way. You need space the miniatures only eighteen inches apart. Fill the holes half full of soil at the start and fill up the depressions gradually as the plants grow. When the stalk has attained a height of eight inches, cut off all but the strongest shoot. If you want exhibition blooms, pinch off the secondary buds on each stem as they form, leaving only the terminal buds.

All but the miniature and pompon varieties need strong support. As you plant the bulbs, place sturdy stakes. Begin tying when the plants are a foot high. You will find green raffia the least conspicuous material and sufficiently strong.

Tie the raffia first to the stake and then to the plant following the universal principle of staking for vegetables or flowers.

In the New York area the last week of May or the first week of June is the proper time to set out dahlias. Cultivate plantings lightly throughout the summer to keep the soil loose and hence preserve moisture around the plants. Water thoroughly in periods of drought. Woody stalks and poor flowering result from lack of cultivation and insufficient moisture.

Wait for a killing frost before lifting your dahlias in the fall no matter how rightly impatient you are to plant your tulips in the space taken up by these summer flowers. Before digging cut the stalks down to within four to six inches of the surface. Lift the whole clump of tubers intact for storage. You cannot take too much precaution in avoiding injury to the brittle necks which join the tubers to the stalk. Damaged tubers are an easy prey to fungus or rot which quickly spreads to healthy roots.

After lifting, lay plants down on the soil surface with the tubers exposed to the sun. When they have dried, the clumps are ready for frost-free winter storage in a box or bin with the roots resting on a layer of sand or peat moss and with three inches of the same material above them to prevent drying out. In the spring each tuberous root with budding eye is ready to be separated from the parent stalk and planted.

Large dahlias are best set out in separate beds or gardens where they can have all the room and special attention necessary for fine development. Seen here in all their glory, it is easy to understand how magnificent specimens like the yellow California Idol, the apricot-blend Amelia Earhart and the pure white Mrs. William Knudsen evoke such enthusiasm. Each huge, handsome flower seems a triumph.

The smaller pompons and miniatures with their branching stems make excellent bedding plants. Inexpensively grown from roots or spring seeding in the open, they may be planted among summer perennials. They will give three months of bloom and a constant supply of lasting cut flowers for the house. The single whites are as lovely as waterlilies and like them may be floated in shallow bowls. The smaller dahlias are also useful along the edge of the shrubbery border provided sufficient sun reaches them there.

Prospective dahlia buyers have a wide range of types from which to choose. For many years the large, globe-shaped ball dahlia reigned supreme. It is still in some demand but its stiff formality is not so appealing today. The informal and twisted petal dahlia is now more popular.

Most dahlias sold today are grouped in the following classifications or variations of them:

Ball varieties include huge round, compact flowers of evenly rolled petals.

Formal decoratives have full, double blossoms with flat rays sometimes rounded on the ends.

Informal decoratives are a little less double. Petal tips are curved.

Cactus varieties are double with the petals rolled and considerably twisted and curled. Semi-cactus sorts are similar but the petals are less twisted.

Singles are open-centered with flat broad rays.

Pompons are small replicas of the ball type, fully double with perfect petals. Their formality is rather appealing in the same manner that a starched collar is cute on a small boy.

Miniatures are dwarf forms of the larger types.

Like gladioli, dahlias grow so rapidly from seed that many small commercial growers become their own hybridizers. There are varieties, however, which have achieved such widespread popularity that their tuberous roots are well worth buying. Some of the more striking of these are listed below:

BALL

Big Ben. Flame orange.
Orchid Ball. Rosy lavender.
Queen of the Yellows. Bright yellow.
Snow Queen. Pure white blossoms borne on long stems.
Supt. Amrhyn. Clear rose pink.

FORMAL DECORATIVE

Dahliadel Gold. Huge flowers of golden yellow.
Darcy Sainbury. Large, showy white.
Jersey's Beauty. True pink, delicately shaded amber.
Ruby Taylor. Carmine.

INFORMAL DECORATIVE

California Idol. Clear, bright yellow.
Fort Monmouth. Crimson maroon.
Jane Cowl. Blend of bronze, buff and apricot.
Kathleen Norris. Rose pink.
Mrs. William Knudsen. Pure white.

CACTUS

American Triumph. Bright red.
Golden Standard. Buff, shaded amber and gold.

SEMI-CACTUS

Amelia Earhart. Apricot-buff with salmon lights.
Miss Elsie Jane. Shrimp pink with cream shadings.
Son of Satan. Bright scarlet.

SINGLE

Lorna Doone. Soft rose.
Newport Wonder. Deep pink.
Purity. Snow white.
Tongo Century. Orange and gold.

POMPON

Bob White. Cream white.
Ila. Blood red.
Iolanthe. Copper orange.
Yellow Gem. Bright yellow.

MINIATURE

Bishop Llandaff. Dark red.
Fairy. Apricot-buff.
Helly Boudweijn. Pure white.
Rosebud. Cream, flushed rose.

CANNAS

Cannas are easily third in general importance among spring-planting bulbs. They produce their huge towers of bloom on strong stems four to five feet tall rising from a mass of broad, heavy leaves. Flowers and foliage combine to produce an effect of imposing strength.

Actually cannas do not grow from bulbs, corms or tubers, but from large fleshy roots. Still by tradition and cultural requirement they deserve to be considered with the spring-planting bulbs. Do not plant cannas before all frost danger is past. Then set them eighteen inches apart to allow for the spread of their foliage and cover them with four to five inches of soil to assure stability of growth. They like open sun and welcome plenty of nourishment. In periods of prolonged drought water them thoroughly.

Cannas provide bloom right up to frost. After the first touch of it, lift the roots but do not expose them to the sun for more than a few hours. If enough soil does not adhere when they are dug, store with a covering of peat moss to prevent drying out. Fifty degrees is safe storage temperature. Like dahlias, canna roots are not divided until spring when they should be sectioned with a sharp knife and one bud allowed each division.

Cannas suggest red swatches in parks or hotel lawns to those of us too young to remember the lozenge-shaped beds in front of Victorian homes which always featured these plants. Their universal appearance in all front yards, no matter how small, for some years caused a general boycott of cannas by gardeners becoming more conscious of landscape proportions. Now cannas are staging a popular return. Gardeners are realizing anew that flowers of such easy culture, moderate cost, long-lasting and magnificent bloom should not be forsaken. To fill this demand growers have developed varieties of softer tones more readily blended with other flowers.

If yours is a really limited garden of small, enclosed beds, omit cannas. But if you have long, deep borders, by all means use these flowers to give strength and power to the planting. The white and salmon tones combine strikingly with such sturdy fall asters as the lavender novi-belgi, Climax. Between groups of summer phlox repeated plantings of cannas in white and yellow and the lighter shades of rose give a lift to the border.

Cannas likewise are handsome when massed in front of shrubbery or evergreens. The new scarlets or whites produce an imposing picture in front of the dark green of hemlocks. A long bed of cannas at the foot of a distant wall makes a telling display.

This short list of varieties merits your consideration:

Ambassador. 5 feet. Cherry red with bronze foliage.
City of Portland. 4 feet. Clear pink, green leaves.
Copper Giant. 4½ feet. Maroon, flushed rose with green foliage.
Eureka. 4 feet. Pure white with green leaves.

King Humbert. 4 feet. Brilliant scarlet with bronze foliage.

King Humbert Yellow. 4 feet. Deep yellow with dark green leaves.

Mrs. Alfred Conard. 4 feet. Salmon pink. Bronze foliage.

Wintzer's Colossal. 5 feet. Pure cerise with deep green leaves.

CHAPTER TWENTY-TWO

More Color in Summer

A LONG procession of riotously colorful summer flowers comes from spring-planting bulbs. Many less familiar than the gladioli, dahlias and cannas are equally charming. The anemone, ranunculus, ixia and sparaxis, for example, can be planted outside in the spring as an alternative to greenhouse culture or to heavily mulched outdoor planting in the fall. The true bulbs of lachenalia, gloxinia and amaryllis, as well as the fleshy roots of agapanthus and calla, are sometimes classed as summer-flowering bulbs. But they are better known as indoor plants which may be moved outside for decoration in the warm months. Besides all these, however, there are many important bulbs, such as cooperias, montbretias and tigridias, whose primary place is in the garden and whose season of planting is in the spring or early summer.

If you are not familiar with the wide variety of spring-planting bulbs for the summer garden make their acquaintance, if only a few at a time and season by season. Let them fill vacant spaces in your perennial beds or use them to brighten shrubbery borders. You will find their cultural demands modest. Although montbretias, hardy begonias and Oxalis adenophella alone are hardy, most of those which need lifting store easily. With proper care they will provide many successive seasons of bloom.

TUBEROUS-ROOTED BEGONIAS

Three months enjoyment of bloom from the lovely tuberous-rooted begonia bloom can be yours. This is true unless you live in the driest regions of the arid Southwest or your garden is so sun-struck that it offers no shady haven for them. The tubers produce twelve- to fifteen-inch plants with large, rich green leaves and many successive flowers. Dinner-plate blossoms are not impossible in Maine and California where the climate is ideal for them. If you live in an area where summers are hot and muggy, you can expect well-grown plants to yield a profusion of flowers four to six inches across.

Despite their usual name these plants grow from tubers, not tuberous roots, since the eyes are formed on the tubers themselves. Plant the saucer-shaped tubers concave side up with a two-inch covering of loamy soil containing plenty of humus. Through protracted dry spells, water them well. Otherwise you will need to give them no further attention, once they are properly set, except to gather the flowers.

Begonias will tolerate neither frost nor the cold wetness of near-freezing soil. Therefore, do not plant them outside until danger of cold weather has definitely passed. This, in the vicinity of New York, is about May fifteenth.

You can start your begonias indoors long before then, however, and thus lengthen the season of bloom. Plant the bulbs in pots or pans in late February, March or April in fairly rich soil. A good mixture consists of half garden soil, one quarter humus and one quarter well-rotted manure. Add enough sand to make it friable even when moist. Set the bulbs one inch below the surface. Water lightly at first, plentifully after growth starts. Place the pots in the light but away from direct sunshine.

Begonias started indoors must not be set outside until two

weeks after the earliest date on which it would be wise to plant tubers outdoors. June first is a safe time in the New York area. At that, the more advanced of the indoor-started begonias will be yielding flowers when the sprouts of the garden-planted tubers are only just beginning to appear.

The same dislike of cold which necessitates late outdoor planting of tuberous begonias dictates early lifting. The end of September or early October before the ground gets really cold is the best time. Bring the plants inside immediately and let them dry off until stems part easily from tubers. Then store them over the winter in flats or bags of dry peat moss. A temperature of approximately fifty degrees is suitable.

Finding a perfect site for tuberous-rooted begonias is usually an easy task. The shady side of the house, the base of a high-branching but deep-rooting tree or a bed beneath a leafy arbor are fine locations. Select a spot where nothing else will grow if you like, but don't let it be under the eaves, behind the rhododendrons or close to a foundation planting. Begonias need shade but they also require air. For that reason, too, they should never be planted under low trees or shrubs. Avoid, also, setting the tubers in a thick mat of roots made by the tree or bush which provides the shade.

Soil is important, too. You may have a shady corner framed by a recess of the house or garden wall where nothing seems to get enough sun. Before deciding that this is just the spot for begonias, examine the soil. If it is the hard, poor quality usually found in such a neglected spot, make haste slowly in planting. Fork in, first, a couple of wheelbarrow loads of mixed topsoil and humus. Then your begonias will have the wherewithal to produce a profusion of green leaves and sparkling flowers.

An unusual but good location for tuberous begonias is in a rock garden where the encroaching shade of a tree is causing high mortality among once-flourishing herbaceous plants. Here, if planted on a nearly level plane (they do not like steep slopes), begonias will give you summer-long beauty. If they are not hardy, nor found in standard lists of rock garden plants, what difference does it make?

Tuberous begonias are generally sold by color and type. Colors range from white through lemon yellow, pink, salmon and apricot to deep copper-orange, scarlet and red. Types vary from single through frilled and crested forms to the fully double, carnation-flowered kinds. There are also pendant forms so effective for hanging baskets, porch boxes and beds along the top of a wall. Named varieties are available in each of the colors and types but when bought this way the bulbs are fairly expensive.

BEGONIA EVANSIANA—HARDY BEGONIA

Begonia evansiana, the so-called hardy begonia, a tuberous species, is a boon to gardeners. Planted in the spring in the densest shade under three or four inches of soil which has even a modicum of organic content, these tubers will send up sturdy plants in a matter of weeks. All summer they make otherwise barren areas attractive with their rich, red-veined leaves. The small pink flowers, resembling those of the fibrous-rooted begonias, appear in the autumn, loosely branching off a long stem.

At least as far north as southern New England, evansiana will winter perfectly if a light mulch of leaves is provided. The following spring plants will not only reappear from the tubers you originally set out but new shoots will arise, since the species multiplies rapidly from bulb offsets. Bulbils also form in the axils of the leaves, fall off and start new growth. I know of one large colony under a tall elm. Started four years ago from ten bulbs, it now numbers hundreds.

Planted under trees and shrubs the hardy begonia stands more interference from low branches than the large-flowered tuberous-rooted kinds. It is fine also as a ground cover for wooded areas where a spring display of mertensia, trillium and bloodroot needs a summer counterpart. As yet the hardy begonia is little grown or available, but as more gardeners discover its wonderful value the demand will increase and growers will increase their stocks.

CHLIDANTHUS—DELICATE LILY

The delicate lily, Chlidanthus fragrans, is an infrequently grown amaryllid of uncommon charm for the summer garden. Its stem is ten inches tall and, like the amaryllis, it bears its trumpet-shaped flowers in a horizontal umbel at the top. Blossoms open in July or August, are four inches long, golden yellow and deliciously scented. Plant chlidanthus in the sun with a three-inch covering of rich soil as soon as possible in the spring, since it sprouts early. Keep the bulbs over the winter in a cool, dry place.

These flowers look well in the border or in low front areas of the rock garden.

COOPERIA DRUMMONDI—RAIN LILY

Opening in late afternoon, the rain lily or evening star, Cooperia drummondi, adds beauty and fragrance to the summer twilight and early evening. On slender eight- to twelve-inch stems, the pink buds open to shallow trumpets, white within, rose tinged without. Plant cooperias in April or May in sunny spots of the border or rock garden. Place a two-inch covering of loose or gritty soil above them. Lift the bulbs in September or October for winter storage in dry soil or peat moss.

GALTONIA—HYACINTHUS CANDICANS

Galtonia candicans, the summer or cape hyacinth, sends up from its large bulb a three- to five-foot stalk bearing a spike of twenty to thirty loosely hung, fragrant, white bells. These lend distinction to the garden when planted between clumps of phlox or delphiniums in repeated groups to the rear of a deep perennial border. They like full sun and rich soil. North of Virginia, galtonia bulbs are usually lifted and stored like gladioli, although some gardeners report successful wintering outdoors under a heavy mulch. In either case the bulbs may not flower two years in a row, preferring to rest the alternate one. It is, therefore, wise to renew stock with some fresh bulbs every year.

GLORIOSA—CLIMBING LILY

Gloriosa rothschildiana, the Rothschild lily or climbing lily, is a vine growing to three feet when planted outdoors. Hitherto confined to the greenhouse gloriosa is now recognized as a beauty for the summer garden. Each plant produces ten or more large, lily-like flowers which open scarlet and yellow and turn all scarlet. Start the tubers indoors as you do begonias or plant them outside in May. Grown in full sun and sheltered from high winds, they produce colorful blossoms from late July to September. A three-inch covering of rich soil is advisable. Lift the tubers in the early autumn and store in dry peat moss.

HYMENOCALLIS—ISMENE, PERUVIAN DAFFODIL

Hymenocallis, still better known as Ismene calathina, the Peruvian daffodil, is the summer gardener's delight. Promptly beautiful, the broad strap-like leaves of bright green are soon followed by fragrant, amaryllis-shaped flowers, white with green centers. These are carried in umbels of three to four on two- to three-foot stems. The attractive foliage lasts weeks after flowering.

You can grow Peruvian daffodils in almost any soil. While they like sun, they will flower in as much as fifty per cent shade. Cover the bulbs with three inches of soil for anchorage. Lift them in September or early October, keeping the fleshy roots intact, and store them in a temperature which does not go below fifty degrees. Bulbs increase rapidly from offsets. Save these for growing on and in a few years you will have a sizable stock from an original purchase of a dozen bulbs.

Hymenocallis are also grand flowers for cutting, while the speed with which they produce bouquets is impressive. Flowering varies with time of planting. This may safely be any time after May first. Later-planted bulbs grow faster, those set out in June flowering in three to four weeks. The Peruvian daffodil is a bulb to count on for a quick and handsome display.

OXALIS

Do not overlook the garden possibilities of the versatile oxalis genus. Members of the wood sorrel family, they grow from tubers, bulbs or creeping rootstocks. They are small, but free-flowering, and the blooming season of certain easily grown and readily obtainable species lasts for several summer months. Some are hardy with a little protection, but most should be treated as tender spring-planting bulbs, to be lifted and stored in dry peat moss over the winter. Many varieties are so inexpensive that gardeners treat them as annuals. A covering of two inches of light soil suffices.

Three species are particularly recommended. Adenophylla produces small lilac-rose flowers with deep pink centers. Stems rise to ten inches from a mass of gray-green foliage. Bloom starts early in the summer and lasts until autumn. This species grows from tubers which may be treated as fall-planting bulbs since, in a sunny location, they are hardy with light protection. Adenophylla is charming to the fore of a border planting. Bowiei in a sunny spot will produce, from midsummer on, ten-inch panicles of bright pink flowers. The flowers follow the sun and the clover-like leaves droop in the shade or on cloudy days. Lasiandra is crimson with large four-leaf clover foliage. The florets are borne on graceful racemes ten inches long. Lasiandra also likes the sun.

POLYANTHES—TUBEROSE

Old-fashioned tuberoses and summer gardens are inseparable. Whether you plant the three-foot tall, waxy Double Pearl or the two-foot Mexican Single of equally pure whiteness, grow at least a few clumps of these scented beauties. Let them fill your moonlit August nights with white loveliness and sweet fragrance.

Plant tuberoses three inches deep in good garden soil. Select a sunny spot and water during dry spells. Renew your stock annually since tuberoses do not bloom satisfactorily from second-year bulbs. Tuberoses started indoors in March or April and transplanted outdoors by May twentieth will blossom a month earlier than those started outside in May.

SPREKELIA—JACOBEAN LILY

Sprekelia formosissima, the jacobean lily, is a large-flowered, deep scarlet member of the amaryllis family which, scattered here and there in the garden, adds beauty and interest. The flowers, carried on stems two feet tall, are curiously formed, suggesting huge scarlet spiders suspended in mid-air. They are six-petaled with the upper three petals branching out like claws. The lower segments are larger and the middle one slightly recurved. Plant sprekelias during May under a three-inch covering of good loamy soil. They usually flower in late June or early July. Bulbs may be stored in the winter like hymenocallis.

TIGRIDIA—MEXICAN SHELLFLOWER

Your summer planting will not be complete without the exotic and exquisite tigridia, or Mexican shellflower. Triangular shaped flowers, often measuring five inches across with brilliantly spotted center cups, are borne on twelve- to sixteen-inch stems. The thin, narrow sword-like leaves rise four or five inches higher.

Tigridias come in soft tones of white, cream and rose and in warmer colors of yellow, flaming orange and scarlet. Because of the delicate texture of the flower petals, the effect is always fragile and ephemeral, no matter what the hue. Tigridias seem more precious because each exotic bloom lasts but a day. You will learn to watch for the burgeoning of each bud so as not to miss its brilliant flowering. Although each blossom ends with the first nightfall, sometimes as many as six or eight flowers appear successively from midsummer to late October.

Plant tigridias in full or nearly full sun in loamy soil high in humus content. A three-inch covering is wise. Water copiously in dry weather. Lift the bulbs after the first killing frost. With careful handling you can save your original stock and also reap the benefit of the increase made through offsets. Attempt no bulb division until spring and save the large roots which may have formed under the bulbs during summer. Prevent drying out by storing the bulbs in damp sand or peat moss at about fifty degrees. When you buy tigridias, examine the bulbs carefully. If kept for any length of time on warm store shelves, they dry out and become worthless.

Tigridias look well in clumps of ten to twenty throughout the perennial beds. Or you can grow them row by row for cutting. They make unusual and charming table arrangements.

The following varieties are worth planting:

Aztec Chief. Blazing scarlet with deep red spots in center cup.
Buccaneer. Orange scarlet with cup of deep maroon, spotted orange.
Canary Queen. Pale yellow petals with white cup almost imperceptibly spotted yellow.

Gypsy Maid. Shining chrome yellow with maroon-spotted centers.

Rose King. Soft rose with wine red spots in center.

Scarlet Giant. Large petals of silky scarlet surrounding cup of pure orange.

Sunset Glow. Brilliant orange petals with center cup heavily spotted dark red.

Vagabond Prince. Pure white petals surrounding cup of clear orange.

TRITONIA—MONTBRETIA

Tritonia, better known as montbretia, is a striking race of cormous plants which now include wonderful hybrids. Somewhat like the gladiolus, the montbretia carries its florets more widely spaced on a three- to four-foot spike which is graceful and arching. Leaves are narrower and lighter, too.

The corms require a moderately rich soil and flourish wherever they get full sun for at least a half day. A three-inch covering is sufficient. Although you plant new bulbs in the spring, old ones may be left in the ground over the winter. A light mulch is advisable in a cold exposure or whenever plantings are made north of southern New England. If, for convenience, you do lift the bulbs in the fall, store them in peat moss. When purchasing, watch out for dryness as you do with tigridias.

Montbretias lend festive color to perennial beds when planted in repeated groups. They are also striking massed in front of green shrubbery or hemlock hedges or colonized in large drifts at the woods' edge. A border of bright montbretia spikes swaying gracefully in front of a white picket fence is a gay sight in late summer.

If you revel in sunset colors and autumn foliage, you will like montbretias. In August, September and October they splash the garden with bright apricot, fiery red, tawny crimson and gold. New light yellow and rose-tinted varieties have also been developed.

Here is a selection of outstanding kinds:

Apricot Queen. Golden apricot. One of the first to flower.
Citronella. Large florets of canary yellow with crimson blotch in the center.
Fire King. Brilliant fiery scarlet, golden center.
George Davison. Pure yellow.
His Majesty. Very broad florets of scarlet with gold markings.
Indian Chief. Crimson with copper-orange center.
Lemon Queen. Yellow with pale yellow center. Short stemmed.
Queen Alexandra. Golden yellow, flushed apricot.
Queen Boadicea. Deep golden orange.
Rosea. Pale yellow, suffused pink.
Star of the East. Tawny orange with a cream center.
Una. Apricot tan with crimson blotches in center.

ZEPHYRANTHES—FAIRY LILY

The zephyr or fairy lily, growing eight to twelve inches high, resembles a small lily or a large species crocus. Bulbs planted in the spring flower freely in successive bursts of bloom from midsummer to frost. They prefer an open sunny situation but will stand light shade. Loamy garden soil is best and a two-inch deep planting. When cold weather ends their season, lift and store the bulbs in peat moss. If stored properly, the same stock can be used for many years.

Use zephyranthes copiously for summer and autumn enjoyment wherever low growing flowers can be planted effectively. Colonize them in masses down the front of the flower borders or in walk beds for recurrent display. Plant them in vacant pockets of the rock garden for August and September bloom there.

Fairy lilies in tubs or pails adorning the porches and terraces of New England homes are a pleasing and familiar sight. Sometimes planted receptacles are buried in flower beds or plunged on either side of the front stoop. Frequently plants are left to ripen in the tubs after the flowering season, then brought indoors for storing.

These species are recommended:

Ajax. Bright yellow. Summer-flowering.
Candida. White. Autumn-flowering.
Carinata. Large bright pink. Midsummer-blooming.
Rosea. Light rose. Autumn-flowering.

CHAPTER TWENTY-THREE

Hardy Bulbs with Autumn Flowers

THE bulb kingdom contains another group which may appropriately be called the summer-planting or autumn-flowering division. Set out in midsummer the colchicum, autumn crocus, hardy amaryllis and sternbergia brighten the landscape during the late summer and early autumn. Few in number, but hardy, they are important in rounding out the season of bulb bloom.

COLCHICUMS

Like giant crocuses in size and shape, colchicums bloom from August to November. White through rosy lilac to violet flowers rise on naked white stems eight to ten inches long. Although no foliage appears during the flowering season, the heavy, round corms two to three inches in diameter produce it abundantly in the spring. Then large masses of coarse, grassy leaves spread over a wide surface around the bulbs and ripen off completely six weeks or so before the first budding flower stem emerges.

You can grow colchicums almost anywhere, although they prefer moderately rich soil with the tops of the bulbs not more than two inches below its surface. Light shade fosters best year to year bloom, but you will get flowers from bulbs

planted in full sun or fairly heavy shade. You need give them
no winter mulch although they naturalize happily where a
light annual fall of leaves is allowed to remain.

The corms have a relatively short dormancy from the time
the leaves ripen until the flower stems emerge. It is during
this resting period that the bulbs are lifted for commercial
handling and for transplanting in your garden. It is always a
race to get new corms to the gardener in time. Colchicums
are insistent bloomers; there is no holding them back. Whether
planted or not the bulbs send forth flowers at the appointed
time. It is not an uncommon occurrence on unpacking a late-
arriving case of colchicums to find bleached blooms attached
to long stems inside. You should, therefore, secure and plant
your corms early in August before sprouts appear or at the
latest early in September, before growth is advanced.

When you select a spot for them, be sure to take into account their lack of foliage while flowering. Provide the white
stems with some low, green background. You will find no better place for them than in meadow grass or in a corner of the
lawn near shrubbery where it is not necessary to mow. They
will colonize well in either spot. Colchicums, if planted in the
midst of a ground cover of vinca, will bring you welcome
autumn color there.

They may be used in rock garden pockets wherever you can
find room to set the large bulbs among low alpines. In the
herbaceous border their use is questionable because of the
bareness of their fall growth and density of their spring foliage. However, I do know one attractive planting with Anchusa
myosotidiflora. In May the large anchusa leaves more than
hold their own against the lusty foliage of the colchicums for
whose colorful autumn blooms they later provide excellent
dark green contrast.

These varieties of colchicums are worth planting:

Autumnale. Rosy lilac.
Autumnale album. Pure white.
Bornmuelleri. Large blossoms of lilac-rose with white base.
Guizot. Violet.
President Coolidge. Lavender.
Speciosum. Crimson-rose.

AUTUMN CROCUSES

To many of you the flowers of the autumn crocus may recall the Austrian or Swiss Alps. There, growing wild in the
valley meadows and on the more gently sloping hillsides, literally millions of them have delighted American visitors each
late summer and autumn. From these mountains and from
other parts of Europe and the Middle East where they are
native, come the species which are so hardy and well adapted
to our gardens.

In size and shape of bulb and flower the autumn crocus is
unmistakable kin to its spring-flowering cousin. In other re-
spects it invites comparison with the larger colchicum. Both
have a color range of white, lavender, rosy lilac and violet.
Both are highly tolerant of soil variation, flower in sun or
shade and like shallow planting.

Plant autumn crocuses at the same time as colchicums but
with even greater promptness to avoid their "blooming in the
bag." Provide the supporting green of grass or other low
plants for their white flower stems, which are entirely leafless
or with only a suggestion of foliage. Expect from autumn crocuses as you do from colchicums a generous spread of leaves
in the spring.

Is the flowering season ushered in for you by cheerful drifts
of crocuses? Then let gay colonies of the autumn kinds end
the season's bloom. Speciosus and zonatus send up successive
flowers from mid-September until late November.

Do not plant autumn crocuses where there is likely to be a *heavy* fall of leaves. Unless constantly raked off, the leaves will hide the lovely blooms. And remember these bulbs are not for the rodent-loving suburbanite. Squirrels dote on autumn crocuses, whose white sprouts seem also to be perfect signposts to guide hungry chipmunks down to each crisp, crunchy corm.

These crocuses will bring you autumn beauty:

Asturicus. Deep violet.
Nudiflorus. Deep purple.
Sativus. Lilac, feathers violet. Bright orange anthers.
Speciosus. Deep lavender-blue.
Speciosus aitchisonii. Large flowers of bright blue.
Speciosus albus. Pure white.
Zonatus. Rosy lilac.

LYCORIS SQUAMIGERA—HARDY AMARYLLIS

The Hardy Amaryllis, sometimes listed as Amaryllis halli, is a summer-planting bulb which lends robust charm to the late garden. Its broad, strap-like leaves, appearing in the spring, ripen off and disappear by early June. A month or so later a stout, leafless flower stalk thrusts two to three feet upward. At its top in mid-August there unfolds a spreading umbel of four to seven large rose-pink flowers, trumpet-shaped and fragrant.

The best time to transplant lycoris bulbs is in late June during the short resting period after the foliage has ripened but before the flowering stem has started. They may also be moved in the fall right after the flower dies down. Fall-dug bulbs kept over the winter may get too late a start for bloom the following summer although you can expect them to return to their foliage-flower cycle the following year.

Lycoris likes good loamy soil. It is perfectly hardy under a four-inch covering and has a tendency to dig itself quite deeply if left undisturbed. Light shade is best.

For good effect in the garden, plant the hardy amaryllis at the shady end of the bed among hostas or Anchusa myosotidiflora. To make the best use of them, naturalize them in light woodland. There they will colonize contentedly among your ferns, returning each August with enchanting color.

STERNBERGIA—YELLOW AUTUMN CROCUS

Sternbergia lutea provides that warm yellow which is lacking among colchicums and autumn crocuses so that the name of the flower whose place it usurps is often used for its common name. And the golden, orange-anthered sternbergia blossom on its five-inch stem does look for all the world like a yellow crocus, although it does not end its bloom by opening out flat. The leaves are also different, of about the same length as the crocus leaves, but broader, thicker and darker green.

Plant sternbergia in August or early September under four inches of loamy, well-drained soil. Unlike the colchicums and autumn crocuses, sternbergias have a rosette of foliage to set off their fall flowers. These leaves winter over, making further growth in the spring and ripening off by June. From June until August is the resting period during which bulbs are lifted for transplanting.

If you live south of Mason and Dixon's line, you can plant sternbergias anywhere in sun or light shade for yearly bloom. In more northerly latitudes you must give them as much sun as possible so as to give the foliage enough time for ripening after the fall blossoming. North of southern New England winter comes so quickly after sternbergia blooms that the bulbs usually have too short a period to ripen properly.

You can naturalize sternbergia bulbs in full southern sun with the protection of wall or shrub on their northern side. They make splendid rock garden plants when set in a southern or southeastern exposure. Their deep yellow contrasts effectively with the blue autumn Crocus, speciosus, or with Colchicum, Guizot.

CHAPTER TWENTY-FOUR

Easy Indoor Flowering

OF ALL the trials of gardening, none is more vexing than the long winter wait for bulbs set out in fall to burst into bloom the following spring. There is a good remedy for this impatient chafing—growing a few of the easier bulbs indoors. This is also a pleasant means of ameliorating the sad lot of apartment dwellers who have no garden for spring flowers.

As every one knows, bulbs are highly adaptable for "forcing." This means they may be brought into flower ahead of their outdoor schedule by giving them a warm temperature earlier than nature would provide it. It is a *spring* not a *summer* temperature which is thus afforded in advance.

It is true that many bulbous plants, like Dutch iris, freesias and most of the May-flowering tulips, need, for successful indoor growing, the skill of the professional or at least the more easily controlled environment of a greenhouse. Fortunately, there are many bulbs which can find conditions to their liking in the home and do not demand undue attention. While they prefer special temperatures and humidity, they tolerate moderate lapses in them.

Simplest to grow are those which will flourish in pebbles and water. Of these none is more justly popular than the narcissi of the tender tazetta division: the snowy Paperwhite, the white and yellow Chinese Sacred Lily and the orange-eyed, yellow Soleil d'Or. By successive plantings bowls of these fragrant polyanthus daffodils can be kept blooming on tables and at windows from before Christmas until after Easter.

Undoubtedly more Paperwhites than all other bulbs put together are grown by window gardeners. Successful bloom should be the rule, but frequently it is the exception. When failure occurs, it is natural to assume that the bulbs were blind. More often it is because the simple cultural procedure was not carefully followed.

Of course it is important to use large firm bulbs. These should come from carefully selected stock of true Paperwhite Grandiflora. Bulbs fourteen centimeters in circumference are the smallest size worth growing, while top size sixteen centimeter bulbs give the best results.

It is a good plan to buy your winter's supply of Paperwhites early in the autumn, but do not start the first lot before the end of October since bulbs are not fully mature before that time. Store the bulbs before planting in an open container (a flat or shallow box is best) in a cool room. Time your plantings so as to use up the last bulbs by the middle of February because an increasingly high percentage lose vitality after that, no matter how carefully you store them. Before planting each group, give them five or six days extra-cool storage in a cold pantry or on the bottom shelf of a refrigerator.

Use containers deep enough to allow the bulbs to be set firmly in pebbles with two inches or more of space below for roots. Fill the bowls with water, at room temperature, up to one-half inch above the bottom of the bulbs. This extra half inch of moisture will soon evaporate. Thereafter try to keep the water level fairly constant at the base of the bulbs by refilling twice a week to replace that lost by evaporation. Put a piece of charcoal in each bowl to keep the water sweet.

Nearly everyone knows that Paperwhites and other polyanthus narcissi should be placed in a cool, dark place for root growth immediately after planting. This is to discourage top growth until after good root systems have developed. Unfortunately, many gardeners, intent on protecting their narcissi from the smallest ray of light, shut them up in such airless closets that blasted buds often result. This lack of air is, I believe, the principal reason amateurs sometimes have poor blooms from these easy bulbs. Pitch darkness is not necessary but good ventilation is essential.

A cool cellar or a shaded pantry shelf in a fifty-five degree temperature is the best place to keep bowls of narcissi during the root-making stage. If you have no such location, place them in your coolest closet, but leave the door open a crack for ventilation. And remember that the atmosphere near the floor is less stuffy than that on the top shelf.

How long it will take the bulbs to make sufficient roots depends on the date of starting. The rooting period varies from three weeks for bulbs planted in October to ten days for those started in February. Bulbs planted later also produce foliage and flowers faster so that, while it takes five or six weeks for Paperwhites set in pebbles in the early autumn to blossom, blooms can be expected in three or four weeks from those planted in the late winter.

When a pencil cautiously poked among the pebbles reveals the bottom of the bowl to be well filled by roots, bring the narcissi to the light. With these plants, *as with all bulbs brought out from a period of dark growing,* avoid direct sun until foliage turns green. Then give the Paperwhites as much bright sunshine as possible to promote quicker growth and hence shorter, sturdier stems. When the flowers actually open, prolong their bloom by moving the bowls out of full sun.

For ideal conditions, the room in which polyanthus narcissi —and most other bulbs grown indoors—produce their foliage and flowers should be a steady sixty degrees. Since this is not feasible in the average house or city apartment, approximate it as nearly as you can. At all events keep the temperature constant, avoiding draughts or sudden drastic changes.

After you have grown the tender daffodils successfully, try some of the hardy poetaz kinds. If not started before November, these cluster-flowering beauties are easy to grow in pebbles and water. Allow three to four weeks for root development. The white and yellow Laurens Koster and the deep yellow, red-centered Scarlet Gem are good ones to start with. The amazing new and still scarce poetaz Cragford grows about as readily in pebbles and water as the Paperwhite. You can have other hardy narcissi indoors but they are best grown in soil.

The tender French Roman hyacinths can also be grown in pebbles and water. These bulbs produce slender, graceful spikes of loosely hung rose, blue or white bells. Let them make roots for eight weeks in the same cool dark place you use for the Paperwhites. Then bring them to the light. They should flower in four more weeks. For variety, try some of the tender French-grown Dutch Roman hyacinths now offered again in white, rose and blue.

The familiar, large Dutch hyacinths are hard to manage in pebbles but can easily be grown in water alone if the special hyacinth glass is used. This is a tall vessel with a cup shaped top to hold the bulb. In using these glasses, fill with only enough water to touch the base of the bulb and keep it at that level by refilling as the water evaporates. After setting the hyacinth in place move the glass to a cool dark spot. It takes the bulb about twelve weeks to fill the lower part of the container with roots, then three or four more weeks of growing in the light to perfect a full bloom. To avoid long, lanky stems give hyacinths all the sun possible once foliage has turned green.

Colchicums and autumn crocuses can also be grown in pebbles and water or just left in a saucer with no water at all! I have never admired colchicums indoors—too much bulb and too little flower it seems to me. A bowl of closely spaced autumn crocuses is effective, though, especially the lavender sativus or the blue speciosus but these are even more charming in a shining white container filled with soil on which a little grass seed has been sown to provide green.

A large number of bulbs may be forced in soil in regulation flower pots or in bulb pans, which are merely shallow clay pots. These or glazed-surface containers may be used with equal success. The glazed pots, having less porosity, require less watering. Their colors can be selected to blend with a decoration scheme. New clay pots should be soaked in water twenty-four hours and dried out before using.

Whatever the container, a proper soil mixture and method of potting remain important. Good soil for indoor bulb growing may be bought from the local florist or prepared at home by combining two parts of well-sifted garden soil and one part humus. Mix in sand until the material crumbles in your hands even when it is moist. The superphosphate-Bovung, or bone-meal-Bovung mixture you use for outdoor bulbs is likewise good for the window garden. Use it at the rate of one tablespoonful per seven-inch potful of soil.

Starting bulbs in clay pots is not difficult. First place an arching piece of broken crock or flower pot over the hole in the bottom and add, for drainage, about an inch of the rough material left in the sieve after the soil has been sifted. Fill in with the potting mixture to the level at which bulbs are to rest. This will vary according to the kind and size of bulb being planted. After placing the bulbs, add more soil but leave one inch of space at the top to receive water.

Bulbs which can be forced in soil may be divided into two

groups: those which may be kept inside for both rooting and flowering and those which are generally buried in their containers outdoors for root growth. Of those which stay indoors the amaryllis yields the showiest blooms for the least attention. Actually many of the bulbs sold under this name are hippeastrums, a closely allied genus, whose culture and appearance are similar. The amaryllis, or hippeastrum bulb you buy in the fall should be just ready to send up its sturdy flower stalk. This generally grows from twelve to fifteen inches tall before the long, swelling bud at its tip unfolds in a branching umbel of three to five large, trumpet-shaped flowers of pink, white, candy-stripe or velvet red.

Keep your new amaryllis bulbs at room temperature before potting them. Exposure to cold before planting is one of the two chief reasons for failure to bloom. The other cause is overwatering in the early stages of growth. Cold inhibits the embryo flower stalk. Too much moisture stimulates foliage growth. The large, strap-like leaves normally make little progress until the plant is ready to bloom. If they make too much early headway because of overwatering or because the nascent flower stalk is retarded by cold, they will literally crowd out the budded stem before it emerges from the bulb.

The amaryllis is also more reliable about blooming if kept somewhat potbound. Therefore, avoid an overly large container. An inch all around between bulb and pot is adequate. Set the bulb firmly at a depth to permit exposure of the top third.

The amaryllis takes about six weeks for root making. Properly, this should occur in a dark or shaded place, but I have had gardeners tell me they left theirs on the living room mantel with just as good results. Wherever it is, water only once a week during the root-making stage. When the bud is well protruded, move the plant to light and sun for four more weeks of growing to bring on the blossom. During the last three weeks water about every third day or as often as the soil soaks up the moisture.

To keep your amaryllis for another winter's flowering do not neglect after-blooming care. Water regularly to encourage the handsome foliage which follows the flower. When summer comes, plunge the plant in a lightly shaded garden spot. There the foliage will continue to flourish until early fall when you should bring the plant indoors. Give it a complete rest until the leaves have dried off. Then retire it for root-making with an occasional watering just as you would a new bulb. In six weeks a bud should appear and the plant be ready again for growing and blooming in the sunlight.

Bletilla hyacintha is another plant you can start indoors for late spring beauty. Pot the bulbs in November and give them eight weeks in a cool, dark place. Then move them to a light, well-ventilated spot where the atmosphere is as close to an even sixty degrees as you can approximate. Expect the flowers to open in March, six to eight dainty, orchid blossoms on a twelve-inch stem. If they grow well, they will yield six weeks of blooms.

Lachenalia, or Cape cowslips, are attractive in the window garden. For bloom within three months, they need only be potted, placed on a sunny window sill and regularly watered. Plant them at the rate of three bulbs per five-inch pot. Eight-inch spikes will be thickly clustered with flowers by Christmas from bulbs started in late September. After the flowers fade, keep watering the plants until the foliage ripens. When this process has been completed, dry off the bulbs and store them until the next fall. They may be planted again for another indoor season.

These are three excellent kinds of lachenalia:

Aurea. Golden yellow. About twenty-five florets to the stem.
Blue Beauty. True blue.
Pendula Superba. Bright red pendulous flowers.

Ornithogalum arabicum, the large-flowered member of the
star of Bethlehem clan, is well worth your growing. You won't
find it difficult, although you cannot hurry it. Even florists
learn to be patient with this plant. Start the bulbs late in
October or November, three to an eight-inch pan. They need
not be in the dark although they must be kept out of bright
sunlight all winter. If you have a table with a lower shelf
near your window garden, this is an excellent wintering place
for them. Water regularly but do not soak them. The long
swinging stems with tight green buds will be well extended
by early March. Then is the time to place the pans on a sunny
window sill. Do not expect flowers overnight. Even after buds
are well developed, it takes four or five weeks more for them
to open. When they do, your patience will be well repaid.
The ten-inch spikes are filled with pure white florets each
with a large, gleaming, black center.

Veltheimia viridiflora is a bold, handsome plant which the
inexperienced gardener can grow with ease. In October pot
the large bulbs in a roomy container with the shoulder and
neck exposed and place them immediately in sunlight. Soon
foliage will appear, a rosette of glossy green leaves twelve
inches long. In January the flower stalk begins its slow rise
to a height of fifteen inches. Throughout its six weeks of
bloom some forty to fifty tubular flowers will open on the
spike. These are about one and one-half inches long and with
an occasional tone of yellow or green. After foliage has ripened
both ornithogalums and valtheimias may be stored for another
season.

The early spring bulbs, muscari, crocuses and even snowdrops can be treated as indoor stayers, too. Start them in late

October in shallow pans with the bulbs a half-inch apart and barely covered with soil. Leave them eight weeks in a cool, dark place. Water them every five days or so. Then bring them to the light for early January or February blooms.

A long indoor display of colorful flowers can also be obtained from the major spring bulbs—tulips, daffodils and hyacinths. These are most satisfactory when they are buried outside in their containers for root growth and brought in successively for continuous bloom. Shallow pans are best for tulips and daffodils. Either pans or individual pots may be used for hyacinths. Avoid new, unsoaked containers.

The best plan is to assemble, on some bright September or October Saturday, your winter's supply of these bulbs for a single half day's task of potting. How many bulbs you need depends, of course, on the number of pans you want to have in bloom at the same time or in succession. Twenty-five to a hundred tulips, about half as many daffodils and one-third as many hyacinths will fill space varying from a small sill to a large, shelf-hung window.

Set your bulbs about an inch apart in the containers with the tips barely exposed. If you have an empty, well-drained cold frame, this may serve as their outdoor residence while rooting. Give one thorough watering. Then place the pots in the bottom of the frame. Fill the spaces between with light soil or peat moss and spread enough on top to provide a four-inch covering for the bulbs. Add an eight- to ten-inch mulch of leaves or salt hay. Leave off the top of the frame so the bulbs will receive moisture from rain and snow.

If you have no available cold frame, dig a narrow trench on the north or west side of the house, or any convenient place that is shady but exposed to rain. Make this trench twelve inches deep with a six-inch layer of cinders in the bottom for drainage. Place the containers, fill in with the covering of soil or peat moss and add the leaves or salt hay. This mulch makes it easier to get at the bulbs during a winter freeze. A paper chart will help you locate the pans you wish to uncover.

The time needed for adequate root-making varies with kind and variety. It is usually safe to wait twelve weeks before bringing in the first batch. If the day is cold, move the pans rapidly from the trench or frame to a cool, shaded place indoors where the temperature is around fifty degrees. Both gardener and bulbs appreciate being out in the freezing air no longer than necessary. Remove soil adhering to the outside of the pots and between the pale sprouts, being careful not to damage growth.

Let the newly lifted bulbs remain in a cool place for at least a week. During this time water them enough to keep them moist but do not soak them. From here on observe three precautions about watering: Water more frequently as growing progresses; water in the morning so that the soil will be fairly dry by nightfall; and use water of room temperature.

As soon as foliage has noticeably spread and budded stems are well started, move the plants into bright light or sunshine. As a general rule, plenty of sun is required to produce sturdy plants and fine blooms. For even blossoming, turn the pans around occasionally to spread the sunlight.

The length of time it takes bulbs to bloom after they are lifted from the trench varies considerably with variety and with environment. You will have to determine this for yourself by experience with your own indoor-growing medium. Until you have done so, don't expect to be able to time blooms with much exactness. Above all, never try to force blossoms by giving them more heat. A slow sixty degrees is best. Since this is probably cooler than you can provide, approximate it as best you can and keep it steady, whatever it is.

Once you have successfully forced your own spring bulbs you are not likely to want to give it up. Those indoor gardeners who labor only with tropicals, but buy their hardy bulbs already potted, are misguided people indeed. Perhaps they lack ambition or interest in variety, but more likely they do not know how easily bulbs can be forced.

The great advantage of forcing your own is that you can enjoy kinds you cannot buy. You can count on the fingers of both hands the standard commercial varieties of tulips and daffodils stocked by the average florist. You can buy shoals of the yellow trumpet Narcissus, King Alfred. But try for yourself the starry giant, Diotima, or the primrose British Monarch. You will never be satisfied with anything less lovely. Grow also, among daffodils, pans of the white trumpets Imperator and Beersheba, bicolor President Lebrun, incomparabilis Fortune and John Evelyn. Do not overlook the lovely white leedsii Silver Star and the apricot-tinted Mrs. R. O. Backhouse. The snowy triandrus, Thalia, is an excellent grower and a perfect companion for the orchid-colored Bletilla hyacintha.

All of the early tulips force well, but you might try Apricot Yellow, blush pink Cullinan, orange DeWet, Pink Beauty, White Hawk and the golden Rising Sun as the best of their respective colors. Among the taller Mendel and Triumph varieties select Kansas, a pure white; Lord Carnarvon, cream, flushed pink; Johanna, a beautiful salmon, and Zenith, a satiny rose. With the May-flowering tulips you are on your own. But when you have gained confidence you might experiment with the long, creamy white Glacier, the rosy Pride of Zwanenberg, the warm yellow Golden Age or others of your outdoor favorites.

Hyacinths are easiest of all. The light rose Crown Princess Margaret is a window beauty rarely found in florist shops.

Small, but appealing, is the salmon-orange Oranjeboven. The dark blue Duke of Westminster and the light blue Perle Brillante contrast effectively with white L'Innocence, although you may have to bring the white variety into light a little later than the blues if all are to flower together.

What to do with bulbs that have been forced is a frequent question. The problem is simple for the tender, pebble-grown kinds. Discard them. They cannot be grown outdoors and they are not satisfactory for a second season of forcing. Save for outside growing the hardy spring bulbs, including your Easter gift plants of daffodils and hyacinths. After the blooms fade continue watering until foliage starts to ripen. Then remove the bulbs from the pots. Plant them in an outside bed immediately. It may be two years before you get good blooms again but the results will warrant saving the bulbs, especially the narcissi and hyacinths.

CHAPTER TWENTY-FIVE

Woodland Plantings

Is your home surrounded by so many trees that you have foregone a garden and left whatever open space there is to a struggling lawn? You may still enjoy the beauty of flowers by making your wooded area a haven for such fall-planting bulbs as daffodils, scillas, snowdrops and dogtooth violets, and for easily domesticated wild flowers like mertensia, trillium and bloodroot.

Many gardeners are fortunate enough to have both a sunny place for a regular garden and a tree covered area for woodland plants. I decided long ago that if I could have only one type of planting it would be the woodland. Although the most luxuriant blossoming of flowers would cease with the end of spring, so would most of my gardening responsibilities.

Bulbs play a vital role in creating woodland beauty as there are far more of them to flourish in the limitations of a shaded area than there are of perennials or annuals. Many bulbs such as the hardy begonia, Galanthus nivalis and Fritillaria lanceolata are at their best with some leafy protection from hot sun. There, if the humus and moisture content of the soil is to their liking, they naturalize happily.

If your wooded area is large enough, plant your bulbs and wildflowers in relation to a path or an indicated path. An indicated path can be made by edging certain of the drifts so that they seem to follow a line. As you and your friends walk through the woods to enjoy the flowers, the actual path will soon be created. Not all, or even a majority of the drifts should border a real or indicated path, of course. Many should be placed to the rear to give depth to the planting. Nor should any walk be continuously lined with plants. Sweeps of bare earth between border and rear plantings give greater effect to patches of bulbs and other flowers. Any woodland area looks best, I think, when from one-quarter to one-half the surface is covered.

Do not suppose that bulbs which can prosper under trees are endowed with some special ruggedness rendering them impervious to all cultural difficulties. Some merely tolerate the shade that others prefer. They must all have that minimum of sunlight each species and variety may require. If the trees are so leafy or close together that no sunshine filters through, they should be thinned out or the branches pruned.

Soil is important. Bulbs in woodland locations must compete with roots for a supply of moisture. If the soil is not naturally full of humus, work in a three-inch layer of such a moisture-retentive substance as leaf mold, peat moss or Hyperhumus in the areas to be planted. A yearly mulch of this material is also advisable. In those spots where you intend to place drifts break up root mats by thorough cultivating with fork or mattock.

Insufficient sunlight for ripening, too little moisture and too much interference from roots are the usual causes for the petering out of bulb bloom in shade. An overly acid soil can be another cause. If shade is provided by oaks, the soil beneath these trees is likely to become too acid for the continued flourishing of most bulbs. Correct this by liming the soil over the plantings. Spread enough hydrated lime on the surface each fall to whiten it. Then add the fertilizer, raking it in lightly so that it will not blow away. Winter rain and snow will ensure its leaching into the earth.

Every year my conviction grows stronger that the effectiveness of a woodland planting is measured by its showing of daffodils. These lovely flowers thickly colonized beneath birches and dogwoods delight the heart as nothing else can. The different types of narcissi, trumpet, incomparabilis, poeticus and jonquil, each in its separate location, provide variety. Kinds with different blooming times, early, medium and late, prolong the season.

Some gardeners, to achieve naturalistic effect, like to fling their narcissus bulbs and plant them where they fall. I have no quarrel with this style of planting but most of the bulbs I fling seem to come to rest on a rock or against a large tree trunk. Others roll to the nearest hollow where they huddle in a round pile. Consequently when naturalizing daffodils or other bulbs, I set them out in drifts before planting. Close placing, three to four inches apart, in the center of the colony and wider spacing, five, six and eight inches apart, toward the irregular edges, give it a more natural look. I save about five per cent of the bulbs for scattering by ones, twos and threes in the empty spaces between drifts. And I frequently add a few clusters of bulbs, like off-shore islands, a foot or so from the edge of the larger patches. Perhaps this is a poor simile because "shore" suggests boundary and I strive to arrange each colony so that you could not draw a line around it if you tried.

For real beauty in the woods buy and plant narcissi in separate named varieties. In this way you can be certain of growing the kinds which look best and which are best suited to this type of culture. Inexpensive mixtures rarely contain the varieties which are the most attractive or culturally best adapted for woodland. And the individual kinds, in the woods as in the garden, always show off far more effectively when planted separately than when mixed.

The most important companion for daffodils is not a bulb but the fleshy-rooted Mertensia virginica, Virginia bluebell. The blue panicles of this flower contrast beautifully with both white and yellow daffodils. Plant them in separate colonies or at the edge of narcissus groups. When they come to you the roots of mertensia look, but do not feel, like short, dry twigs. Plant them horizontally under two inches of soil.

Among other wildflowers excellent for supplementing your bulb planting are Sanguinaria canadensis or bloodroot, and the various species of trillium or wake robin. Both are readily obtainable and easy to establish if planted with the crowns just under the soil surface. Bloodroot opens its daisy-like blossom in March or early April. The three-petaled blooms of trillium appear in late April or early May.

Try making a home for additional native plants when you have successfully established mertensia, sanguinaria and trillium. Arisaema triphyllum or jack-in-the-pulpit colonizes without difficulty. It may already be growing wild in your woods. Aquilegia canadensis or wild columbine, Delphinium tricorne or rock larkspur, and Dodecatheon meadia or shooting star, are all worth adding. Of course you will want to experiment with the pink Cypripedium acaule or moccasin flower and the yellow Cypripedium pubescens or downy ladyslipper.

Dicentra eximia or fringed bleedingheart is an excellent companion for spring bulbs and an attractive foliage plant through the summer. Moreover it colonizes abundantly. Plant native ferns, especially maidenhair, leatherwood, Christmas and cinnamon fern, for the summer-long beauty of their green fronds. Establish patches of Myrrhis odorata or sweet cicely to cover with its anise-scented leaves the areas left bare by the disappearing foliage of spring bulbs. Familiarize yourself with soil and other cultural requirements of these wild flowers before setting them out. Most of them come to you in the form of plants which should be reset to the depth of their old soil line.

Bulbous plants which prefer or tolerate a shady location are legion. Start the season with Galanthus nivalis, the shade-loving species of snowdrop. Follow it with blue sheets of chionodoxas and squills. For fascinating April bloom do not omit colonies of dogtooth violets. The May scillas or wood hyacinths are almost as indispensable as daffodils. At the woods edge certain tulipas, particularly eichleri, fosteriana Red Emperor, kaufmanniana and australis, will establish themselves in splashes of color as will the flaming Fritillaria imperialis or crown imperial. Alliums, Begonia evansiana, camassia and the native lilies will give you late spring and summer beauty of both foliage and flowers.

The following species and varieties of shade-growing bulbs are all worth trying. Correct planting depths, suggested distances apart, approximate heights and blooming times are given as are the amounts of shade in which each flower will thrive. Some explanation of the different terms defining shade is advisable. Twenty-five per cent or less shade I always consider as amounting to full sun. Plants growing together in open garden beds shade each other so that rarely does one receive more than three quarters of the day's full sunlight. For the purposes of this list of woodland bulbs I would define anything from twenty-five to fifty per cent shade as light, from fifty to sixty-five as medium and from sixty-five to eighty as heavy shade. Shade so dense that it will admit less than one-fifth of the day's sun will permit few bulbs to flourish. Woodland shade is always measured by the amount of sunlight kept from the earth *after* trees are in leaf.

WOODLAND BULBS, ALL HARDY

	Height in Inches	Light Shade Medium Shade Heavy Shade	Month of Bloom in N.Y. Area	Inches of Soil Covering	Distance Apart in Inches
Allium					
acuminatum	12	LS	May	3	4
cernuum	15	LS	June	3	4
moly	12	LS	June	3	4
Anemone quinquefolia	4	LS	April	3	3
Begonia Evansiana	14	MS/HS	July-Sept.	4	6
Calochortus					
albus	18	LS	May	3	4
amabilis	16	LS	May	3	4
venustus citrinus	15	LS	May	3	4
Camassia leichtlinii	18–36	LS	May	4	6
Chionodoxa					
gigantea	6	LS/MS	March	2	3
luciliae	4	LS/MS	March	2	3
luciliae alba	4	LS/MS	March	2	3
Claytonia virginica	5	LS/MS	April	3	3
Crocus					
vernus (all varieties)	5–6	LS	Mar.-April	2	3
biflorus	4	LS	March	2	3
imperati	6	LS	April	2	3
korolkowi	5	LS	April	2	3
sieberi	4	LS	March	2	3
susianus	4	LS	March	2	2
tomasinianus	4	LS	March	2	2
Dicentra					
canadensis	10	LS/MS	April	3	5
cucullaria	10	LS/MS	April	3	5
Erythronium					
californicum	10	LS/MS/HS	April	3	4
grandiflorum	12	LS/MS/HS	April	3	4
hendersonii	12	LS/MS/HS	April	3	4
revolutum, Pink Beauty	14	LS/MS/HS	April	3	4
revolutum, praecox	12	LS/MS/HS	April	3	4
Fritillaria					
imperialis (all varieties)	36	LS	May	4	8
lanceolata	18	MS	April	3	4
meleagris alba	8	LS	April	3	4
meleagris (mixed)	8	LS	April	3	4
recurva	15	MS	April	3	4
Galanthus nivalis	4	LS/MS	February	3	3
Leucojum					
aestivum	12	LS	April	3	5
aestivum gravetye	16	LS	April	4	5
vernum	6	LS	March	3	4

WOODLAND BULBS, ALL HARDY—*Continued*

	Height in Inches	Light Shade Medium Shade Heavy Shade	Month of Bloom in N.Y. Area	Inches of Soil Covering	Distance Apart in Inches
Lilium					
canadense	48	LS	June	5	8
philadelphicum	36	LS	June	4	8
superbum	48	LS	July	5	8
Lycoris squamigera	24	LS	August	4	8
Muscari					
armeniacum	8	LS	April	3	3
botryoides album	7	LS	April	3	3
plumosum	9	LS	May	3	3
Narcissus trumpet					
all yellow:					
Aerolite	18	LS	April	4	6
Emperor	16	LS	April	4	5
all white:					
Lovenest	16	LS	April	4	5
Narcissus incomparabilis					
with yellow perianth:					
Carlton	14	LS	April	4	5
Dorine	16	LS	April	4	5
Fortune	24	LS	April	4	5
Havelock	20	LS	April	4	5
Jalna	18	LS	April	4	5
Red Cross	20	LS/MS	April	4	5
Yellow Poppy	18	LS	April	4	5
with white perianth:					
Dick Wellband	22	LS	April	4	5
Francisca Drake	16	LS	April	4	5
John Evelyn	14	LS	April	4	5
Narcissus barrii with yellow perianth:					
Afterglow	18	LS/MS	April	4	5
Marion	16	LS	April	4	5
Norman	16	LS	April	4	5
with white perianth:					
Adler	14	LS	April	4	5
Alcida	14	LS/MS/HS	April	4	5
Firetail	18	LS/MS	April	4	5
Lady Diana Manners	18	LS	April	4	5
Narcissus leedsii					
giant crowned:					
Daisy Schaeffer	16	LS	April	4	5
Mrs. R. O. Backhouse	14	LS	April-May	4	5
Silver Star	22	LS/MS	April	4	5
small crowned:					

WOODLAND BULBS, ALL HARDY—*Continued*

	Height in Inches	Light Shade Medium Shade Heavy Shade	Month of Bloom in N.Y. Area	Inches of Soil Covering	Distance Apart in Inches
Hera	12	LS/MS/HS	April-May	4	5
Mrs. Nette O'Melveny	16	LS/MS	April	4	5
White Lady	18	LS/MS/HS	April	4	5
Narcissus triandrus					
Agnes Harvey	14	LS/MS	April	4	4
Elizabeth Prentice	14	LS	April	4	4
Moonshine	12	LS	April	4	5
Queen of Spain	14	LS	April	4	4
Thalia	18	LS/MS	April	4	5
Narcissus cyclamineus					
February Gold	12	LS	March	4	4
March Sunshine	12	LS	March	4	4
Narcissus jonquilla					
Golden Sceptre	16	LS/MS	April	4	5
Trevithian	16	LS	April	4	5
Narcissus poetaz					
La Fiancée	16	LS	April	4	5
Orange Cup	16	LS	April	4	5
Scarlet Gem	16	LS	April	4	5
Red Guard	16	LS	April	4	5
Narcissus poeticus					
Crenver	18	LS	April	4	5
Recurvus	10	LS/MS/HS	May	4	4
Narcissus double					
albus plenus odoratus	12	MS	May	4	4
Cheerfulness	14	LS/MS	May	4	5
Daphne	16	LS	April	4	5
Ornithogalum nutans	10	MS	April	3	4
Scilla					
autumnalis	8	LS	August	3	3
bifolia	5	LS	April	3	3
campanulata alba	12	LS/MS/HS	May	3	4
campanulata Blue Queen	12	LS/MS	May	3	4
campanulata coerulea	12	LS/MS/HS	May	3	4
campanulata Excelsior	16	LS/MS/HS	May	3	4
campanulata Rose Queen	12	LS/MS/HS	May	3	4
nutans alba	10	LS/MS/HS	May	3	4
nutans coerulea	10	LS/MS/HS	May	3	4
nutans rosea	10	LS/MS/HS	May	3	4
sibirica alba	4	LS	April	3	3
sibirica coerulea	4	LS	April	3	3
sibirica, Spring Beauty	8	LS	April	3	3

WOODLAND BULBS, ALL HARDY—*Continued*

	Height in Inches	Light Shade Medium Shade Heavy Shade	Month of Bloom in N.Y. Area	Inches of Soil Covering	Distance Apart in Inches
Tulipa					
australis	12	LS	May	6	5
eichleri	10	LS	April	6	5
fosteriana, Red Emperor	16	LS	April	6	5
kaufmanniana	6	LS	Mar.-April	6	5
kaufmanniana Brilliant	8	LS	April	6	5
Zygadenus freemonti	24	LS	May	4	6

CHAPTER TWENTY-SIX

Bulbs for Rock Garden and White Garden

SPECIES and varieties of bulbous plants are to be found for almost any type of garden. Two fairly prevalent planting styles requiring by their nature a restricted selection of plants are rock gardens and white gardens. For both these situations bulbs provide such a wealth of material as to warrant separate consideration of the manner in which they can be used and special listing of the species and varieties suitable.

No group of plants provides more beautiful or dependable blooms for the rock garden than bulbs. This is true whether it is carefully designed or merely a bank in which well-placed rocks retain the soil. From the first white snowdrop to the last blue autumn crocus, bulbs light up the spaces between dwarf evergreens, sedums and creeping phlox.

Most rock garden pockets furnish excellent drainage for bulbs. If the soil is not already full of humus, this material can be added in the form of peat moss or leaf mold. Pockets must have sufficient depth of soil to prevent winter heaving and to provide proper covering for the different species and varieties.

There are more bulbs suitable for rock gardens than even

a very large one can accommodate. All of the early spring bulbs thrive here: snowdrops, crocuses, chionodoxas, winter aconites, squills and others. Their short stems and small flowers are appropriate in an area where dwarf plants are the rule. Species daffodils and tulips find no better place to display their beauty than in rock gardens. They like the baking sun usually afforded there and they will blossom for years if their ripening leaves are not deprived of strong sunlight by the foliage of other plants. If a long rock bank is your only available site for flowers, plant there also the large varieties of the major bulbs. Daffodils, tulips and even hyacinths will flourish if the slope is not too steep.

Spring offers the greatest profusion from rock garden bulbs. But some kinds brighten the summer months too. There are alliums to flower in June and July; lilies for the same months; cooperia, oxalis and zephyranthes for July and August; colchicums, crocuses and sternbergias for September and October. All of the spring-flowering kinds are hardy, but many of the summer-blooming bulbs are tender and need to be lifted each fall.

Most rock gardens are sunny, but occasionally there are shaded corners or ends. Bulbs can also fill these sunless spots with flowers. Here you can grow Scilla campanulata or wood hyacinths and dogtooth violets in the spring and tuberous-rooted begonias in the summer.

In the list of recommended rock garden bulbs which follows at the end of the chapter approximate heights and blooming times are given. Taller-stemmed plants should always be placed at the base of the rock garden or in the lower pockets. The higher planes should be filled with dwarf plants and miniatures. Bulbs which have the same blooming period should be placed throughout the whole area so as to afford a balanced appearance in each season.

Correct planting depths and suggested distances apart are also stated as are the preferences of the various kinds for sun, light or heavy shade. For the purposes of this list from twenty-five to fifty per cent shade is considered as light and from fifty to seventy-five per cent as heavy shade. Less than twenty-five per cent shade is considered as full sun. The list is divided into two groups: the hardy bulbs and the tender.

In the case of many of the small bulbs closer planting is recommended for rock gardens than for woodland plantings.

White flowers always have a special appeal. They seem such an effortless achievement of purity and perfection. Cool and reposeful during the hot midday, a garden of white flowers is filled with ethereal but exciting beauty through twilight and evening.

If your space permits only a single area for flowers, you may tire of only one effect but if you have room for two gardens by all means have a white one. It may be only a corner or bay off the main garden. It need not be large. In fact, it is better to have it too small for a noisy crowd.

For me the perfect white garden is an area surrounded by tall cedars, hemlocks or pines. Beneath the lofty evergreens are white azaleas and rhododendrons whose blossoms add to the floral display during their season and whose foliage provides handsome green during the rest of the year. The center space is a lawn. A narrow border in front of the low azaleas and the rhododendrons provides the only space for flowers.

Plants for the border should be selected with great care. Every flower will not do just because it is white. It must have good substance, purity and clarity. The habit of growth may be informal but never undistinguished. Gossamer babys-breath lends grace, for example, but white nicotiana, in my opinion, lacks quality for the white garden, however lovely it is in the mixed border.

Many bulbous plants are excellent for white borders but here too it is wise to be selective. Hyacinths, daffodils, tulips and scillas are invaluable. Hyacinthus candicans is too tall and lanky and requires too deep a bed.

The bulbs in the third following list are recommended for the white garden. They are grouped according to time of bloom. Approximate heights are given. Hardiness or non-hardiness is indicated as well as correct planting depths and distances apart.

HARDY BULBS FOR THE ROCK GARDEN

	Height in Inches	Sun Light Shade Heavy Shade	Month of Bloom in N.Y. Area	Inches of Soil Covering	Distance Apart in Inches
Allium					
acuminatum	12	S/LS	May	3	4
flavum	10	S	June	3	4
moly	12	LS	June	3	4
ostrowskianum	10	S	June	3	4
purdomii	5	S	June	3	4
pulchellum	12	S	July	3	4
Brodiaea					
capitata	8	S	May	3	2–3
lactea	10	LS	May	3	2–3
uniflora violacea	6	LS	May	3	2–3
Bulbocodium vernum	4	LS	March	3	3
Calochortus					
amoenus	8	LS	May	3	3
benthamii	5	LS	May	3	3
maweanus major	6	LS	May	3	3
Chionodoxa					
gigantea	6	S/LS	March	2	3
luciliae	4	S/LS	March	2	2
luciliae alba	4	S/LS	March	2	2
sardensis	4	S/LS	March	2	2
Colchicum					
autumnale	8	S/LS	Sept.-Oct.	2	4
autumnale album	8	S/LS	Sept.-Oct.	2	4
bornmuelleri	8	S/LS	Sept.-Oct.	2	4
Guizot	8	S/LS	Sept.-Oct.	2	4
President Coolidge	8	S/LS	Sept.-Oct.	2	4
speciosum	8	S/LS	Sept.-Oct.	2	4
Crocus					
vernus (all varieties)	5–6	S/LS	Mar.-April	2	3
biflorus	4	S/LS	March	2	3
imperati	6	S/LS	April	2	3
korolkowi	5	S/LS	April	2	3
sieberi	4	S/LS	April	2	3
susianus	4	S/LS	March	2	2
tomasinianus	4	S/LS	March	2	2
asturicus	4	S/LS	Sept.-Oct.	2	2
nudiflorus	4	S/LS	Sept.-Oct.	2	2
sativus	4	S/LS	Sept.-Oct.	2	2
speciosus	4	S/LS	Sept.-Oct.	2	2
speciosus aitchisonii	4	S/LS	Sept.-Oct.	2	2
speciosus albus	4	S/LS	Sept.-Oct.	2	2
zonatus	4	S/LS	Sept.-Oct.	2	2

HARDY BULBS FOR THE ROCK GARDEN—*Continued*

	Height in Inches	Sun Light Shade Heavy Shade	Month of Bloom in N.Y. Area	Inches of Soil Covering	Distance Apart in Inches
Eranthis					
cilicica	5	S	Feb.-March	2	3
hyemalis	4	S	Feb.-March	2	3
Erythronium					
californicum	10	LS/HS	April	3	3
grandiflorum	12	LS/HS	April	3	3
hendersonii	12	LS/HS	April	3	3
revolutum, Pink Beauty	14	LS/HS	April	3	3
revolutum, praecox	12	LS/HS	April	3	3
Fritillaria					
meleagris alba	8	LS	April	3	4
meleagris (mixed)	8	LS	April	3	4
lilacea	8	S	April	3	4
pudica	8	S	April	3	4
Galanthus					
elwesii	6	S	February	3	2
nivalis	4	LS	March	3	2
Iris reticulata	8	S	Mar.-April	4	4
Leucojum					
aestivum	12	LS	April	4	5
vernum	6	LS	March	3	4
Lilium					
concolor	18–24	S	June-July	4	6
pumilum (tenuifolium)	18–24	S	June	4	6
Muscari					
armeniacum	8	S/LS	April	3	3
azureum	8	S	Mar.-April	3	3
botryoides album	7	S/LS	April	3	3
conicum	8	S	April	3	3
neglectum	8	S	April	3	3
neglectum rosea	8	S	April	3	3
plumosum	9	S/LS	May	3	3
racemosum	8	S	April	3	3
Narcissus					
trumpet minimus	4	S	February	4	3
trumpet minor	6	S	March	4	3
triandrus albus	5	S	April	4	3
triandrus, Agnes Harvey	14	S/LS	April	4	4
triandrus calathinus	8	S	April	4	3
triandrus, Elizabeth Prentice	14	S/LS	April	4	4
triandrus pulchellus	8	S	April	4	3
triandrus, Queen of Spain	14	LS	April	4	4

HARDY BULBS FOR THE ROCK GARDEN—*Continued*

	Height in Inches	Sun Light Shade Heavy Shade	Month of Bloom in N.Y. Area	Inches of Soil Covering	Distance Apart in Inches
cyclamineus (type)	6	S	March	4	3
cyclamineus, February Gold	12	S/LS	March	4	4
cyclamineus, March Sunshine	12	S/LS	March	4	4
cyclamineus, Turn A'Penny	10	S/LS	April	4	4
jonquilla campernelle	12	S	April	4	3
jonquilla simplex	8	S	April	4	3
bulbocodium conspicuus	6	S	April	4	3
bulbocodium citrinus	6	S	April	4	3
juncifolius	6	S	April	4	3
Puschkinia scilloides	6	S	Mar.-April	3	3
Scilla					
autumnalis	8	S/LS	August	3	3
bifolia	5	S/LS/HS	April	3	3
campanulata alba	12	S/LS/HS	May	3	3
campanulata, Blue Queen	12	S/LS/HS	May	3	3
campanulata coerulea	12	S/LS/HS	May	3	3
campanulata, Excelsior	16	S/LS/HS	May	3	3
campanulata, Rose Queen	12	S/LS/HS	May	3	3
nutans alba	10	S/LS/HS	May	3	3
nutans coerulea	10	S/LS/HS	May	3	3
nutans, Rose Queen	10	S/LS/HS	May	3	3
peruviana	12	S/LS	May	3	3
sibirica alba	4	S/LS	April	3	3
sibirica coerulea	4	S/LS	April	3	3
sibirica, Spring Beauty	8	S/LS	April	3	3
Sternbergia lutea	5	S	Aug.-Sept.	4	3
Tulipa					
australis	12	S/LS	May	6	4
biflora	3	S	Mar.-April	6	3
chrysantha	6	S	May	6	3
clusiana	10	S	May	6	4
cornuta stenopetala	15	S	May	6	3
dasystemon	5	S	April	6	4
eichleri	10	S/LS	April	6	4
fosteriana, Red Emperor	16	S/LS	April	6	5
kaufmanniana	6	S/LS	Mar.-April	6	5
marjoletti	12	S/LS	May	6	4
persica	5	S	May	6	4
praestans	12	S/LS	April	6	4
sprengeri	9	S	May	6	5
sylvestris	14	S	April	6	4

TENDER ROCK GARDEN BULBS

	Height in Inches	Sun Light Shade Heavy Shade	Month of Bloom in N.Y. Area	Inches of Soil Covering	Distance Apart in Inches
Anemone					
Blue Poppy	12	S	May	3	3
His Excellency	12	S	May	3	3
Quinquefolia	4	LS	May	3	3
The Bride	12	S	May	3	3
Begonia, Tuberous-rooted	12	HS	July-Sept.	2	8
Chlidanthus fragrans	10	S	August	3	5
Cooperia drummondi	10	S	July-Aug.	2	6
Oxalis					
adenophylla	8	S	July-Aug.	2	3
bowiei	10	S	July-Aug.	2	3
lasiandra	10	S	July-Aug.	2	3
Zephyranthes					
ajax	10	S	July-Aug.	3	4
candida	10	S	Aug.-Sept.	3	4
carinata	10	S	July-Aug.	3	4
rosea	10	S	Aug.-Sept.	3	4

BULBS FOR THE WHITE GARDEN

	Height in Inches	Hardy or Non-Hardy	Inches of Soil Covering	Distance Apart in Inches
February-March:				
Galanthus elwesii	6	H	3	2
Chionodoxa luciliae alba	4	H	2	2
Hyacinth				
Arentine Arendsen	12	H	4	8
L'Innocence	12	H	4	8
Leucojum vernum	6	H	3	4
Early and mid-April:				
Crocus vernus, Snowstorm	5	H	2	3
Narcissus				
trumpet—Beersheba	14	H	4	5
leedsii—Silver Star	16	H	4	5
Single Early Tulip, Lady Boreel	13	H	4½	5
Double Early Tulip, Schoornoord	11	H	4½	5
Scilla sibirica alba	4	H	3	3
Late April:				
Leucojum Aestivum Gravetye	16	H	4	5
Muscari Botryoides Album	7	H	3	3

BULBS FOR THE WHITE GARDEN—*Continued*

	Height in Inches	Hardy or Non-Hardy	Inches of Soil Covering	Distance Apart in Inches
Narcissus				
trumpet				
Roxane	12	H	4	5
Mrs. E. H. Krelage	12	H	4	5
leedsii				
Gertie Millar	13	H	4	5
Hera	12	H	4	5
triandrus				
Agnes Harvey	14	H	4	4
Elizabeth Prentice	14	H	4	4
Moonshine	12	H	4	4
Thalia	18	H	4	4
double				
Daphne	12	H	4	5
Irene Copeland	12	H	4	5
Triumph Tulip, Kansas	24	H	4½	5
Parrot Tulip, Gemma	20	H	4½	5
May:				
Narcissus double, Cheerfulness	14	H	4	5
Darwin Tulip				
Annie Speelman	28	H	4½	5
Duke of Wellington	30	H	4½	5
Glacier	28	H	4½	5
Helen Eakin	30	H	4½	5
Mrs. Grullemans	28	H	4½	5
White Giant	32	H	4½	5
Cottage Tulip				
Carrara	25	H	4½	5
Mt. Erebus	30	H	4½	5
Double Late Tulip, Mt. Tacoma	22	H	4½	5
Scilla campanulata alba	12	H	3	3
June:				
Gladiolus				
Maid of Orleans	36	NH	3	6
Vredenburg	36	NH	3	6
Hymenocallis (Ismene) Calathina	24	NH	3	6
Lilium				
candidum	60	H	2	8
martagon album	60	H	3	8

BULBS FOR THE WHITE GARDEN—*Continued*

	Height in Inches	Hardy or Non-Hardy	Inches of Soil Covering	Distance Apart in Inches
July:				
Begonia, Tuberous-rooted				
camellia, crispa, fimbriata white	12	NH	2	8
Dahlia				
pompon, Bob White	30	NH	5	10
miniature, Helly Boudweijn	30	NH	5	10
Gladiolus				
Maid of Orleans	36	NH	3	6
Snow Princess	36	NH	3	6
Vredenburg	36	NH	3	6
Hymenocallis (Ismene) Calathina	24	NH	3	6
Lilium centifolium hybrids	60	H	6	10
August:				
Begonia, Tuberous-rooted				
camellia, crispa, fimbriata white	12	NH	2	8
Dahlia				
pompon, Bob White	30	NH	5	10
miniature, Helly Boudweijn	30	NH	5	10
Gladiolus				
Maid of Orleans	36	NH	3	6
Snow Princess	36	NH	3	6
Vredenburg	36	NH	3	6
Hymenocallis (Ismene) Calathina	24	NH	3	6
Lilium speciosum album	50	H	6	10
Tuberose, Double Pearl	45	NH	3	8
September:				
Begonia, Tuberous-rooted				
camellia, crispa, fimbriata white	12	NH	2	8
Colchicum autumnale album	8	H	2	4
Crocus speciosus albus	4	H	2	2
Dahlia				
pompon, Bob White	30	NH	5	10
miniature, Helly Boudweijn	30	NH	5	10
Gladiolus				
Maid of Orleans	36	NH	3	6
Snow Princess	36	NH	3	6
Vredenburg	36	NH	3	6
Lilium formosanum, wilsonii	60	H	5	8

Month by Month Reminders

JANUARY

For the outdoor gardener this month brings freedom from chores and perhaps time for a trip to Florida or Southern California. The flora of these regions is exotic and beautiful, but not more beautiful than that which you will see in your own garden a few months hence. If you stay at home, spend part of the time enjoying the early spring catalogues.

Should you, in January, come upon any bags of tulips, daffodils or other spring-flowering bulbs, through some mischance left unplanted, by all means get these into the ground during the first thaw. Do not, under any circumstances, consider keeping the bulbs until next fall because fall is normal planting time. Such procedure would be like finding overlooked bottles of milk on the doorstep at noon and leaving them there until the next morning because morning is the time to bring in milk. Bulbs kept for a year out of the ground will be in no better condition than milk left outside for a day's sunning. Discard all of the overlooked bulbs which appear soft or dried out but plant the others. They may not flower well the first spring, but you will have saved the bulbs for possible future development.

For the indoor gardener January is a month for enjoying a harvest of bloom from bulbs planted earlier. Paperwhites started in December will flower now. Continue the planting of new bowls of polyanthus narcissi at two- or three-week intervals. The following bulbs will be ready now to be moved into the light from their root-making stay in the cool dark: Bletilla hyacintha, amaryllis or hippeastrum hybrids and Dutch hyacinths in glasses.

Bring in pans of tulips, daffodils and hyacinths that have spent at least twelve weeks making roots outside in a trench or cold frame. Leave the bulbs for a week in a cool, shaded place where the temperature is as close to a steady fifty degrees as you can manage. Then gradually bring them into strong light and water more plentifully.

FEBRUARY

The outdoor gardener can still relax. If you are in Florida, remain, unless toward Washington's Birthday you must see whether your tulips and daffodils are coming through and if your snowdrops have started to bloom. If you are at home, you can spend time perusing catalogues.

Indoors the display of bulbs continues. Narcissi are in flower from bulbs started in January. The richly, colored veltheimia is at its height. Amaryllis buds are fascinating as they prepare to burst into vivid blossom. Pans of daffodils and hyacinths brought in the previous month fill the window ledge with color and fragrance.

Early this month you can place in pebble-filled bowls the last of the Paperwhites since they will deteriorate if kept longer. Continue to bring in pans of tulips, daffodils and hyacinths from their outdoor root-making station. Cut off the flower stalk of the amaryllis as it finishes blooming, but continue to water the plant to keep foliage flourishing until the pot can be plunged outside for the summer.

The end of February is not too soon to start tuberous-rooted begonias destined for shaded areas outdoors in summer. Use rich soil in pots or pans and set the tubers one inch below the surface. Water sparingly at first, plentifully after growth shows. Keep the growing plants in the light but not in direct sunlight.

MARCH

This is the month when winter aconites, early crocuses, chionodoxas and snowdrops rush into bloom at the first sign of retreating winter. Don't miss these blossoms and don't let any winter mulch or covering of leaves hide their beauty. If later-blooming bulbs are planted in perennial beds which are entirely mulched, remove this covering gradually from the bulb areas as the ground thaws. Unless the season is very late, shoots of tulips and daffodils will be visible by the end of March.

The first warm days stimulate moles into feverish activity so, if you are plagued with these rodents, start your campaign against them without delay. Watch for the first appearance of runs, then set traps or place poison tablets. After light spring rains, go hunting with the pitchfork or sharp pointed stick where heaving turf gives evidence that moles are at work.

If you have not done so before, order now all the new bulbs of gladioli, montbretias, ismene and other summer flowers which you wish to add to your collection of bulbs. It is too soon to plant these, but any lilies you may have on hand for spring planting should be put into the earth as soon as it is sufficiently thawed.

Indoors the last tender narcissi planted in bowls of pebbles and water will be blossoming. Bletilla hyacintha which you started in November will reward you with blooms. Tulips, hyacinths and daffodils brought indoors in February will also be in flower. You can now bring indoors the last pans to force for April bloom. After these flower, save the bulbs for the outside garden. Either move the plants to the garden as soon as the earth is workable, there to let them ripen, or let them dry off in the pots. Later you can remove them and store for fall planting. At the beginning of this month move your Ornithogalum arabicum to full sun and let it stay there until it finishes flowering. If you did not pot tuberous-rooted begonias in February, do so at once so they can be transplanted later to the garden as well-started plants.

APRIL

During the first week of April make sure that all spring-flowering bulb areas are free of any remaining mulch or garden debris. Unless a frozen winter crust persists, give bulb plantings their spring fertilizing and cultivating. Dust the surface of the soil thoroughly but not heavily with the half-and-half mixture of superphosphate and Bovung. Gently work it into the soil between the young shoots with a hand claw. Wash off with a fine spray any quantity of this fertilizer which lodges in leaf axils.

The last half of the month is the time to make first plantings of gladioli. The ones set out this month are not likely to suffer serious thrip damage since they make their growth and bloom before hot weather sets in.

Other spring-planting bulbs which may be put into the ground from the fifteenth to the thirtieth of April are montbretia, Begonia evansiana or hardy begonia, the various oxalis species, galtonia or summer hyacinth, Chlidanthus fragrans and Cooperia drummondi. If you live in a region where there is no danger of a heavy freeze after the middle of this month, also plant tigridias and tuberoses. Neither like severe cold, but the earlier you plant tigridias the less chance there is for them to dry out. The sooner tuberoses get a start the better their chances of a full season of bloom before autumn frosts. Shoots from bulbs planted in late April are not likely to appear above ground until the season for heavy frosts is past.

The display of bulbs grown indoors draws to a close in April. The last pans of tulips, daffodils and hyacinths are blossoming and the black-eyed ornithogalum you have waited all winter to see is at last in glorious flower. When this plant has finished blooming, allow the foliage to ripen, then remove the bulb and store it in a cool, dry place until fall. Early this month is your last opportunity to pot up begonia tubers if they are to make headway before being transplanted outdoors.

MAY

With the continuing bloom of the later daffodils and the arrival of May-flowering tulips, the spring bulb season is at its height this month. The flowers are lovely at any hour of the day but most beautiful when early morning sun strikes the dew-covered blossoms and again at sunset. Morning and early evening are also the best times for gathering them for the house. Always make a slanting cut and plunge stems in cold water nearly up to the blossoms for a few hours before arranging flowers in containers. Frequent change of water and the occasional snipping off of a half inch more of stem helps to keep them fresh. To prolong the life of tulips indoors cut them before flowers have reached full size but after buds have shown color for three days.

If May brings drought and hot sun, soak the tulip beds with a spray from the garden hose, being careful not to splash blossoms. This may prolong the blooming period in an abnormally hot, dry season for as much as a week.

As flowering ceases, remove the wilted flowers. Catch them

before they scatter if you can, otherwise pick up the petals from where they have fallen. Break off the tops of flower stems to prevent formation of seed pods.

Leave the foliage of all spring bulbs to ripen undisturbed for best development of the crop underneath. If you feel that you must free certain spaces occupied by tulips, daffodils or hyacinths, or if you wish to rearrange plantings, lift the bulbs after blooming and heel them in or transplant them to their new location. If the bulbs are heeled in, let their foliage ripen before bringing them indoors for summer storage.

When cultivating among your perennials, watch out lest your garden implement decapitate heads of lilies which may be growing right under the soil surface. Most varieties will break through and reveal their presence by the end of this month.

May is the month to plan your spring garden and to order your bulbs for next year. Go among your tulips and daffodils while they are still blooming and make notes of the changes you desire and of the places for which you will need new bulbs next year. As a guide for fall planting make a chart showing the intended locations for new bulbs or place five-inch wooden labels deeply enough so they won't be conspicuous, but protruding sufficiently so they can be found when you rake off the leaves in the fall. Nothing is more hopeless than trying to figure out in October, as you stare at the bare surface of a flower bed, which were the empty spaces in the spring.

Plant in May all the summer bulbs which could have gone in during April but which you were too busy to plant then. It is time now to set out the following additional bulbs: hymenocallis or ismene, Sprekelia formosissima, zephyranthes and, at the end of the month, cannas. May fifteenth is the time for outside planting of the tuberous-rooted begonias which have not been potted for a head start indoors. Continue your successive plantings of gladioli but from now on be sure to give the corms a pre-planting immersion in Lysol solution as precaution against thrips.

JUNE

The summer procession of lilies commences this month with the flowering of candidums and testaceums. Early in June place stakes for any lilies which will require support.

If you plan to lift tulips and hyacinths for division and storage until autumn, the middle of June is the time. As soon as the bulbs have dried, remove earth and old skins and store the new bulbs and offsets in shallow wire-bottomed bins or trays where the temperature is not likely to go above seventy, but where the air is not damp and conducive to mildew. Daffodils still ripening in the garden will probably not be ready for this lifting and storing until July, but all bulbs that you heeled in during May should now be taken up and stored.

Plant dahlias during the first week of June. Place stakes for the large varieties at the same time you plant the tuberous roots. Begin tying when plants are a foot high.

Gladioli may be planted up to July first for latest blooms. To ward off thrips corms planted now should be first immersed in the Lysol solution and, for complete safety, the plants should receive a twice-a-month spray of nicotine solution beginning when shoots are six inches high.

June first is a safe date to move well-started tuberous-rooted begonias to their garden location. Plant Hymenocallis (Ismene) calathina for quick production of foliage and flowers. If you have not already set out canna roots, do so early this month. Plant Lycoris squamigera now for August blooms.

JULY

The spring bulb gardener can at this time enjoy a summer rest. No gardening chores need keep you from a two months vacation in the cool North Woods unless you are planning to lift and divide your daffodils. If so, these will have finished ripening by the middle of the month and will be ready to be taken up and stored with the same care you gave tulips and hyacinths similarly lifted in June.

If you have not done so earlier, order your bulbs for fall planting now. In any season, no matter how abundant the crop, there is never enough of the good varieties.

The summer-flowering bulbs should be making a fine display for you to enjoy from shaded terrace or porch. A bi-weekly spray for the gladioli, watering the dahlias in dry weather and pinching off all but their terminal buds, are light tasks to remember if you grow these plants.

AUGUST

This is another easy month for the spring bulb grower. Continue to ignore bulbs left in the ground, although you might check on the stored bulbs to make sure they are not baking or mildewing.

Plant now colchicums, autumn crocuses and sternbergias for fall blooms. If you receive the bulbs in time, set out Lilium candidums or madonnas at the end of the month.

SEPTEMBER

Early in September plant the madonna lilies, colchicums, sternbergias and autumn crocuses that you may not have received or had time to plant in August.

The last half of September is the time for replanting your

old daffodil bulbs which may have been lifted and stored, together with any new narcissi received by this time. The little species narcissi should surely be planted in September. This is also the best time for setting out eranthis, fritillarias, such western bulbs as erythroniums and brodiaeas, and native trilliums, mertensia and sanguinaria.

Tuberous-rooted begonias should be lifted this month as they do not like cold wet soil. After they have dried, store the tubers in peat moss in a temperature approximating fifty degrees. Late September is not too soon for lifting gladioli and other tender bulbs for winter storage in the environment each species prefers. Dahlias, however, should be left until after the first killing frost.

September is also the month for making a start for the indoor bulb season. Secure your winter's supply of paperwhites now, but do not plant the bulbs until late October in order to give them time to mature. In late September start pebble-filled bowls of Roman hyacinths and pots of lachenalia for Christmas blooms. At the same time place large Dutch hyacinths in glasses and remove them to a dark, cool place for root making.

OCTOBER

October is the busiest month for the fall bulb planter. Frost nipped annuals are ready to be removed from areas destined for tulips, hyacinths and daffodils. If you are a busy gardener, able to devote only one time to planting, make it the middle of October. This will not be too late for daffodils, eranthis or winter aconites, erythroniums and other bulbs which prefer a September planting and not too soon for tulips which, if convenience permitted, would rather be planted in November. Before planting place eranthis bulbs in wet sand overnight or until the tubers become plump.

New fall bulbs or old ones being replanted should go in soil already prepared. Fertilizer should be scattered this month over all bulbs left in the ground, whether they are in the garden or naturalized in woodland or meadow. The half-and-half mixture of superphosphate and Bovung is satisfactory for this purpose. It should be broadcast over the surface at the rate of approximately one hundred pounds per thousand bulbs and lightly raked in.

Remember, this month, to cover your montbretias and hardy begonias with a light mulch of leaves or peat moss.

Lift for winter storage any remaining tender bulbs. After heavy frost blackens their foliage take up the dahlias, first cutting stalks down to four or six inches. Lay the plants on their sides to expose roots to the sun. After they have dried, store the tubers with the clumps intact.

October is also the time for planting many bulbs which will flower indoors. During the latter part of the month the first pebble-filled bowls of Paperwhites should be arranged. Continuous bloom from these and other polyanthus narcissi can be enjoyed by making successive plantings every two or three weeks until early February. Each lot of bulbs must remain in a cool, dark place for root-making before being brought out into the light.

The first or second Saturday of October is a good time for potting your winter's indoor supply of tulips, daffodils and hyacinths. Fill shallow clay pans with these bulbs and remove them to the cold frame or special trench for outdoor root-making. Wait for twelve weeks before lifting the first lot. You can bring in pans every two or three weeks thereafter for continuous blooms from January to April.

Veltheimia viridiflora and Ornithogalum arabicum should also be started now. Both must be grown in soil but need not be moved outside or to a dark room.

NOVEMBER

The first week of November is the best time for planting tulips. The weather is cool enough to discourage top growth. Most lily bulbs have now been delivered to you. Plant these as soon as possible after they arrive. If you have not yet set out crocuses, daffodils, scillas and other spring bulbs which prefer September or October planting, do so as soon as you can this month. Examine the bulbs carefully. If still sound they will probably flower satisfactorily despite late planting.

Indoors it is time to pot new amaryllis bulbs and move them to the cool dark for six weeks. Old bulbs should be watched for signs of sprouting. When this occurs, replace the top layer of soil, fertilize and start watering. Bletilla hyacintha should be potted now. If you find you ordered a few too many tulips, daffodils or hyacinths for the garden, use the remainder for indoor pans. Do not remove these late-started bulbs from their outside resting place until February. Any remaining French Roman hyacinths should be started now. They will produce flowers in January.

DECEMBER

By the first of December your outdoor bulb gardening tasks will have been completed and you can relax in your fireside chair in pleasant anticipation of spring bloom to come. This will be true unless, as frequently happens to me, you are so rushed with other tasks during the autumn that you must do in December the planting unharassed gardeners have accomplished in the preceding three months. If you are so delayed, all I can say is, finish your planting as soon as you can and pray that winter, with its bitter cold and snow, will stay its hand.

Late-arriving lilies may not be delivered to you before December. Plant them on arrival or at the first chance unfrozen ground permits rather than keep them until spring. You can make sure the earth stays frost free by forehanded mulching of the areas for which these bulbs are intended. A twelve-inch covering of leaves is not too much.

During this month continue to make successive plantings of Paperwhites. Blooms of these narcissi planted in November, Roman hyacinths that were retired for root-making in September, large Dutch hyacinths in glasses and lachenalias will now be filling your window garden with colorful blooms. They will be sure to make your Christmas merrier.

Glossary

Annual. Plant which completes its life cycle in one year. It grows from seed, produces foliage and flowers, forms new seed and dies. From the standpoint of the bulb gardener annuals like forget-me-nots are indispensable companions for bulbs; others, such as petunias, excellent follow-ups.

Anther. Pollen-bearing sac or head of stamen in flowers. The large, colorful anthers of certain flowers like tulips and lilies have more than botanical significance. Together with petals they give the flower its total effect.

Axil. Upper angle where leaf, leaf stem or branch joins main stalk of plant.

Blind. A bulb which contains no embryo flower, usually because it is immature.

Broken. Physiological change in individual bulb, especially tulip, of a clone, probably caused by mosaic. The self-colored or blended tulip "breaks" into a patchwork of the original color on a white or cream background. Each bulb offspring of the altered individual will thereafter produce blooms which are identical with the new color pattern.

Bulb. Form of modified stem in which certain plants live in their dormant state. It consists of approximately concentric layers of flesh or scales usually surrounding an embryo flower.

Bulbil. Small bulb offspring formed by plant in leaf axil. It requires at least one year's cycle of growth before it develops into a bulb mature enough to contain an embryo flower.

Bulb Pan. Shallow clay pot used for indoor growing of bulbs.

Clone. Collective term for all the asexually produced off-spring of a plant originally raised from a seed. All the bulbs of a hybrid variety, wherever located, are part of the same clone.

Corm. Form of modified stem in which certain plants, gladioli for example, exist in their dormant state. It is composed of a solid starchy substance without an embryo flower in its center.

Cormel. Small offset in cormous plants attached to base of new corm. It needs to be grown for several years before developing into a flowering-sized corm.

Cottage Tulips. One of the three principal classes of tall, May-flowering tulips. The term is often misapplied to short-stemmed Single Early tulips.

Daffodil. English word for narcissus.

Floret. The individual flower forming part of a floral spike or cluster.

Forcing. Bringing bulbs into bloom ahead of their outdoor schedule by giving them a warm temperature earlier than nature would provide it.

Genus. Division of plants having common chacteristics, ordinarily including several species. Plural *genera.* The flower itself as we familiarly know it, whether by its English or Latin name, is usually the genus. Thus tulips, daffodils, crocuses, lilies, gladioli are all genera. Wood hyacinth, Scilla campanulata, is, however, a species or subdivision of the genus, scilla. Groups of genera with allied characteristics are classified by botanists in *families.* The family is known by the name of a distinctive genus member. The family which includes the garden hyacinth, lily and tulip is known as the lily family. This does not mean that tulips and hyacinths are subdivisions or descendants of lilies. All three are co-equal genera of the same family, Liliaceae.

Growing On. Process whereby small bulb offspring complete under cultivation several yearly cycles of growth, from bulb to foliage plant to bulb again, until they become large enough to produce good flowers.

Heeling In. Setting living plants with rootstocks down in a temporary location, usually a trench, until they can be moved to their permanent garden site. Bulbs lifted right after flowering can be heeled in until their ripening has completed.

Hybrid. Seedling cross between two varieties or species, sometimes accidental, usually by design.

Inflorescence. Type or manner of flowering, particularly the arrangement of florets on a spike or in a cluster.

Jonquil. One type of narcissus or daffodil. Fragrant, golden yellow, small-cupped. The jonquil and its hybrids constitute one of the eleven divisions in the presently accepted classification of the narcissus genus.

Laciniated. Term describing petal edges which are deeply serrated or indented.

Narcissus. Latin word for daffodil.

Naturalize. To plant so that flowers will have appearance of natural growth or colonization. Bulbs naturalized are not given annual lifting and resetting.

Panicle. Flowers borne in a loose, branching cluster at the top of a stem. Mertensia virginica and Brodiaea coccinea produce their flowers in panicles.

Papillae. Protuberances on flower petals such as those on speciosum lilies.

Perennial. Plants whose rootstocks live in the ground for two or more winters while the tops die down each year. Perennials make attractive companions and follow-ups for bulbs. Thus Phlox divaricata is a good associate for tulips, summer phlox a fine successor.

Plunge. Sinking a plant up to the rim of its pot in soil, ashes or moss.

Raceme. Loose arrangement of florets on a stem. The small flowers of Dicentra cucullaria, or dutchman's breeches, branch loosely off the stem in the form of a raceme.

Ripening. Maturing of plant foliage which sends nourishment down to the bulb or bulb divisions at its base.

Root Base. Bottom of bulb from which new roots will grow at the proper time if sufficient moisture is present. The root base is frequently identifiable as a ring of ridges.

Seedling. An individual plant raised from seed. Most available bulbs are grown from divisions whose parents were first raised from seed ten to fifty years ago. The term is also used to indicate descent of one variety from another. Thus Narcissus trumpet Tresserve is spoken of as a King Alfred seedling.

Species. Subdivision of genus as it is found in nature. Species may differ from one another in form, color, habit of growth and blooming time, yet their inclusion in the same genus can be as evident to the amateur as to the botanist. Thus the white Lilium candidum, blooming in June, is very different from the red-spotted Lilium speciosum which flowers in early August. But any gardener can tell that both are lilies.

Spike. Type of flowering in which florets are arranged along a straight and usually stiff stem. Gladioli are familiar spikes.

Sport. Physiological change in an individual bulb of a clone, aside from breaking. The change is usually noticeable as an alteration of color or form or both in the flower. The individual which has sported will produce bulb offspring whose flowers are identical with the new color pattern. All bulbs of Parrot tulips are offspring of individuals which have sported.

Stamen. Male part of the flower consisting of stem-like filament and pollen sac, or anther. The filament may be short as in the case of a tulip, or long as in the case of a lily.

Truss. Type of inflorescence in which stiff spike is surrounded by closely spaced bell-shaped florets carried horizontally. The hyacinth blossom is generally called a truss.

Tuber. Type of modified stem in which certain plants exist in their dormant state. Tubers are fleshy substances bearing eyes from which new plant stalks grow. Tuberous begonias are typical examples of tubers.

Tuberous Root. Type of modified stem. They are like tubers except that the eyes from which new growth starts are located on the necks. These join the tuberous roots to the base of the old plant stalk.

Umbel. Type of flower cluster in which florets of equal size branch out from the top of a stem so that the cluster forms a regular surface which may be flat, concave or convex. Florets are held erect in the case of some of the alliums. They are pendant in the case of Fritillaria imperialis, crown imperial.

Variety. Term used to designate individuals of the same species. Most varieties are hybrids but the word is also used to indicate various forms in which species are sometimes found in nature. In a plant name the genus comes first, followed by the species then by the variety. Thus in Scilla campanulata, Excelsior, scilla is the genus, campanulata the species and Excelsior the variety.

Index